ECONOMICS FOR DEMOCRACY IN THE 21ST CENTURY

A Critical Review of Definition and Scope

Government of the people, by the people, for the people, shall not perish from the Earth.
Abraham Lincoln

KHANDAKAR QUDRAT-I ELAHI PH.D.

Economics for Democracy in the 21st Century
Copyright © 2021 by Khandakar Qudrat-I Elahi

All rights reserved. No part of this publication may be reproduced, distributed, or transmitted in any form or by any means, including photocopying, recording, or other electronic or mechanical methods, without the prior written permission of the author, except in the case of brief quotations embodied in critical reviews and certain other non-commercial uses permitted by copyright law.

Tellwell Talent
www.tellwell.ca

ISBN
978-0-2288-5401-2 (Hardcover)
978-0-2288-5399-2 (Paperback)
978-0-2288-5400-5 (eBook)

Table of Contents

PROLOGUE vii

I INTRODUCTION 1

II WHY ECONOMISTS DISAGREE:
AN EMPIRICIST INSPECTION 8

2.1 Introduction 8
2.2 Why Economists Disagree: State-Of-The-Art 12
2.3 Epistemology and Social Science 23
2.4 Conclusion 50

III MARSHALL, JNK, ROBBINS, JMK,
AND SAMUELSON: MOTIVES AND MORALS 52

3.1 Alfred Marshall 52
3.2 John Neville Keynes 55
3.3 Lionel Robbins 58
3.4 John Maynard Keynes 58
3.5 Paul Anthony Samuelson 62
3.6 Concluding Commentary 67

IV ALFRED MARSHALL:
DEFINITION AND SUBSTANCE OF ECONOMICS 71

4.1 Introduction 71
4.2 The Growth of Free Industry and Enterprise
(Appendix A) 72
4.3 The Growth of Economic Science (Appendix B) 80
4.4 The Scope and Method of Economics (Appendix C) 92
4.5 Uses of Abstract Reasoning in Economics (Appendix D) ... 100
4.6 Introduction (Chapter I) 104
4.7 The Substance of Economics (Chapter II) 112
4.8 Conclusion 129

V JOHN NEVILLE KEYNES: SCOPE AND METHOD OF ECONOMICS ... 134

5.1 On the Relation of Political Economy to Morality and Practice (Chapter II) ... 134
5.2 On the Character and Definition of Political Economy Regarded as a Positive Science (Chapter III) ... 141
5.3 Conclusion ... 146

VI ROBBINS: ENDS, MEANS, AND SCARCITY ... 148

6.1 The Subject Matter of Economics (Chapter I) ... 148
6.2 Ends and Means (Chapter II) ... 173
6.3 The Relativity of Economic "Quantities" (Chapter III) ... 205
6.4 Conclusion ... 212

VII JOHN MAYNARD KEYNES: GENERAL THEORY AND THE SCOPE OF ECONOMICS ... 214

7.1 Introduction ... 214
7.2 The General Theory (Chapter 1) ... 216
7.3 The Postulates of Classical Economics (Chapter 2) ... 217
7.4 The Principle of Effective Demand (Chapter 3) ... 227
7.5 Critical Commentary ... 230

VIII PAUL SAMUELSON: SCARCITY, EFFICIENCY, AND MIXED ECONOMY ... 249

8.1 Introduction ... 249
8.2 The Central Concepts of Economics (Chapter 1) ... 250
8.3 The Modern Mixed Economy (Chapter 2) ... 254
8.4 Basic Elements of Supply and Demand (Chapter 3) ... 260
8.5 Critical Commentary ... 264

| IX | ECONOMICS FOR DEMOCRCAY IN THE 21ST CENTURY: A PARADIGM SEARCH | 289 |

9.1 Introduction 289
9.2 Definition and Scope of Economics 291
9.3 Summary 300
9.4 The Fundamental Cause of Definitional Debate 301
9.5 Democracy in the 21st Century: The Political Paradigm ... 308
9.6. Economic Paradigm of Modern Democracy 332

| X | CONCLUSION | 339 |

BIBLIOGRAPHY 347

PROLOGUE

Theories of modern economics and modern democracy are not consistent.

Introduction

The definition and scope of an academic discipline are supposed to clarify its nature and confine the boundary of its inquiry. In its most ordinary usage, the definition of a word or phrase is simply a statement of its meaning or signification. From an intensional perspective, definition describes the denotation/connotation of the term, while it lists the objects referred to or implied by this term from the extensional perspective. Thus, in social science, the extensional definition is understood as the scope of the discipline, which distinguishes it from other similar disciplines. It is vitally important to note this critical connection between two significations of the definition of an academic discipline: intensional definition defines its scope not the other way around. This connection is the causal relationship between the two terms, which is often overlooked. It is even worse when they are treated synonymously, i.e., intensional and extensional perspectives are confounded. Lionel Robbins represents a classic example in this regard, which we will examine in Chapter VI.

To the community of economists, economics is the royal discipline among those belonging to the social sciences. This claim is not irrational because political economy was the first social science separated from moral and political philosophy. Then, the methodology of science is more accurately applicable in economics compared to other social sciences like sociology and political science.

Despite these truths, generations of economists have distinctly differed on their discipline's precise and concise definition over the past two centuries. This agreement is critical for confining the scope of its investigation. Unfortunately, the professional disagreement has reached such an extent that some economists are convinced that it is now time to forgo the debate for good because a reasonable agreement is unattainable and unnecessary.

This state of debate has inspired this research. Is it true that we are unable to agree on the definition and scope of our discipline? This book dares an exploratory attempt to address this question.

We can have little doubt about the complexity of the controversy that is going on for centuries. Therefore, the pertinent point is for us to explore how to address this issue. Fortunately, some of our trusted authors have left clues about how to deal with research situations. First, Karl Marx developed his own version of classical economics by rejecting the general methodology pursued by classical economists, including Adam Smith, David Ricardo, J.S. Mill, J.B. Says, and Pierre-Joseph Proudhon. He argued that one could not criticize political economy by using its own methodology. Second, in his masterpiece, *A History of Western Philosophy*, Bertrand Russell (1945) suggests that we ought to follow a new approach in analyzing this type of controversy as the conventional approach would lead us nowhere. Finally, we can quote Albert Einstein from the internet:

> We cannot solve problems by using the same kind of thinking we used when we created them.

These authors suggest that we need a new approach to address the Herculine controversy like the one we are dealing with in this book. Accordingly, this book has chosen the approach that Aristotle applied to investigate the nature of the state and government in a civilized society in his classic, *Politics*:

> He who thus considers things in their first growth and origin, whether a state or anything else, will obtain the clearest view of them. In the first place, there must be a union of those who cannot exist without each other; namely, of male and female, that the race may continue ... and of natural ruler and subject, that both may be preserved. For that which can foresee by the exercise of mind is by nature intended to be lord and master, and that which can with its body give effect to such foresight is a subject, and by nature a slave; hence master and slave have the same interest. Now nature has distinguished between the female and the slave. For she is not niggardly, like the smith who fashions the Delphian knife for many uses; she makes each thing for a single-use, and every instrument is best made when intended for one and not for many uses (Aristotle 350 BCE).

His successors, particularly political philosophers, have passionately practiced this recommendation. For example, we owe to John Locke for the model of democracy currently practiced worldwide. The origin of this model is the *Social Contract Theory*, which justifies how human beings transited to the civil system of government from their natural conditions in the wilderness. Without this theory, we can never establish the people as the sovereign authority of the state.

As a social science, political economy was pioneered in the 18th century to study human activities related to production, distribution, exchange, and distribution of commodities necessary for survival and comfortable living. The fundamental purpose of economics is commodity consumption. For fulfilling this purpose, humans must produce. This production is a unit of activity around which all other departments of economics revolve. Exchange facilitates the disposal of commodities produced while distribution determines who consumes them.

Without demand, no supply will turn up in the economic sense. The consumption of certain commodities ensures our survival; everything else becomes meaningful after this. This physical activity begins with the birth of a baby and continues until its death.

We can argue that the fundamental difference between the orthodox approach of modern economics and the approach of this book lies on this point. All living citizens of a country are consumers, but not all of them are producers. To see the point more clearly, we can divide the entire life period into three age categories—junior and dependent, mature and independent, and senior and retired citizens. The dependent and retired citizens are not involved in producing and exchanging commodities, meaning they cannot claim any share of the commodities produced and exchanged in an economy. This is the reason these two categories of consumers are excluded from the economic theory of distribution.

This distributional feature of modern economics raises some puzzling questions: Who should be responsible for feeding these people? Who will bear the costs of schooling of the dependent citizens? Who will take care of the medical needs these people need most?

It is critical to note that these questions were irrelevant during the time of Aristotle. In his theory, the idea of distribution is nonexistent because the Greeks used slaves to carry out all kinds of household-related activities, including agriculture. During the 18th and 19th centuries, when the theory of distribution was developed as part of the free-market or laisse-faire economics in Europe, those three questions were not still very critical because poor people living in rural areas were serfs, while those living in urban areas were wage-labourers in industry or affluent households. As the role and significance of slavery dramatically declined, the economic bondage of the working people got transformed into a serf and wage-labour relationships. This was possible because monarchs and nobles controlled governments; ordinary people were their subjects, not citizens.

David Ricardo (1817) portraited this sociopolitical scenario in his masterpiece *Principles of Political Economy and Taxation* by classifying all factors of production into three kinds—land, labour, and capital. In this model, the total output of a commodity produced by applying these factors is distributed among their owners—landlords, labourers, and capitalists. Each factor's share is fixed by its price determined by the interaction of the forces of demand and supply in the free market.

Today, addressing those three questions is relevant and vital because the political scenario has dramatically changed. The dignity of humankind guaranteed by universal suffrage affirms that human labour, irrespective of its nature, cannot be considered as an input in the production. For it will violate the UN's principles of fundamental human rights and the principle of equal citizenship on which the system of democratic government is founded.

This argument is not empty as it rests on some genuine scientific reasons and rationales. First and foremost, all modern production activities require different kinds of human resources, ranging from the general labourers to the CEO, the top decision-making authority of the firm. Because different skills embody different levels of merit, training, and investment, their market value must be different, i.e., the general workers and the CEO should receive the lowest and highest compensation packages, respectively. This inequality in human labour compensation is natural, i.e., expected or desirable, for which it conforms with the principles cited above.

Second, the existence of expected inequality among different kinds of labour skills underlines the fact that human labour is not a homogenous commodity, which contradicts the assumption of our basic market model. This supply characteristic of labour supposedly encourages the demand side to discriminate among different kinds. This issue is serious because the demand-side of labour is highly concentrated, violating another condition of perfectly competitive market structure.

Third, only labour can claim a share of net value-product or surplus value of the commodity produced. For labourers not only contribute to the production of goods and services, but are its ultimate consumers. The remaining two, being non-human inputs, cannot claim any share of the surplus value. They are purchased inputs that are included in the firm's costs of production itinerary to determine the exchange value. Land, a natural gift, is converted into a tangible asset by applying human labour. Similarly, capital, the monetary value of physical and financial assets, is the surplus value created in previous productions. Since no production is possible without the application of human labour, a rational theory of distribution is supposed to apportion the net value of the output among the various kinds of human resources used by the firm in the production process. Land and capital represent sunk costs, meaning their owners should receive fees for lending their services to the firm, which borrows them to execute its business plan.

Ricardo did not consider this line of reasoning because, in his time, human labour was an input like all other non-human factors of production, bought and sold in private markets. Marx recognized this defect, discrediting the classical distribution theory. However, he did not point it out because he wanted to abolish the political system that legalizes the institution of private property. Instead, he demonstrated, with scientific rigour, what happens to ordinary people when their labour is treated as a purchased input, i.e., commodity. However, treating low-skill labour as an input today not only misinterprets facts from an academic perspective, but also violates the principles of governance from a democratic perspective. In a democracy, we are all equal citizens, all discriminatory laws are un- and anti-democratic. When human labour is treated as an input, it loses its right to claim a share in the surplus value, which makes the job contract discriminatory.

All this explanation leads to one single point: The modern theory of distribution conflicts with the democratic system of governance. This conclusion is of little consequence if we do not review modern economics in light of democratic governance. It is not entirely illogical to argue that modern economists are teaching and preaching economics, violating the laws that give them this opportunity.

Nevertheless, we cannot ignore scientific implications of this practice. The issue we are dealing with here is ordinarily discussed in microeconomics. Both partial and general equilibrium micro models are founded on the premise of closed economy, which is created by default with the establishment of a sovereign state. The ideas of state and government are inseparable as we cannot imagine the existence of one without the presence of the other. The basic difference between the two is that the state belongs to the citizenry, while government is a political institution, which exercises the state's sovereignty on behalf of its owner—the people.

The country's constitution, written or unwritten, guides the government in performing this solemn responsibility. All this suggests that public policies, including those related to economy, formulated and executed by the government, are supposed to be consistent with the fundamental principle of democracy—equal citizenship. This line of reasoning directly points to the conclusion that the basic model of modern economics contradicts the fundamental principles of democratic governance: The principle of democratic governance says that all contracts, private or social, that discriminate one citizen viz-a-viz the other are undemocratic and hence illegal. Modern economics ignore this democratic principle and legal prescription. To remedy this deficit, we need to reformulate the premises, which makes modern economics controversial.

The title of this book—*Economics for Democracy in the 21st Century*—has been chosen for this reason—making the theories of modern economics and modern democracy harmonious. The subtitle, *A Critical Review of Definition and Scope*, underlines that the book's approach is to achieve this objective; it critically evaluates definitional discussions of five outstanding authors of modern economics.

The book has been divided into ten chapters. To set the stage for its detailed discussion, this prologue intends to describe how our political and economic systems are connected to each other. In this regard, we have used Thomas Kuhn's critical concept of the paradigm shift.

Paradigm of Democratic Governance

Two human organs—heart and head—regulate our physical and mental body functions. The function of the heart is to circulate blood throughout our body, which keeps us alive. The head controls our nervous system, which helps us live like human beings. Any coarse connection between the two organs might paralyze our regular activities. Our social life is organized in the same way. A democratic government is supposed to formulate and execute law and order in society to guarantee three inviolable rights of its citizens: security to life, liberty, and pursuit of happiness. Under the clause, pursuit of happiness, citizens enjoy the right to own and accumulate private property. Thus, the third clause of the "Preamble of the American Constitution" is the foundation of the economic system of a democratic political system. Accordingly, we can formulate the fundamental paradigm of democratic governance in the 21st century by paraphrasing the American *Declaration of Independence* on July 4th, 1776:

We, the people living in an internationally recognized territory, have chosen democracy as the principle of governance to protect and promote our security that concerns "life, liberty, and the pursuit of happiness." Security regarding life concerns protection against all kinds of physical and natural violence, including crimes and diseases. Liberty refers to freedoms under the law concerning pursuing different types of activity in the territory. Finally, pursuing happiness in life requires that the government provide all the necessary goods and services that citizens need in different phases of life. For we all seek happiness in life, but the nature of our need and desire differs decisively between different stages. The children pursue happiness through passing their time in playful activities, while the seniors pursue happiness by resting and socializing. However, independent adults seek happiness by realizing their ambitions. The government is constitutionally obligated to cater to these needs and desires of all citizens, not just those who can create wealth. To pursue happiness, junior citizens need schooling facilities. In contrast, all citizens need healthcare, suggesting that the democratic government must deliver these two services as a constitutional obligation.

If these policies are not pursued in a country, it is not a democratic government, no matter how old and stable its electoral system is. The country is not ruled based on the theory of democracy. On the contrary, politicians and their vested-interest friends use the voting mechanism to materialize their economic and social ambitions.

Paradigm of Democratic Economy

As noted above, the institution of private property is the fundamental pillar of a democratic economy or economy of a democratic country. Therefore, economists in this country are supposed to study its operation by developing models and theories that are consistent with the principles of democratic governance. The institution of private property is concerned with three fundamental components of economics—production, distribution, and exchange. These are also the economic activities that involve mature and independent citizens. On the other hand, all citizens—dependent, independent, and retired—are consumers. This modelling feature creates a serious problem in modern neoclassical economics in that the dependent and retired citizens cannot be included in the demand function as they have little or no purchasing power. More specifically, the consumption of junior citizens depends entirely on their parents/guardians, which include two most critical services—education and healthcare. On the other hand, the consumption of senior citizens depends on retirement incomes from different sources. The critical point to be noted here is that these respectable nationals—who had contributed to the economy according to their professional powers—need regular healthcare services. However, their retirement incomes are too meagre to cover these costs.

The four compartments of economics form a close-circuit continuum in which the market economy operates. Accordingly, modern economics is, at best, a partial study of the economy of a democratic country. This point highlights the difference between modern economists and their ancestors. Aristotle did not have to deal with this issue because the Greek households owned all property and were responsible for the subsistence of everyone belonging to them. We do not know whether Adam Smith thought about this issue. However, he could say little about it because the society was politically, socially, and legally stratified based on the possession of private property. David Ricardo accepted this social stratification and developed the theory of distribution accordingly.

However, modern economists have few excuses to uphold and upgrade this classical orthodoxy. Developed democracies in the western hemisphere have been consistently improving their social security systems in various ways since the end of WWII. Consider Canada. First, all medically required healthcare services are free for Canadian citizens and permanent residents since 1984. Second, the Canadian parliament enacted a Canada Child Tax Credit program in 1989 to help low-income families eradicate child poverty. Under this program, mothers of all Canadians and permanent residents receive a specific federal government tax-free contribution each month until their offsprings celebrate their 18ᵗʰ birthday. Third, currently, all senior citizens (65 years and above) receive guaranteed income supplements as their old age security if their annual incomes fall below a benchmark level. This program is the modern version of the law enacted in 1927, under which the federal and provincial governments jointly financed an old-age pension program for Canadians over 70 years old. It was meant to help retired Canadians avoid poverty. Finally, the free primary and secondary education policy, which dates back to the late 1800s when universal free education for the elementary level was introduced.

None of these issues receive consideration in the basic model of modern economics. Therefore, the argument—the fundamental paradigm of modern economics is inconsistent with the country's social policy—cannot be brushed aside without due justification. Thus, to make modern economics relevant for a democratic country and help the economic profession accomplish its citizenship duties, the paradigm of modern economics needs to be reformed in line with the political paradigm of democratic governance stated above.

This is a Herculine task that requires the genius of the sharpest minds of our generations. Hopefully, this initiative will come spontaneously someday soon. However, this book makes an insignificant exploratory attempt to argue that some of the impressions on which methodology of modern economics is founded need to be reformed to make the study of economics consistent with its political system.

The orthodox approach in this regard is to appeal to the authority of the father of our discipline, Adam Smith. Unfortunately, for at least two reasons, this orthodoxy cannot help this inquiry. First, Adam Smith lived about two and a half centuries ago. The society we are living in today is diagonally different from his. The only thing that has not changed is our native nature: we are selfish. Not only that, this human selfishness has multiplied with the miraculous improvements in science and technology by which we achieve our ambitions. Therefore, any assistance we take from our professional father is susceptible to complicate the situation further instead of resolving it.

Second, the economics profession seems to agree only on one point about Adam Smith—he is the founding father of economics. Other than this point, he is a highly controversial figure, which is not self-created culpability. Being original and accepted by the elite classes in the western hemisphere, promoters of economic freedom and mixed economy equally praise and use his authority. The economic consequences of the policy regimes suggested by the two schools, as experienced over the past several decades, are very different, meaning appealing to his authority is nothing less than inviting controversy in our discussion.

To avoid this confusion and controversy, we will follow the Ancient Greek aphorism—know thyself—one of the Delphic maxims inscribed in the pronaos (forecourt) of the Temple of Apollo. Instead of imagining assumptions and ideas on which the new economic paradigm ought to be founded, we will look at our social life and determine the assumptions and ideas that need to be used in the modern context. This rectification is expected to transform economics from its current status of pseudoscience to true social science.

We are citizens of a democratic political society. Our story of social life begins with our birth and ends with death. During this cycle, we pass through three stages as described above. When we are dependent citizens, our parents and the government share the burden of nursing, guiding, and training us to become mature and independent citizens. We begin our independent social life in the same way our parents did—we work, find a life partner of the opposite sex, procreate babies, and eventually retire from the workforce to prepare for our journey to eternity.

Thus, our functions in social life are pretty much predetermined. We might vary the nature and extent of each stage of social life, but we can never escape this natural progression and culmination.

In our lifetime, we get involved in two kinds of activities—production and consumption. We are consumers throughout our life, but we are producers mainly during the middle phase of our life, as described above. The methodology of microeconomics overlooks this fact, which is a serious modelling mistake. Since we are allowed to own and accumulate private property, we are supposed to generate enough income/wealth during the second stage of life to support our offsprings, pay taxes for running the government businesses, and provide for our retirement. This production responsibility must be understood in the collective sense, not in the individual one. For, we collectively, not individually, own the state. Moreover, collectivity is a requirement of equal citizenship.

Thus, the first impression that we must modify is the idea of our economic man or *homo economicus*, who is understood as a Robinson Crusoe ruled by his natural instincts. This Robinsonade premise might have been appropriate during the time of Aristotle and Adam Smith, but not today. It no longer describes the mature independent citizen of a modern democracy. For as an equal citizen, it has both rights and obligations. Its rights include pursuing its own happiness under law, which also requires it to give similar rights to others. In other words, our *homo economicus* being an independent citizen of a democratic country must be treated equally with others who want to hire its skills for any production purpose.

Second, when we accept the first premise, we can no longer treat labour as an input like other non-human factors of production. Since the inception of economics in the 18th century, the jargon, labour, signifies physical strengths and skills supplied by ordinary workers in the production process. By political status, these people were subjects acting as serfs or wage-earners. This political status has dramatically changed in modern times. In a democracy, they enjoy equal citizenship status by virtue of the "Universal Declaration of Human Rights." Thus, a job contract that treats labour supplied by some individuals as purchased input while that of others as the claimant of surplus value violates the equality clause of democratic governance. This point, it may be noted, is immaterial or worthless if we do not tie the economy with its political society. Since the 18th century, when economics was introduced as a separate branch of moral sciences, successive generations are passionately upgrading the discipline based on this idea.

If we modify these premises, a possibility beams forth to make political and economic governance paradigms harmonious. First, we will not invent the model of our economic system. For our choice of political system has supplied one already. Political governance is in the driver's seat, not economic governance. This point becomes crystal clear when we curiously read Chapters I and II of Milton Friedman's (1962) *Capitalism and Freedom*. Once we put political governance in the driver's seat, all factors/instruments of production become divisible into two kinds—human and non-human. Non-human factors are purchased inputs, meaning they are simply costs of production, not claimants of the surplus value created through the production process. However, human resources involved in the production process are not purchased inputs, meaning they are genuine claimants of surplus value. Their share in the production process is supposed to be determined based on their skills. More specifically, these shares are not supposed to be determined in the same manner that prices of non-human inputs are determined in the factor markets. Instead, the rewards of different kinds of labour would be determined based on their market valuation. This is, perhaps, one way out to rectify incurable imperfections in the human resources market.

This lengthy discussion is needed to justify the new economic paradigm being suggested in this book. Alterations made in the impressions on which modern economics is founded are fundamental and far-sighted. First, we reject Adam Smith's view of free enterprise because it makes the private sector overwhelmingly responsible for navigating the economy. This policy prescription was not wrong in his time because the democracy we practise nowadays did not exist at that time. Since the people are now the state's sovereign authority, the government, which exercises this authority, must assume specific responsibilities toward its citizens, particularly those who belong to the dependent and retired categories.

Second, since the beginning of the last century, the economics profession seems to be averse to political considerations. We will better understand this point if we carefully examine the writings of those authors who promote economic freedom against political freedom. This is mainly a political issue because it ultimately concerns the role of government in protecting and promoting the interests of ordinary citizens. They are victims of the business class's greed, as Debertin (2012) tells his young readers of *Applied Microeconomics: Consumption, Production and Markets*. However, there is another explanation for avoiding political considerations in economic theorizing. Mainstream economics nowadays mainly mean positive economics, which Friedman (1953) defined in his controversial essay, *The Methodology of Positive Economics*. Positive economics is concerned with "what is" issues, which means economists are supposed to be disinterested scientists for the sake of constructing a body of principles that will guide public policy issues.

This impression is objectionable on the three grounds. First, we live in a democratic country, meaning the public policy is supposed to guide the construction of positive economics, not the other way around. To see this point clearly, we might want to examine the Paretian efficiency criterion of welfare economics: *A new policy is Pareto efficient if it does not make anyone worse off but at least one person better off.*

The Pareto criterion is derived under the stringent conditions of a perfectly competitive market structure. All decisions concerning production and exchange are optimal, i.e., they have no tendency to deviate from the equilibrium point unless some external factors cause them. *This requirement of a perfectly competitive market suggests that the initial income distribution in Pareto's model is optimal by default.*

To see the implication of this assumption, let us apply Pareto's principle to the fiscal policy debate in the US. The US economists are deeply divided along with the party lines concerning this critical economic policy: As their economic philosophy, Republicans favour supply-side economics, which involves reducing income and corporate taxes to boost economic growth and downsize the public sector. Democrats, on the contrary, favour demand-side economics, which argues that imposing progressive tax rules is critical for improving the welfare of low-income households.

The Bush Tax Cut (2001 and 2003) program is used here to show the implication of the Pareto welfare criterion. In his 2000 presidential beat, Republican candidate Gorge W. Bush promised tax cuts across all income brackets. With both the components of Congress under Republican control, he easily fulfilled his promise. He signed two tax-cut legislation into law under the titles, "Economic Growth and Tax Relief Reconciliation Act of 2001" and "Jobs and Growth Tax Relief Reconciliation Act of 2003." The details of these legislations are reported in Table 1.

Since the tax rate is related to taxable income, the higher income groups became bigger beneficiaries of the legislation. For example, the top 1% of the US households received an average tax cut of over $570,000 between 2004-2012, which increased their after-tax income by more than 5% each year (Horton 2017). Compare this figure with the income increase of the people earning less than $17,000 per annum. Their after-tax income increased by only $550, meaning the top 1% of households gained 1036 times more from the tax cut than the lowest-income households. It is difficult to imagine how we can convince ourselves that this tax policy is equitable to all income groups unless we assume that the initial income distribution was optimal. Nevertheless, the Bush Tax-cut legislation is Pareto optimal because it benefits every income group in the US!

Table 1.
Income Tax Rate Reductions Under the 2001 and 2003 Tax Cuts

Taxable Income	Previous Rate	New Rate
Below $17,000	15%	10%
$17,000 — $68,000	15%	15%
$68,000 — $137,000	28%	25%
$137,000 — $209,000	31%	28%
$209,000 — $374,000	36%	33%

Source: Horton 2017.

This example is meant to highlight the consequences of policy changes based on positive theories. The so-called disinterested or apolitical attitude might be one of the causes why and how we have gotten into the current chaos of diabolic income/wealth distribution. To get out of this economic chaos, the conventional wisdom of economics needs to be reformed to allow economists to play a dual role in studying economic science. Economists are citizens of a democratic country. Therefore, their first role is policy-related. They are supposed to approve and admire only those economic policies that promote the fundamental principle of democratic governance. Put it differently, the normative of economics is supposed to guide the construction of the basic model of positive economics. However, this argument raises other vexing questions: Is the current methodology of normative economics consistent with the present model of democratic governance? Is public/social choice theory a right approach to choosing public policies? Does crime economics belong to the scope of economic investigations?

However, economists' fundamental role involves developing and refining the science of positive economics—to produce a body of principles and theories that can help formulate and execute desirable economic policy in the country. The profession is performing this job rather poorly because Robinson Crusoe represents our economic man. We can no longer make this deductive premise because we are citizens of a democratic country and collectively its sovereign authority. Thus, the methodology of positive economics is supposed to be dictated by perception as a citizen of an advanced democracy.

Finally, we reject the conventional wisdom of tripartite income distribution because this wisdom can no longer be sustained and supported in this era of globalization. As already noted above, all factors of production are divided into two kinds—human and non-human. Non-human factors are purchased inputs; they cannot claim any share of the surplus value created by a team of individuals contributing their skills and commitments. Thus, all individuals have the rights to share the surplus value, which is supposed to be proportional to the market valuation of their skills.

It is time to end this monotonous discussion and offer a definition of economics for the 21st century advanced democracy: *Economics is a social science that studies production, exchange, distribution, and consumption of wealth following the fundamental principles of democratic governance.* Human behaviour, which seems a typical phrase in most famous definitions, seems unnecessary because all social sciences study this topic. Their field is distinguished by the broad categories of the social subjects under inquiry. Thus, economics studies human behaviour concerning production, distribution, exchange and consumption of wealth, while political science studies the same aspect concerning politics and governance.

To appreciate the signification of this definition, we may be reminded that it is conceived by changing impressions of some fundamental premises on which modern economics is founded. However, these changes seem to boil down to eventually one point: Instead of treating our economic man Robinson Crusoe as a natural self-seeking person, it should be treated as a citizen of an advanced democratic society who pursues happiness by honouring laws of the land.

This book was conceived as a simple idea of criticizing Robbins's definition of economics in light of Marshall's substantive one. The analysis gradually guided the inquiry in a very different direction, which was particularly influenced by Thomas Kuhn's (1962) theory of paradigm shift. He defined scientific paradigm as a universally recognized scientific achievement that, for a time, provided model problems and solutions for a community of practitioners, i.e., what is to be observed and scrutinized.

In social sciences, this paradigm is ordinarily implied by the definition and the discipline's subject matter. This research indicates that the current controversy over the definition and scope of economics cannot be resolved without surveying the developments in the conceptions of the influential economists since the late 19th century. To complete this survey, the study first included the two great British economists John Neville Keynes and his son John Maynard Keynes along Marshall and Robbins.

However, after WWII, most significant theoretical and empirical developments in economics have taken place in North America. Accordingly, Paul Samuelson was included in the research as the final author since he was truly the pioneer in revolutionizing the methodology of economics.

The book has eventually turned out to be a story about how the definition and scope of economics have evolved over the last century and why these conceptions are no longer appropriate for analyzing the economic issues with which the advanced democracies are currently grappling. As noted above, this is a job for the economic giants of our generation. Nevertheless, this insignificant effort is submitted for critical review by those who truly believe in democracy and are ready to take a fresh look to find out what is really wrong with the state of our discipline.

Postscript

The author does not owe any academic or financial support, which he can acknowledge. However, he got both inspiration and book-publishing help at the final stage of this project, which he will acknowledge below.

First, the author acknowledges his inspiration from his granddaughter, Zara, who will be two this November. Her innocent smile and natural responses to physical and mental needs helped him see the world of economics from a very different perspective. What he overlooked during his student and professional life stood crystal-clear before him: The science of economics, since its birth in ancient Athens, is a partial study of individual behaviour and political systems. It is concerned only with the middle part of individual life, which is directly involved with producing goods and services. By this activity, they also become claimants of the wealth created in society. By the same logic, the junior and senior citizens are not claimants of this wealth as they cannot be a part of the labour force. The junior citizens only consume but are not "consumers" by the definition of the neoclassical demand theory. The senior citizens, whose most pressing need is medical care, are basically consumers, not labour suppliers. This partial study is no longer appropriate in a democratic society in the 21st century because it contradicts the first principle of democracy–equality of citizenship.

The second person the author is grateful to is the Tellwell editor Tereza, who took enormous interest in making the manuscript free of grammatical and typing errors. Because of her untiring efforts, the author expects readers to find the book easier to skim and scan. However, he alone remains responsible for all the remaining errors. Finally, he cannot thank the Project Manager, Redjell Arcillas, who was always available to help him through the process of book publishing. Last but not least, he wants to thank the whole Tellwell team involved in this project. He congratulates them all on their professionalism.

Khandakar Qudrat-I Elahi Ph.D.
Guelph, Ontario, Canada
15 August 2021

CHAPTER I
INTRODUCTION

Soon after the *Wealth of Nations* publication in 1776, the definition and scope of economics have become subjects of critical controversy. A closer look at this nearly two-and-half century-old debate reveals that this situation, though disappointing to some, no longer surprises many modern economists. However, to a layperson, it is a common-sense curiosity: How could professionals of this discipline claim to be "economists" if they cannot agree on the meaning of their profession's title?

Although this disagreement's history can be traced back to the time political economy was developed as a branch of social science, this book will date it from 1932 primarily for convenience and practical importance. In that year, Lionel Robbins, Professor and Head of the Department of Economics at the London School of Economics and Politics, published his overtly assertive treatise titled *An Essay on the Nature and Significance of Economic Science*. At that time, the ruling thoughts on these topics were Alfred Marshall's *Principles of Economics,* which was considered the economics Bible worldwide. In *An Essay on the Nature and Significance of Economic Science,* Robbins attacks Marshall without giving him the appropriate credit. In 1983, he upheld the opinions articulated in the *Essay* in his invited lecture at the American Economic Association's 93rd annual conference.

In the beginning, Robbins's radical conceptions were not respectfully received in the profession (Backhouse and Medema 2009a and 2009b). Nevertheless, his ideas eventually formed the foundational concepts of modern economics. The working definition of the discipline he derived in the *Essay* is this: *Economics is the science that studies human behaviour as a relationship between ends and scarce means that have alternative uses.* Most, if not all, modern introductory textbooks copy Robbins's critical concepts, and instructors illustrate them eloquently in introductory courses.

This pedagogical practice has developed in the absence of a satisfactory resolution to the controversy, a phenomenon that is truly unfortunate for a discipline like economics. The state-of-the-art has persuaded some economists to conclude that the continuation of this definitional debate is neither necessary nor useful:

> Modern economists do not subscribe to a homogeneous definition of their subject. At a time when economists are tackling subjects as diverse as growth, auctions, crime, and religion with a methodological toolkit that includes real analysis, econometrics, laboratory experiments, and historical case studies, and when they are debating the explanatory roles of rationality and behavioural norms, any concise definition of economics is likely to be inadequate. *This lack of agreement on a definition does not necessarily pose a problem for the subject* [emphasis added]. Economists are generally guided by pragmatic considerations of what works or by methodological views emanating from various sources, not by formal definitions: To repeat the comment attributed to Jacob Viner—economics is what economists do— ... adhering to a specific definition may constrain the problems that economists believe it is legitimate to tackle and the methods by which they choose to tackle them (Backhouse and Medema 2009a, 231).

This is the definition and scope of economics that will be the subject matter of this book. In this regard, the first weakness of the concerned literature is that it grossly ignores the views of John Neville Keynes (1904), a Cambridge economist and the father of the famous John Maynard Keynes. He wrote two treatises on the nature, methodology, and scope of economics. Neville's first work, *Studies and Exercises in Formal Logic*, was published in 1884, which, for the first time, showed the role of formal logic in economics without using its inherent mathematical symbolism. However, his second book, *The Scope and Method of Political Economy*, published in 1891, was a landmark in this debate's history. Here he addressed the nature and source of disagreements among economists concerning the different economic issues.

These arguments and opinions are about a century old, meaning they are interesting to us mainly for historical reasons. However, the world has changed dramatically in all respects since then—culture, education, and politics. Therefore, this historical debate is more than an academic exercise unless we connect it with our current research and teaching. Accordingly, this book will also review Paul Samuelson's contribution to economics, who is correctly called the father of modern economics. He introduced his mathematically smart idea in his 1941 Ph.D. thesis, *Foundations of Analytical Economics*, which came out as a book in 1946 under the title *Foundations of Economic Analysis*. Besides this methodological approach, he must be credited for dividing economics into two independent but impermeable compartments—micro and macroeconomics. Through his introductory textbook, *Economics*, he achieved this spectacular success, which has gone through twenty editions since it was published in 1948.

However, Samuelson cannot be understood adequately without first understanding JMK's (1936) contribution to modern economics, although he did not categorically address issues of the definition and scope of economics. He fathered macroeconomics and is rightly regarded as the most significant neoclassical economist. Accordingly, his contribution to economics will be discussed before assessing Samuelson.

Finally, it seems important to note that the five authors have used different terminologies to highlight their ideas about the boundary of the economic discipline: Marshall—substance;

JNK—scope; Robbins—subject matter; JMK—general theory; and Samuelson—scarcity and efficiency. We will discuss them under a general vocabulary—*the scope of economics*.

Three novel ideas form the foundation of this book. First, in social sciences, economists are most dis-reputed for their legendary disagreements, which are often highlighted by quoting the late British Prime Minister Winston Churchill—*You put two economists in a room, you get two opinions unless one of them is Lord Keynes, in which case you get three opinions*. The disagreements concerning the definition and scope of economics will be treated as part of broader research issue: Why economists disagree.

Second, this book will examine the nature of these disagreements from the perspective of John Locke and David Hume's empiricist philosophy. Marx once commented that one could not criticize political economy by accepting its basic premises. The same is true in our case. All the debates and discussions are taking place under the framework laid down by Adam Smith and David Ricardo. If we accept their theoretical framework, we might be able to make minor improvements as Marshall and JMK did, but we will never be able to dig out the factors responsible for the confusion and controversies.

Accordingly, this book will examine the definitional debates from the perspective of John Locke and David Hume's empiricist philosophy—a branch of epistemology. All scientists are engaged in discovering the cause-and-effect relationships among variables in their concerned fields. Economists are no exception. Therefore, without the help of epistemology, the economists' mission will remain incomplete. More specifically, this book intends to examine the arguments and opinions of Marshall, JNK, Robbins, JMK, and Samuelson from Locke and Hume's empiricist philosophy.

Finally, this book will take a diagonally different approach to examine the definition and scope of economics. The economic model, developed and refined over two and half centuries, treats the *economic man* as a Robinson Crusoe, a natural person who pursues self-interests without any regard to the country's laws, let alone the welfare of their fellows. Because of this feature, this approach has been severely accused of being immoral and antisocial, which is typically undermined as a value-judgment. As a science, economics is free from all kinds of subjective judgments.

It is then a challenge before the current generation of economists to prove that this orthodox premise of economic inquiry is unscientific. It is, indeed, interesting to note that the answer to this challenge lies in the very model being practiced for about two and a half centuries. This model is conceptually incorrect because it contradicts its primary premise used to formulate the laws of economics. The present model is founded on the assumption that all economic activities in the economy occur under the institutional framework of private property. Nowadays, it is indeed a supposition, but it was not in ancient Greece from where comes both the systems of governance and the production of the means of subsistence and comforts. In ancient Athens, which first experimented with democracy, the economy was privately owned and run by slave labour.

Modern democracies have substantially changed the management and ownership patterns of private property. To some, this conversion is just a little more than replacing physical slavery with wage slavery, which is an economic jargon that describes complete economic dependence on wages or a salary for livelihood. In this sense, it closely mimics the reality of all Western economies, which well-serves the public policy objectives of these governments. However, from a theoretical viewpoint, this idea suffers from insurmountable difficulties. It does not explain the distribution of profits of private enterprises according to the theory of private property in democracy.

Therefore, this book will understand the livelihood conditions of ordinary people as economic slavery, which one might criticize as Marx's view about the relation between wage, labour, and capital. This criticism will not be entirely untrue. However, the purpose of the approach taken in this work is entirely different from that of Marx. *Marx analyzed the economic exploitation of the labour class under capitalism to establish a socialist superstructure. This book will highlight the deficiencies in the current approach to help the economic system of a democracy fulfil its principles and promises.*

For achieving this objective, the only point we need to reckon with is that the fundamental pillar of the democratic economic system is the "institution of private property." Owning and accumulating private wealth is an inviolable individual right, which the government must protect and preserve in light of the two fundamental principles of democracy—equality and liberty. Thus, the approach taken in this book is this: *the government formulates and executes laws of private property according to the modern theory of democracy. Economists develop economic theory and laws consistent with the political theory. The economic man will have the liberty to create and accumulate wealth according to Locke's theory of property so that the principles of distribution in modern economics can be reformulated accordingly.*

This book has been organized into ten chapters: Chapter II—*Why Economists Disagree: An Empiricist Inspection*—summarizes Locke and Hume's empiricist philosophy of human knowledge. This chapter is intended to highlight the shift in the conceptual methodology in this commentary. In Chapter III—*Marshall, JNK, Robbins, JMK, and Samuelson: Motive and Morals*— this new line of reasoning is applied to examine their objectives (motives) for defining and delimiting the scope of economics and the value-judgment (morals) which guided them. Chapter IV—*Marshall: Definition and Substance of Economics*—critically reviews Marshall's arguments and opinions presented in the concerned chapters and appendices of his *Principles*. Similar analyses are done in Chapters V, VI, VII, and VIII, respectively, for JNK, Robbins, JMK, and Samuelson. Chapter IX—*Economics for Democracy in the 21st Century: A Paradigm Search*—summaries thoughts concerning the definition and scope of economics examined in the previous chapters to present the views of this author. The book is concluded in Chapter X with some closing comments.

CHAPTER II
WHY ECONOMISTS DISAGREE: AN EMPIRICIST INSPECTION

2.1 Introduction

The modern system of democratic governance has evolved from the ideas presented in John Locke's *Second Treatise on Government*. For that reason, social scientists, including economists, view this philosophical masterpiece as a political document. This seems to be a half-truth because democracy, no matter how elegant the theory is, is of little consequence as a social organization unless it helps individuals and society prosper economically. In his memorable book, Locke recommends a formal framework for the economy of his cherished governance system founded on the institution of private property. In his political society (civil society), owning and accumulating property is treated as an inviolable individual right. Thus, the institution of private property constitutes the fundamental pillar of the economy of a democratic country. In this regard, Locke was the first philosopher who described a complete model of the state under democratic governance. The relevant sections of Chapter V are quoted below to understand better his philosophy of the economic system, which today is wrongly referred to in several terms, including capitalism, market economy, and free-market economy.

> Whether we consider natural reason, which tells us that men, being once born, have a right to their preservation, and consequently, to meat, drink, and such other things as nature affords for their subsistence: or revelation, which gives us an account of those grants God made

of the world to Adam, and Noah and his sons, it is very clear that God, as King David says, Psal. cxv. 16. has given the earth to the children of men; given it to mankind in common. But this being supposed, it seems to some a very great difficulty, how anyone should ever come to have a property in anything. I will not content myself to answer, that if it is difficult to make out a property, upon a supposition that God gave the world to Adam, and his posterity in common, it is impossible that any man but one universal monarch should have any property upon a supposition, that God gave the world to Adam and his heirs in succession, exclusive of all the rest of his posterity. But I shall endeavour to show how men might come to have a property in several parts of that which God gave to mankind in common and that without any express compact of all the commoners.

God, who hath given the world to men in common, hath also given them a reason to make use of it to the best advantage of life and convenience. The earth, and all that is therein, is given to men for the support and comfort of their being. And tho' all the fruits it naturally produces and beasts it feeds belong to mankind in common, as they are produced by the spontaneous hand of nature; and nobody has originally a private dominion, exclusive of the rest of mankind, in any of them, as they are thus in their natural state: yet being given for the use of men, there must of necessity be a means to appropriate them some way or other, before they can be of any use, or at all beneficial to any particular man. The fruit, or venison, which nourishes the wild Indian who knows no enclosure and is still a tenant in common, must be his, and so his, i.e. a part of him, that another can no longer have any right to it before it can do him any good for the support of his life.

Though the earth, and all inferior creatures, be common to all men, yet every man has a property in his own person: this nobody has any right to but himself. The labour of his body, and the work of his hands, we may say, are properly his. Whatsoever then he removes out of the state that nature hath provided, and left it in, he hath mixed his labour with and joined to it something that is his own and thereby makes it his property. It being by him removed from the common state nature hath placed it in, it hath by this labour something annexed to it, that excludes the common right of other men: for this labour being the unquestionable property of the labourer, no man but he can have a right to what that is once joined to, at least where there is enough and as good, left in common for others.

He that is nourished by the acorns he picked up under an oak, or the apples he gathered from the trees in the wood, has certainly appropriated them to himself. Nobody can deny, but the nourishment is his. I ask then, when did they begin to be his? When he digested? Or when he eats? Or when he boiled? Or when he brought them home? Or when he picked them up? And it is plain if the first gathering made them not his, nothing else could. That labour put a distinction between them and common: that added something to them more than nature, the common mother of all, had done, and so, they became his private right. And will anyone say, he had no right to those acorns or apples, he thus appropriated, because he had not the consent of all mankind to make them his? Was it a robbery thus to assume to himself what belonged to all in common? If such a consent as that was necessary, man had starved, notwithstanding the plenty God had given him. *We see in commons, which remain so by compact, that it is the taking any part of what is common, and removing it out of the state nature leaves it in, which begins the property; without which the common is of no use* [emphasis added]. And the taking of this or that part does not depend on the express consent of all the commoners. Thus, the grass my horse has bit; the turfs my servant has cut; and the ore I have dug in any place, where I have a right to them in common with others, become my property, without the assignation or consent of anybody. The labour that was mine, removing them out of that common state they were in, hath fixed my property in them (Locke 1689, 11-12).

The general principle of the economic system of a democracy, which follows from the above paragraphs, is that humans create property from natural gifts by using their labour—both physical and mental. This process is natural in that human beings have been created in that way. Therefore, no political system can prosper without protecting and promoting the institution of private property.

Locke did not describe how the institution of private property fulfills both individual ambitions and social goals because that was not his objective. Adam Smith, a Scottish scholar of moral philosophy, accomplished the job. He carried forward the leads made by Aristotle, Locke, and his friend David Hume in this regard. In his 1776 ground-breaking classic, Smith lucidly describes how and why an economy founded on the institution of private property should prosper by producing necessities and conveniences for both individuals who supply labour in the production process and government, which depends on that wealth.

Following Smith's lead, several able economists, including David Ricardo (1772 – 1823), Jean-Baptiste Say (1767 – 1832), John Stuart Mill (1806 – 873), and Robert Torrens (1780 – 1864), made significant contributions to expand both the descriptive and normative aspects of the new social science.

However, these developments were not uncritical. Economic experts differed concerning both theoretical and policy issues of the new discipline. The most remarkable example of this disagreement is Thomas Malthus's (1798) *Essay* on population, in which he predicted a gloomy picture about the effects of population increase on economic growth and development. Malthus's population theory inspired Scottish historian Thomas Carlyle to characterize political economy as a "dismal science."

Karl Marx pushed the nature of this disagreement to its pinnacle. Unlike Adam Smith, he saw everything wrong in this institution of private property. With Marx, the study of the political economy became divided into two categories— the classical political economy, which describes the nature of the economic system of the non-socialist political system, firmly founded on the institution of private property. The second, Marxist political economy, describes how the wealth accumulation process of the classical political economy would lead to its collapse and help establish a socialist superstructure, which would severely restrict the ownership of private property and accumulation of private wealth.

The subject of this book falls under the general category of economic disagreements. The specific issues concern the definition and scope of modern economics taught and studied in democratic countries worldwide. As noted, the five authors who have made pioneering contributions in this debate constitute the subject of our investigation, conducted from the perspective of Locke and Hume's empiricist philosophy. The nature of current disagreement literature is briefly summarized below to introduce this new approach.

2.2 Why Economists Disagree: State-Of-The-Art

The disagreement literature may be divided into two kinds— theoretical and empirical. The first step in developing any science is discovering theories, which are then applied to analyze the real-world data to solve practical issues. From the theoretical perspective, the debate's origin may be dated from JNK's famous book, *The Scope and Method of Political Economy* (1904). Following the paths travelled by Adam Smith, David Ricardo, JS Mill, and Alfred Marshall, he defined political economy, founded on the institution of private property, as the study of production, distribution, exchange, and consumption of wealth. To delineate the different aspects of these theories, he divided this scientific stock of knowledge into three compartments—positive, normative, and art.

Positive economics is a systematic body of knowledge derived from analyzing the real-world data, i.e., "what is" situations. This part of the political economy is primarily concerned with theory development. Because economic theories are developed using information concerning experience or fact, they are supposed to be free from value-judgments. For example, positive science includes the theories of market demand and supply of a commodity, which respond negatively and positively to changes in its price under the *ceteris paribus* condition. On the other hand, the normative part of the political economy is concerned with predicting the effects of different policy scenarios. Therefore, economic policies suggested by economists must incorporate value judgments, meaning normative economics is a systematic body of precepts or ideals. These value judgments are supposed to be made based on the political system of the economy under investigation. Thus, the price policy, which is most appropriate for a democratic country, could be most inappropriate for a socialist country. Finally, as an art, economics is a system of rules applied to attain planned objectives. Thus, Keynes argues that disagreements among economists necessarily arise when these distinctions are overlooked. While there is little scope for controversy to continue for long in positive economics, the disagreements involved in normative economics may never be resolved.

After WWII, Milton Friedman (1953) pushed this theoretical disagreement debate to its zenith. This debate, which has now entered its sixth decade, is the most controversial piece of literature ever produced on the methodology of economics. While some economic methodologists are full of admiration about Friedman's *Essay*, others are very conservative, commenting that Friedman's methodological *Essay* does not suggest any methodology for the discipline (Mäki 2003). In his controversial *Essay*, Friedman recommended using abstract theory in economic analysis to argue that a theory's adequacy should be judged by its ability to explain the phenomena under investigation, not by the "realism of its assumptions." Although critical about his argument's inconclusiveness, philosopher Ernest Nagel (1953) approved Friedman's opinion arguing that discarding a sound conclusion due to faulty assumption is more harmful. However, Samuelson (1963) described Friedman's methodological stance as the F-twist.

Thus, the debate on theoretical disagreements continues unabated because the F-twist has not been resolved satisfactorily. One reason is that the debate completely ignores the logic that a conclusion involving a factual issue cannot be derived from a non-factual assumption or premise. For example, all economic theory assumes perfect competition, which is an imaginary idea. However, this fiction is well-intentioned and well-reasoned because it provides a guideline about what could happen in a market if the concerned commodity is produced and consumed by the private people. In the real world, the theory works in dramatically different ways, indicated by the elasticities of demand (consumption theory) and supply (market structure). For starving individuals, procuring food is their only concern. Here, the price, around which whole microeconomics revolves, is not the issue; the issue is affordability, i.e., income. The elegant exchange theory will make little sense to an entire community if its affordability is reduced to solely buying enough food to survive. Famines that occurred throughout history constitute the best evidence to justify this deductive conclusion.

The empirical debates on economic disagreements include differences of opinion among eminent economists on specific policy issues. Fritz Machlup (1965) explains the nature of these disagreement debates with an excellent study conducted in 1964 by the International Finance Section, Department of Economics, Princeton University. In 1963, Douglas Dillon, the American Secretary of the Treasury, formed a committee to thoroughly examine the international monetary system under the understanding that the central bankers had lost confidence in the academic economists due to their differing views and recommendations and decided to ignore them in formulating policies regarding international monetary matters. Professor Fritz Machlup was asked to organize the study. Machlup, who was also an accomplished expert on the international monetary system, organized a committee of professors to prove that theoreticians are "very well able to agree on certain principles." He then invited experts from central banks and other non-academic institutions to participate in meetings of this group. This committee, consisting of 32 academicians and central bank representatives, was called the Bellagio Group. It now consists of academics and officials from G20 countries who meet annually to exchange views and discuss major international economic and financial issues.

To capture the nature of differences among the chosen thirty-two "money doctors," the study focused on four monetary issues: the price of gold, foreign exchange rates, foreign reserves held by national monetary authorities, and targets of domestic monetary policy. Machlup catalogues the differences of their responses under four headings—word meanings, logic, factual assumptions, and value judgments, and draws the following conclusion:

> The first two—semantic and logical differences—can be easily resolved. Differences as to facts can be resolved in principle if the needed empirical evidence is available, but all too often, it is not. Normative differences cannot usually be resolved. However, even where facts cannot be

ascertained and value judgments cannot be reconciled, the mere identification of the differences can serve an important purpose (Machlup 1965, 2).

Machlup's arguments and opinions are crucial for understanding the nature and significance of disagreements among economists. These are critically discussed below.

2.2.1 Machlup on the Economist's Disagreement

2.2.1.1 Word Meanings

One of the primary reasons for disagreements in economic science is that it contains a few universally accepted terminologies. In this project, some important terms include money, money supply, demand for money, the velocity of circulation, hoarding, dishoarding, and currency. These concepts, Machlup says, meant "different things to different economists." Nevertheless, these disagreements are apparent, not permanent, because they are supposed to disappear when the word meanings are clearly understood. This is because this situation does not constitute an issue like the Tower of Babel. Economists can make an ad hoc agreement on the glossary in a particular discussion.

Thus, according to Machlup, different word meanings used in an academic debate do not constitute a critical cause of economic disagreements. This opinion is susceptible to criticisms for at least two reasons. First, it is a requirement of all academic debates that the debaters first agree on the meanings of the key terms used in the discussion. For example, if we want to discuss the subject matter of economics, we must first agree on what economics means so that all debaters can argue based on the agreed-upon definition. This does not seem to be the case in the context of the definitional debate examined in this book.

All debaters undoubtedly agree that economics is the oldest branch of social sciences. After this, all agreements disappear.

They disagree on a boundary line between economics and other social sciences and on the economic activities to be studied under the discipline. For example, all criminal activities are illegal, meaning society does not want these activities to occur. However, the science of economics nowadays consists of well-articulated crime theories, which assume that criminals are rational economic agents like everyone performing economic activities to make their livelihoods and fulfill their ambitions. Evidently, the debaters cannot agree on economics' supposed subject matter because they have assigned different meanings to the term.

Second, Machlup's maxim is contestable for two reasons. Firstly, the disagreements here are published statements, not oral opinions, meaning Machlup's statement is not entirely accurate. Secondly, knowledge in science is generated by a methodology that involves observation, experimentation, analysis, and verification. Naturally, all disagreements concerning word meanings and logical fallacies are supposed to be dispelled during the inquiry process—a truth that directly challenges the validity of Machlup's claim. David Hume answers this dilemma, which will be discussed below.

2.2.1.2 Logical Reasoning

We have no real differences in logic—the rules of *formal logic* [emphasis added]—are the same for all of us, but there may be logical fallacies behind some of the disagreements. This may happen when two or more of the factual assumptions on which an argument is supposed to rest are inconsistent with one another. However, the inconsistency becomes manifest only after some of the hidden implications of the assumptions are laid bare in an analytic process that calls for even more theorizing skills than many trained economists can muster.

Here is an example: Some economists contended that a country would develop a deficit in its trade balance if money incomes in foreign countries were increasing at a slower rate than labour productivity and that the conditions of supply and demand might be such that a devaluation of the currency of the deficit country would not cure the deficit. It was later demonstrated that the conditions under which the deficit would develop and the conditions under which it could not be cured by devaluation are mutually inconsistent. *Disagreements due to such logical flaws will not persist among competent economists. As soon as the inconsistencies are demonstrated, the argument in question is withdrawn* [emphasis added] (Machlup 1965, 2-3).

The above paragraphs are directly quoted to avoid any risk of misinterpreting Machlup's opinions on the nature of "different logical reasoning." First, he ignores the scientific truth that, in logic, all reasoning is divided into deductive (formal) or inductive.

The Greek philosopher Aristotle was the original author of this system, whose book *The Organon* outlines a syllogism method that consists of two propositions, respectively called the major premise and the minor premise, and one conclusion. In formal or deductive logic, the truth of the conclusion is guaranteed if the major premise is right and the minor premise is consistent with the major.

The Aristotelian system of logic dominated the intellectual world until the 17th century, when the European Enlightenment or the Age of Reasons was introduced, known as the Long 18th century (1685-1815). This historical era began with Francis Bacon's classic *New Organon, Or True Directions Concerning the Interpretation of Nature*, published in 1662. This book, titled after Aristotle's *Organon*, details a new system of logic that is more suitable to study modern science, while deductive logic is more appropriate for studying philosophy. In contrast to Aristotle's "deduction method," Bacon (2011) suggested "reduction" for studying empirical issues. Consider heat, which is a natural experience. To find the real causes of heat, one should make three different lists describing three different situations: (i) where heat is produced; (ii) a similar situation where there is no heat; and (iii) where heat varies. The actual causes of heat are those that are always present in the situation (i); absent in the situation (ii), and vary in the situation (iii). Heat, being an impression of sensation, means there are few reasons for us to differ about its meaning. Therefore, all experiments conducted at different places are supposed to reach a similar conclusion about the nature and causes of heat. In this academic experiment, all fallacies are revealed during the research, which leads to the disappearance of all disagreements. This is how natural sciences create knowledge.

However, social sciences are different. Here the objects of scientific research are human beings whose personal and social characteristics vary dramatically both within and between societies. Therefore, the possibilities of disagreements over logical reasoning methods and the results obtained are always higher here compared to natural sciences. Disagreements in social sciences will continue unresolved if the researchers attach different meanings to the critical terms of the debate. For example, Adam Smith and Karl Marx differed fundamentally about the supposed effects of "private property" on economic development. This disagreement is non-reconcilable because there is no fallacy issue here; the disagreement is due to their different beliefs. Similarly, Marshall and Robbins had very different opinions about the reasons for studying economics in a democratic society, which set them apart in terms of the meaning and subject matter of economics.

Therefore, Machlup's conclusion grossly overlooks the theoretical and empirical causes of disagreements among economists:

It goes without saying that disagreements due to such logical flaws will not persist among competent economists.

As soon as the inconsistencies are demonstrated, the argument in question is withdrawn (Machlup 1965, 3).

2.2.1.3 Factual Assumptions

Factual assumptions are the most abundant source of disagreements in economics. These assumptions might concern the past, present, and future. *Past factual assumptions usually relate to matters on which no historical evidence is available*; those about the present may be similar. However, assumptions about the future are the most critical source of disagreements because they typically involve predictions about future outcomes based on the past and current courses of action. These assumptions may refer to:

1. Extrapolations and projections of past reactions (behaviour functions).
2. Predictions of events or conditions are regarded as probable for a variety of stated or statable reasons.
3. Sheer forecasts based on insights of several unspecified kinds.

Thus, economists deal with issues on which reliable knowledge is a scarce commodity. In this situation, they must assume what they think would most likely happen. Then, different experts make different judgments about the probability of their predictions. Therefore,

Economists need not feel ashamed about their ignorance of an unknowable future. They can do no better than make assumptions, and it would be an inexcusable deception of the public if, in the face of extreme uncertainty, they conspired to make the same assumptions. Without such collusion, however, it is most unlikely that they will make the same assumptions; consequently, they will arrive at different conclusions and different recommendations (Machlup 1965, 4).

This debate on the factual assumption in economics goes back to Friedman's 1953 essay on the methodology of positive economics. Questions have been raised about the soundness of this Friedmannian prescription, but few good arguments have been marshalled against it. This is because the critics do not explain *why* economists make different assumptions under different circumstances. What factors make them predict the future based on past information? For example, why did Adam Smith believe that a decentralized decision-making process under private property institutions would bring about both stability and prosperity in society, which Marx criticized ferociously? A sensible answer to this question is the objective of this chapter. However, Machlup's statement that past factual assumptions usually relate to matters on which no historical evidence is available demands critical note because it seems to clash with Hume's empiricism to be discussed below.

2.2.1.4 Value Judgments

Even twin assumptions of fact, Machlup argues, would not generate agreeable recommendations if the "advisers" foster different values concerning the policy's objectives. In this situation, economists would likely cause semantic confusion or logical fallacy because of the factual assumptions. This idea is ordinarily expressed by the Latin maxim, *De gustibus non disputandum*, which, in English, means the absence of disputes in the matters of taste. This maxim implies that personal preferences are subjective choices that cannot be right or wrong and, therefore, are not subjects for scientific analysis. Nevertheless, a discussion on differences in value judgment may be useful, as Machlup argues, because sometimes individuals change their position on an issue, realizing that most of their values are "instrumental" to achieve specific objectives; only a few are "ultimate" or "terminal."

Machlup's recognition that value judgments are a critical cause of economic disagreements is entirely consistent with conventional wisdom. As mentioned above, J.N. Keynes first used the idea to compartmentalize the study of political economy into three distinct areas—positive, normative, and art. Friedman took Keynes's idea further by arguing that a positive approach is the primary methodology of economic science. Machlup accepts the general theme of the proposition. However, his arguments, founded on the division of the value judgments into instrumental and ultimate, are contestable. He argues that the nature of compromise or adjustment in individual value judgments is temporary or transitory, which contradicts the facts as some economic disagreements are continuing for centuries.

The debate on the role of value judgments in economic theorization is indeed remarkable but seems somewhat irrational. The word value, an abstract noun, has two principal significations in standard dictionaries—one economic and the other moral. In the economic sense, it means the amount of money that something commands during the exchange. However, from a moral perspective, the term refers to the principles of right and wrong behaviour, i.e., value implies the principles of right and wrong by which individuals live their lives.

From the moral sense, value refers only to human beings, not to other animals, let alone materials. If this is so, questions necessarily arise as to how individuals can make them entirely value-free in their reasoning process. The phrase, disinterested analyst, is often used in social science, particularly in economics. How is it possible to be disinterested in conducting social research when we are part of it? The methodology literature, which has developed under the title philosophy of economic science, completely bypasses this question, meaning we cannot get any help from economists in this regard. Accordingly, the following sections summarize the empiricist theories of John

Locke and David Hume to see if some clues can be obtained to address the long-lasting controversies in economics.

2.3 Epistemology and Social Science

The preceding section argues that the existing methodological approaches are inappropriate or inadequate to address why economists disagree, an inference that is supposed to inspire us to rethink the methodology we employ to investigate the nature and causes of our disagreements. Academic disagreements are the outcome of intellectual enterprises—cognitive activities that are meant to produce knowledge. Cognition is the process of acquiring knowledge employing the faculty of understanding that thinks and reasons. Since the faculty of understanding is a compartment of the mind, no one knows its contents until communicated orally or with the written word. In other words, this part of the knowledge production process is wholly internal to the concerned individual. Therefore, all our arguments and counter-arguments are expressed with words, conveying the ideas the mind contains. Since these words are the universal means of communication among human beings, we assume that they also convey the same ideas. This is an indubitable mistake that explains why disagreements over theoretical and policy issues in economics often continue unresolved. Thus, the new approach we are looking for in our economic research must begin with an intensive survey of the cognitive activities of the mind of an academic, and epistemology is the branch of philosophy that will help us to do this.

Though coined only two centuries ago, the origin of epistemology is almost contemporaneous to the birth of philosophy. During this long history, different philosophers had underlined different facets of the subject. Plato wanted to understand what "knowing" truly means and how knowledge is good for the knower. On the other hand, Locke's epistemology was an attempt to comprehend the operations of the faculty of human understanding. Hume extended Locke's theory of human understanding to human nature's affective aspects—passions and morals. Kant (1788) investigated the conditions of possibility of human understanding, while Russell's epistemology attempted to understand how modern science could be justified by appealing to the sensory experience.

Much of the recent works in formal epistemology constitute an attempt to understand how the evidence rationally constrains the confidence levels. However, in all these cases, epistemology seeks to understand cognitive successes, which define and measure the rationality of human understanding.

This chapter intends to highlight the nature of the cognitive process that remains confined to the concerned individuals. For this purpose, Locke's theory of human understanding articulated in his classic, *An Essay on Human Understanding*, is summarized first. The discussion in this section is completed by summarizing Hume's philosophy expressed in his classic, *A Treatise on Human Nature*.

Before discussing the philosophy of these two memorable masters, a few words about different epistemological approaches used in philosophy might be worthwhile. Epistemology comes from two Greek words: episteme, meaning knowledge or understanding, and logos, meaning argument or reason. Thus, it is a branch of philosophy that studies the nature, origin, and limits of human knowledge. The principal elements of this investigation are *ideas* that imply anything existing in the mind. Based on the significance they attach to the origin of those ideas, epistemologists are divided into two camps called rationalists and empiricists. Rationalists, like René Descartes, Baruch Spinoza, and Gottfried Leibniz believed that the fundamental source of knowledge is innate ideas. They claim that some innate or *koinai ennoiai* principles are naturally implanted in the human mind, by which knowledge is created. Thus, in rationalism, the reasoning is deductive, i.e., *a priori*.

Empiricists, on the other hand, argue that sense-perception is the primary source of ideas. The principal empiricists include John Locke and David Hume, who claim that nothing but the human experience is the trustworthy source of human ideas and knowledge. The primary difference between the two schools of thought may be described as follows: Rationalists believe in innate ideas, reason, and deduction, while empiricists believe in sense perception, reasoning, and induction.

2.3.1 John Locke: The Origin of Ideas and the Nature of Human Understanding

The philosophy of empiricism is often described by the Latin phrase *tabula rasa*, which roughly means blank slate in English. This theory holds that individuals are born without built-in mental contents, meaning all ideas come from experience or perceptions. During Locke's time, the era of entitlement, both natural and social philosophy had been changing very fast, yet the theory of reasoning remained the same old rationalism. In this context, Locke undertook the epistemological project in 1670 that matured after some two decades.

The subject matter of Locke's *Essay* is the faculty of human understanding. Understanding, Locke says, is the quality of human beings that makes them superior to all other creatures. This quality also enables them to think, reason, and generate knowledge. Accordingly, he set out in his inquiry to examine the original, certainty, and extent of human knowledge together with the reasons and extents of belief, opinion, and assent. He accomplished these objectives in four books. First, Locke rejects the rationalist theory of innate ideas in Book I.

> It is an established opinion amongst some men that there are in the understanding certain innate principles; some primary notions, characters, as it were, stamped upon the mind of man, which the soul receives in its very first being; and brings into the world with it (Locke 1690).

After proving this conventional wisdom scientifically invalid, he describes how ideas originate from human experience in Book II. Individuals are conscious of these ideas as they work with them continuously while awake. However, all these happen within the human mind, which implies that the new ideas created by the mind are of little use to humanity until communicated in public. Accordingly, in Book III, Locke discusses words and languages by which ideas and propositions of human understanding are made public. Finally, he investigates the nature and grounds of faith or opinion, i.e., the assent given to any proposition as accurate, although its truth has not yet been confirmed (Book IV). The following paragraphs summarize Locke's arguments and opinions.

2.3.1.1 Book II – Of Ideas

Ideas are the primary raw materials of human understanding expressed by words like whiteness, hardness, sweetness, thinking, motion, man, elephant, army, drunkenness, etc. Therefore, the first job of an epistemologist is to know the origins of these ideas. To this purpose, Locke says:

> Let us then suppose the mind to be, as we say, white paper, void of all characters, without any ideas: How comes it to be furnished? Whence comes it by that vast store which the busy and boundless fancy of man has painted on it with an almost endless variety? Whence has it all the materials of reason and knowledge? To this, I answer, in one word, from EXPERIENCE. In that all our knowledge is founded; from that it ultimately derives itself. Our observation employed either about external sensible objects or about the internal operations of our minds perceived and reflected on by ourselves is that which supplies our understandings with all the materials of thinking. These two are the fountains of knowledge,

from whence all the ideas we have, or can naturally have, do spring (Locke 1690).

Locke calls these primary sources sensations and reflections. First, our senses convey distinct perceptions of things to our mind that affect our external organs in various ways. For example, we feel the heat when our body comes close to fire, or our tongue feels sour when we eat bitter gourds. In other words, the source of all the ideas is the effects that external objects produce on our body and mind, which Locke names sensations. The operation of our mind is the other source of ideas in Locke's epistemology. Our brain is a vast repository of ideas derived from sense experience. The human mind, like the heart, is never idle while awake. It reflects on the ideas of sensation and perceives a whole new set of ideas, such as thinking, doubting, believing, reasoning, knowing, willing, etc., that were never experienced by our body or soul.

> This source of ideas every man has wholly in himself, and though it be not sense, as having nothing to do with external objects, yet it is very like it, and might properly enough be called internal sense. But as I call the other SENSATION, so I call this REFLECTION, the ideas it affords being such only as the mind gets by reflecting on its own operations within itself (Locke 1690).

Locke then divides all ideas present to the mind into two categories—simple and complex. Ideas, which enter the brain in unmixed manners are called simple. Simple ideas, the building blocks of all human knowledge, are "suggested and furnished" to the mind by the methods mentioned above. Once the understanding has access to these ideas, it has the power to repeat, compare, and unite them in an almost infinite variety. However, it cannot either create or destroy them. The most important quality of simple ideas is that the mind is entirely passive in receiving them while fully active in creating complex ideas. It performs this process in three ways: (i) combining several simple ideas into a compound one, i.e., creating complex ideas; (ii) setting two ideas, simple and/or complex, side by side without uniting them in one, giving the mind ideas of relations; and (iii) separating similar ideas of real existence from all others. This is called abstraction, the process by which all general ideas are created.

2.3.1.2 Book III – Of Words

The preceding sub-section concludes that complex ideas are the primary raw materials for human reasoning. However, all ideas remain hidden in the human mind until communicated in public, suggesting that human knowledge is created in two distinct phases. The first phase involves the mind's operations on conceiving complex ideas, called "private knowledge." This phase has been explained in Book II. The second phase consists of communicating these complex ideas to the public, in which sense it will be called "public knowledge." This section summarizes Locke's theory about how private knowledge is made public.

The literature we are reviewing does not note the existence of private knowledge. By definition, it ought to be the primary source of all academic controversies because the public is not aware of its nature. Thus, disagreement results when our understanding substantially differs from what the author(s) wanted us to understand. When we agree with the meaning of a word or groups of words, we can never differ for long because the human mind thinks alike. Without making this premise, human communication is impossible.

Signification of Words

Words are articulated sounds that humans make to communicate their ideas. This is the critical feature of human communication because if concerned parties do not understand the same ideas by the words used, it will result in confusion and controversy.

In this regard, general and abstract words play critical roles in human understanding.

General and Abstract Words

All things present in the universe are specific or different, suggesting that they must have specific names to distinguish one from another. Proper nouns, which signify a single entity like Adam, America, Ottawa, and Microsoft, have been invented to represent these names. However, communications among human beings, ordinary or intellectual, would be virtually impossible with these kinds of words. Thus, most words used in human communication are general words or terms:

> Words become general by being made the signs of general ideas: and ideas become general by separating from them the circumstances of time and place and any other ideas that may determine them to this or that particular existence. By this way of abstraction, they are made capable of representing more individuals than one, each of which having in it a conformity to that abstract idea, is (as we call it) of that sort (Locke 1690).

For example, "men and women" are general words, but "Adam and Eve" are specific words. Thus, "men and women" are abstract words, representing abstract ideas, while "Adam and Eve" are concrete words, representing concrete ideas. Abstract words refer to ideas or concepts with no physical referents, while concrete words signify objects or events accessible to our senses. Abstract ideas are the essence of genus and species that result from the skillfulness of the faculty of human understanding.

2.3.1.3 Book IV – Of Knowledge and Opinion

In the previous three books, Locke explains how, and from where, the human mind gets raw materials for understanding the relations among complex ideas and processing them into knowledge using the principles of logic. In this final book, he completes his mission by defining knowledge and distinguishing its key features. The book begins with this statement:

> Since the mind, in all its thoughts and reasonings, hath no other immediate object but its ideas, which it alone does or can contemplate, it is evident that our knowledge is only conversant about them. Knowledge then seems to be nothing but the perception of the connection of an agreement or disagreement and repugnancy of any of our ideas. In this alone, it consists. Where this perception is, there is knowledge, and where it is not, there, though we may fancy, guess, or believe, yet we always come short of knowledge. For when we know that white is not black, what do we else but perceive that these two ideas do not agree? When we possess ourselves with the utmost security of the demonstration, that the three angles of a triangle are equal to two right ones, what do we more but perceive that equality to two right ones does necessarily agree to, and is inseparable from, the three angles of a triangle (Locke 1690).

Locke lists four kinds of agreements or disagreements, which are briefly described below to identify the type of knowledge to which this book refers.

Identity or Diversity

Whenever the mind gets any sentiment or idea, its first job is to perceive the image or object to ensure we know exactly what it is. This perception is necessary because there could be no knowledge, reasoning, imagination or distinct thought without this perception as we would not be able to distinguish one idea from another. This perception indicates that each idea in our mind agrees to itself, meaning all distinct ideas present in the mind disagree. This is the general truth, which raises some vexing questions about the terminologies used in social sciences.

Consider, for example, the concept of "capitalism," which implies different ideas to different people. How is this possible? We know that many words have several meanings but do not create any confusion in understanding when used. This is because they are used in different contexts. However, they represent a single idea in a single context. Then how can capitalism mean different ideas when the context used is the same—economic system of a democratic society?

Relation

The second kind of agreement or disagreement the mind perceives concerns relations between two or more ideas. This kind of knowledge constitutes the heart of all scientific investigations.

> For, since all distinct ideas must eternally be known not to be the same, and so be universally and constantly denied one of another, there could be no room for any positive knowledge at all, if we could not perceive any relation between our ideas, and find out the agreement or disagreement they have one with another, in several ways the mind takes of comparing them (Locke 1690).

Co-existence or Necessary Connection

This kind of knowledge implies that certain types of objects have properties that always accompany them. For example, consider gold—a yellow, malleable, ductile metallic element specifically used in manufacturing jewelry and other costly items. This means that these properties are co-existent with the metal. Similarly, water is produced when two molecules of hydrogen and one molecule of oxygen are combined. This is a necessary connection. Investigating this connection is the sole purpose of all sciences, including economics.

Real Existence

The fourth and last kind of agreement or disagreement concerns the existence of God. The existence of God cannot be proved by factual evidence, which does not suggest God's non-existence. Here our knowledge is subject to the degrees of belief.

All sorts of agreement or disagreement, which we can perceive in our life, are comprehensible within these four categories:

> Thus, blue is not yellow is of identity. Two triangles upon equal bases between two parallels are equal is of relation. Iron is susceptible to magnetic impressions is of co-existence. God is of real existence. Though identity and co-existence are nothing but relations, they are such peculiar ways of agreement or disagreement of our ideas that they deserve to be considered distinct heads and not under the relation. This is because they are such different grounds of affirmation and negation, as will readily appear to anyone who will but reflect on what is said in several places of this (Locke 1690).

The main messages of Locke's theory of human understanding, penned down above, may be summarized as follows: Knowledge consists of agreement or disagreement among ideas present in our mind, which are of two kinds—simple and complex. The mind is passive in receiving simple ideas but active in generating complex ideas. Finally, all knowledge, i.e., agreements and disagreements among ideas, is classified under four categories. The first category is called identity and diversity; here, the mind perceives its ideas for "knowing what they exactly are" to distinguish all its ideas from one another. This category is also the first stage in creating all the remaining kinds of agreements and disagreements because, without this knowledge, no further understanding and reasoning are possible.

2.3.2 David Hume: Understanding, Passions, and Morals

The full title of Hume's book is *A Treatise of Human Nature: Being an Attempt to Introduce the Experimental Method of Reasoning into Moral Subjects*. This title demands our attention to appreciate Hume's purpose for composing this historical masterpiece. By the time he published this book, the Scientific Revolution in Europe had been complete in which the key figures were Nicolaus Copernicus, Galileo Galilei, and Isaac Newton. This revolution was not confined to only the field of natural philosophy; it also revolutionized both religious and philosophical thoughts of the time. It established the notion that all claims to knowledge must be supported with proofs, which influenced Europe's religious and political beliefs on the authority of the Church and monarchs without question.

In this regard, the contributions of Isaac Newton were overwhelming. With his book *Mathematical Principles of Natural Philosophy*, he showed that mathematics and human reason could be applied to prove scientific laws. The intellectual community, consisting primarily of philosophers, began to believe that human nature operates according to certain defined principles or laws, which social thinkers can discover by analyzing facts through reasons. Thus, human history came to be understood as a logical, observable process that unfolds according to nature's universal law. In moral and social subjects, this universal natural law is synonymous with human nature.

Locke has already solidified the foundation of the empiricist approach. However, his discussion was confined to the faculty of human understanding. Hume expanded Locke's theory to include the whole province of human nature, freeing reasoning methods from the domain of deductive logic. He used the experimental methods of science to derive the general principles of human reasoning and the nature of knowledge created through the process.

It is evident that all the sciences have a relation, greater or less, to human nature: and that however wide any of them may seem to run from it, they still return by one passage or another. Even Mathematics, Natural Philosophy, and Natural Religion are in some measure dependent on the science of MAN; since they lie under the cognizance of men and are judged by their powers and faculties. It is impossible to tell what changes and improvements we might make in these sciences were we thoroughly acquainted with the extent and force of human understanding and could explain the nature of the ideas we employ and the operations we perform in our reasoning (Hume 1739-40).

Hume underlines that the knowledge of social sciences is critically dependent on human nature. The purpose of logic is to explain the principles and operations of the rational part of the human mind. The sciences of morals and criticism are concerned with individual tastes and sentiments, while politics consider humans, united in society, as dependent on one another. The sciences of Logic, Morals, Criticism, and Politics include almost everything related to the "improvement or ornament of the human mind."

The *Treatise* is divided into three books, each dealing with a distinct subject related to human nature. These distinct subjects are understanding, passions, and morals. The following paragraphs attempt to summarize the principal arguments of each book and show how they are connected.

2.3.2.1 Of Human Understanding

Locke (2012) said that "understanding" is the mind's power of thinking. Therefore, to generate propositions, the faculty of human understanding thinks and reasons by employing the principles of logic. Hume composes his first book by consenting to Locke's conceptions and empiricist propositions, as stated above. The fundamental conceptual differences between the two great philosophers lie in Hume's approach to human nature, consisting of three analytical principles—copy, causation, and necessity (Morris and Brown 2020).

Copy Principle

Unlike Locke, Hume calls the mind's contents perceptions, which can be divided into two broad categories—impressions and ideas. The intensity of force and liveliness by which they hit the mind and make their way into our thought or consciousness indicates the nature of the distinction between them. Impressions strike the mind with force and violence, which gradually decays over time, leaving a faint memory or image of these impressions in the brain. Hume calls these depreciated feelings or faint impressions "ideas." For example, when we cut our finger, we feel the pain in our mind; this is an impression. After a few days, when the cut has healed, we no longer feel the pain but have a perception or image of the pain. This perception, called an idea, is the subject of human reasoning. Thus, Hume's copy principle states that all ideas of the human mind are copies of impressions.

Causation Principle

Hume divides all objects of human reason into two categories—relations of ideas and matters of fact. The first kind includes the concepts of geometry, algebra, and arithmetic, where every affirmation is either intuitively or demonstratively certain. On the other hand, matters of fact cannot be ascertained in the same manner because all propositions regarding them have contrary possibilities. Human reasoning concerning this topic is the subject matter of Hume's philosophy, which he begins with a summary statement:

> All reasoning concerning matter of fact seems to be founded on the relation of Cause and Effect. Using that

relation alone, we can go beyond the evidence of our memory and senses. (Hume 1748).

This is the theory of causation, which Hume calls "the discovery of relations between objects of comparison." In other words, the relation between the matters of fact is employed in the human reasoning process to obtain less than demonstrative knowledge of the world beyond our immediate impressions (Lorkowski 2019).

Hume describes his theory with the following example: Here is a billiard ball lying on the table and another ball moving toward it with rapidity. They strike, and the ball which was formerly at rest now acquires a motion. This is as perfect an instance of the relation of cause and effect as any which we know, either by sensation or reflection. Let us, therefore, examine it. It is evident that the two balls touched one another before the motion was communicated and that there was no interval betwixt the shock and the motion. *Contiguity* in time and place is, therefore, a requisite circumstance to the operation of all causes. It is evident, likewise, that the motion, which was the cause, is prior to the motion, which was the effect. *Priority* in time is, therefore, another requisite circumstance in every cause. However, this is not all. Let us try any other balls of the same kind in a like situation, and we shall always find that the impulse of the one produces motion in the other. Therefore, here is the third circumstance, viz. that of *constant conjunction* betwixt the cause and effect. Every object, like the cause, always produces some object like the effect. Beyond these three circumstances of contiguity, priority, and constant conjunction, I can discover nothing in this cause (Hume 1748).

The above example establishes two truths. First, all our reasoning concerning the matters of fact is founded on the relation of cause and effect. Second, this causal relation is founded on experience. Since all the matters of fact theories predict some causal relations between two or more variables, the last point naturally raises questions about the certainty of conclusions we draw from experience. More specifically, all matters of fact, i.e., the cause-and-effect relations, are founded on supposing that the future will be conformable to the past. This is the tendency in human understanding, which, according to Hume, is primarily the effect of custom or habit:

> In reality, all arguments from experience are founded on the similarity which we discover among natural objects and by which we are induced to expect effects similar to those which we have found to follow from such objects ... From causes that appear similar, we expect similar effects. This is the sum of all our experimental conclusions (Hume 1748).

This custom principle states that repetition of any act or operation produces a propensity in the human mind to expect the same act or operation in the future with no influence from any reasoning, i.e., the process of understanding. Thus, Hume concludes:

> Custom, then, is the great guide of human life. It alone is what makes our experience useful to us and makes us expect future sequences of events to be like ones that have appeared in the past. Without the influence of custom, we would be entirely ignorant of every matter of fact beyond what is immediately present to the memory and senses. We would never know what means we should adopt in order to reach our ends; we couldn't employ our natural powers to produce any desired effect. There would be an end of all action and of most theorizing (Hume 1748).

However, custom alone is incapable of exciting our willpower to act on the matters of fact. For, our imagination can create infinite varieties of ideas from the original stock furnished by internal and external senses. Nevertheless, only some of these ideas of fiction or vision influence our thought process that eventually leads to action, i.e., movements of our body parts. Hume calls these fictions and visions our beliefs. They do not depend on our willpower as they cannot be summoned at pleasure; they exist in some sentiment or feeling of our heart or soul. Like other sentiments, they are excited by nature and arise from a situation where the mind is placed at any particular juncture.

> I say, then, that belief is nothing but a more vivid, lively, forcible, firm, steady conception of an object than what the imagination alone is ever able to attain. This variety of terms, which may seem so unphilosophical, is intended only to express that act of the mind that renders realities, or what is taken for such, that causes them to weigh more in the thought and gives them a superior influence on the passions and imagination (Hume 1748).

Necessary Connection

This is the final principle that Hume develops in his philosophy of human understanding, which the Hume experts consider most original. For being so original, it has also become a subject of enduring controversy (Russell 1945).

To comprehend this principle, let us first recapitulate the chain of Hume's logic illustrated so far. Ideas, the basic raw materials of human reasoning, are copies of impressions received internally or externally. All reasoning concerning matters of fact is founded on cause-and-effect relations. Since the past cannot be accepted as full proof of the future event, the last proposition is based on the supposition that the past will replicate precisely in the future. This supposition is the effect of our custom or habit. The principle of custom holds that repetition of any act or operation produces a propensity in our mind to expect the same act or operation in the future with no influence from any reasoning or the process of understanding. Hume calls this propensity a belief—a more intense, animated, violent, firm, steady conception of an object compared to the one that our imagination alone can make us feel.

This line of reasoning establishes two truths. First, all scientific knowledge concerning matters of fact is uncertain or probable; the degree of uncertainty varies among the nature of objects studied. The degree of uncertainty in natural sciences is supposedly less than that of social sciences. Second, belief in any matter-of-fact relation is not a new idea; it just perceives or feels the existing relationships differently. However, the reasoning is an intentional or deliberate act of the mind, meaning there must be some other "impression" that the custom creates on the mind, which persuades it to ignore all uncertainties in the relation and place complete faith in its eventuality. The theory that explains this eventuality is called Hume's principle of necessary connection.

Experts differ about the contributions that Hume has made in the field of epistemology. For example, Bertrand Russell thinks that Book I is Hume's most critical contribution to epistemology, although he is fully aware that by Hume's testament, Book III is his most important contribution. However, we might be interested to know how Hume's philosophy of human understanding relates to the methodological debate in economics.

J.N. Keynes divided the study of economics into three departments—positive, normative, and art—and argued that disagreements among economists mainly arise because they fail to distinguish between them during the reasoning process. Today, this positive-normative distinction is differentiated as theoretical and policy studies in economics. Being empirical, positive economics deals with "what is" issues, while normative economics deals with "what ought to be" issues as they concern making public policies.

"What is" and "what ought to be" are now the catchphrases in economics. However, seldom have we ever paid enough attention to understand what the catchphrase "what is" implies. If we look from Hume's perspective, then there is no confusion about the subjects of positive science because all ideas, the raw materials of human understanding, are obtained from impressions. If these ideas do not come from our impressions, they do not qualify to be "what is" ideas, which seems to challenge Friedman's methodology of economics as a positive science. His assertion that assumptions' realism is not a required criterion for sound theory demands critical criticism because it is logically impossible to derive a sound scientific theory based on fictitious premises.

2.3.2.2 Of Passions

The empiricist theory of human understanding explains how knowledge is generated and what it signifies in the empirical sciences. According to Locke, human knowledge is merely an agreement or disagreement between two or more ideas. However, he does not explain why these agreements or disagreements must lead to actions, i.e., movements in the body and mind. Hume closes this reasoning gap by arguing that human knowledge is the belief in cause-and-effect relations among matters of fact. Thus, movements in both body and mind are necessary conditions for generating knowledge.

Nevertheless, beliefs, which are the prerequisites of all moral actions, are alone incapable of exiting the mind to perform or prevent the suggested action. In other words, there must be some forces in human nature that persuade the mind to exert its energy. These forces, according to Hume, are passions discussed in Book II.

All impressions are divisible into original impressions (of sensation) and secondary impressions (of reflection). Original impressions arise without antecedent perception, while the secondary impressions proceed from some of these original ones, either immediately or by their idea's interposition. All original impressions include impressions of senses and bodily pains and pleasures, while the second includes all passions and other emotions resembling them. Passions or reflective impressions, objects of Hume's investigation, are again divided into direct and indirect passions. The direct passions arise immediately from the perception of pain or pleasure, but the indirect ones proceed from the same principles but by the conjunction of other qualities. The indirect passions include pride, humility, ambition, vanity, love, hatred, envy, pity, malice, and generosity. On the other hand, direct passions include aversion, grief, joy, hope, fear, despair, and security, which are the subjects Hume produced in the *Treatise*.

Finally, Hume divides direct passions into productive and responsive ones to distinguish between their causes and objects. All passions are related to feelings of pain and pleasure. Nevertheless, the relationships between specific passions and these feelings are not always the same. Like hunger, thirst, and sexual appetite, some passions are caused by these feelings; they are called productive passions. These passions, which arise in the human soul from natural impulses of instinct, produce the feeling of bodily pain and pleasure. These passions are of little interest from the perspective of moral investigations. However, the impressions of reflections do not cause bodily pain and pleasure; instead, they respond to these stimuli. These impressions, which constitute the main topics in Hume's inquiry, are named responsive passions.

In performing the thinking and reasoning activities, the mind merely responds to the feelings of pain and pleasure. This natural mechanism raises two issues of inquiry. First, the mind has an almost infinite ability to conceive different ideas by combining simple ones. However, it does not believe in all the ideas it creates; neither does it consider all of them equally useful or essential. In other words, an overwhelming portion of these ideas is passive because the mind does not take notice of them. Thus, the responsive passions, in a way, screen out the non-important ideas from our reasoning process.

The second issue concerns the psychological factor that inspires the faculty of human understanding to respond to these specific ideas. In answering this question, Hume begins his analysis by first examining the prevailing philosophy about the relationship between reasons and passions. The object of human reasoning is to discover the truth, a virtue. The prevailing philosophical theory argues that virtue and reasoning are synonymous.

> Nothing is more usual in philosophy, and even in common life, than to talk of the combat of passion and reason, to give the preference to reason, and assert that men are only so far virtuous as they conform themselves to its dictates. Every rational creature, it is said, is obliged to regulate his actions by reason; and if any other motive or principle challenge the direction of his conduct, he ought to oppose it, till it be entirely subdued, or at least brought to a conformity with that superior principle (Hume 1739-40).

The most significant part of both ancient and modern philosophy is founded on this method of thinking. However, this popular notion is contestable because reason does not alone inspire any action or raise any desire. Therefore, this faculty is not capable of stopping any desire or combating any penchant with passions. This is a necessary consequence of human actions.

> 'Tis impossible reason could have the latter effect of preventing volition, but by giving an impulse in a contrary direction to our passion; and that impulse, had it operated alone, would have been able to produce volition. Nothing can oppose or retard the impulse of passion, but a contrary impulse; and if this contrary impulse ever arises from reason, that latter faculty must have an original influence on the will and must be able to cause, as well as hinder any act of volition. But if reason has no original influence, 'tis impossible it can withstand any principle, which has such an efficacy or ever keep the mind in suspense a moment. Thus, it appears that the principle, which opposes our passion, cannot be the same

with reason and is only call'd so in an improper sense. We speak not strictly and philosophically when we talk of the combat of passion and reason. *Reason is, and ought only to be the slave of the passions, and can never pretend to any other office than to serve and obey them. As this opinion may appear somewhat extraordinary, it may not be improper to confirm it by some other considerations* [emphasis added] (Hume 1739-40).

To appreciate the meaning Hume attaches to the relation between reason and passion, we need to clarify the role of the will in moral actions. However, discovering this role from Hume's thoughts seems extremely difficult because he did not detail the nature and functions of the will in a way that the readers could quickly grasp. Hume does not consider this feeling as a passion. Instead, he defines will as the internal impression we feel and are conscious of when we knowingly give rise to any new motion of our body or new perception of our mind (Hume 2012). Nevertheless, this mental quality persuades the mind to respond to the outputs of the faculty of understanding. By this line of reasoning, Hume raises the critical question about human nature regarding its operations in moral subjects: If the will is not passion and reasoning alone cannot excite responsive passion, then what factor persuades the human mind to undergo utmost suffering based on beliefs generated by the faculty of human understanding?

2.3.2.3 Of Morals

Hume answers this question in Book III, which the Hume scholars have ignored in their studies. For this unwarranted omission, only Hume must be held accountable. First, he has composed his monumental treatise to criticize the arena of moral philosophy. Accordingly, he presented topics that his readers find difficult to connect. For example, in Book II, his point was to explain how the operations of human understanding are related to human passions, which alone cause our body and mind to action. If Hume had done his job at all, he has done it very unsatisfactorily.

Second, Hume's original plan, outlined in the introductory chapter, tying up the three faculties of the human mind—understanding, passion, and morality—was to show their combined effect on human reasoning and knowledge that results from that process. However, he raised serious skepticism about this plan through advertisements in two volumes of the *Treatise* published separately: Volume I (Book 1 and Book 2) and Volume II (Book 3).

Advertisement to Volume 1:

MY design in the present work is sufficiently explain'd in the introduction. The reader must only observe that all the subjects I have there plann'd out to myself are not treated of in these two volumes. The subjects of the understanding and passions make a complete chain of reasoning by themselves, and I was willing to take advantage of this natural division in order to try the taste of the public. If I have the good fortune to meet with success, I shall proceed to the examination of morals, politics, and criticism, which will complete this treatise of human nature. The approbation of the public I consider as the greatest reward of my labours, but am determin'd to regard its judgment, whatever it be, as my best instruction (Hume1739-40).

Advertisement to Volume 2:

I THINK it proper to inform the public, that tho' this be a third volume [book 3] of the *Treatise of Human Nature*, yet 'tis in some measure independent of the other two, and requires not that the reader shou'd enter into all the abstract reasonings contain'd in them. I am hopeful it may be understood by ordinary readers, with as little attention as is usually given to any books of reasoning. It must only be observ'd that I continue to make use of the terms, impressions, and ideas in the same sense as formerly; and that by impressions I mean our stronger perceptions, such as our sensations, affections, and sentiments; and by ideas, the fainter perceptions, or the copies of these in the memory and imagination (Hume 1739-40).

When reading these advertisements, one may rationally doubt the conceptual connection among the conclusions reached in Hume's three books. However, this commentary ignores these issues and tries to connect the books' themes to have a complete and consolidated picture of human nature that affects knowledge generated in our intellectual industry.

To conclude Hume's empiricist theory of human nature, we need to identify the moral factors that persuade passions to act, as suggested by the understanding faculty. The final subject of Hume's investigation is the faculty of morals whose sole purpose is to make judgments between moral good and evil and virtues and vices. These judgments are perceptions like all others that occupy the mind. However, the following question needs to be answered to determine the nature of these judgments: Are they ideas or impressions by which the mind distinguishes between vice and virtue and pronounces an action blamable or praiseworthy?

Hume argues that moral judgments can never be treated like ideas, which are the subjects of human reasoning:

Reason is the discovery of truth or falsehood. Truth or falsehood consists of an agreement or disagreement either to the real relations of ideas or to real existence and matter of fact. Whatever, therefore, is not susceptible of this agreement or disagreement, is incapable of being true or false, and can never be an object of our reason. Now it is evident our passions, volitions, and actions are not susceptible of any such agreement or disagreement, being original facts and realities, complete in themselves, and implying no reference to other passions, volitions, and actions. It is impossible, therefore, they can be pronounced either true or false and be either contrary or conformable to reason (Hume 1739-40).

This argument is of double advantage to our present purpose. For it proves DIRECTLY that actions do not derive their merit from a conformity to reason, nor their blame from a contrariety to it. It also proves the same truth more INDIRECTLY by showing us that as reason can never immediately prevent or produce any action by contradicting or approving of it, it cannot be the source of moral good and evil, which are found to have that influence. Actions may be laudable or blameable, but they cannot be reasonable: Laudable or blameable, therefore, are not the same as reasonable or unreasonable. The merit and demerit of actions frequently contradict and sometimes control our natural propensities. But reason has no such influence. Moral distinctions, therefore, are not the offspring of reason. Reason is wholly inactive and can never be the source of so active a principle as conscience or a sense of morals (Hume 1739-40).

Hume concludes that reasoning or the faculty of human understanding has little to do with moral judgments, which, in turn, suggests that moral distinctions are derived from moral senses.

Our decisions concerning moral rectitude and depravity are perceptions, and as all perceptions are either impressions or ideas, the exclusion of the one is a convincing argument for the other. Morality, therefore, is more properly felt than judged of; though this feeling or sentiment is commonly so soft and gentle that we are apt to confound it with an idea, according to our common custom of taking all things for the same, which have any near resemblance to each other (Hume 1739-40).

The preceding argument raises the next question concerning identifying the nature of these impressions and describing how they operate in the mind. Here the answers seem simple: Impressions arising from virtue are agreeable, but those proceeding from vices are disagreeable. The agreeable actions produce pleasure, while the disagreeable cause pain. An action, sentiment, or character is virtuous because its view causes pleasure in our mind, while the same could be considered vicious as they cause a particular uneasiness.

In giving a reason, therefore, for the pleasure or uneasiness, we sufficiently explain the vice or virtue. To have a sense of virtue is nothing but to feel a satisfaction of a particular kind from the contemplation of a character. The very feeling constitutes our praise or admiration. We go no farther; nor do we enquire into the cause of the satisfaction. We do not infer a character to be virtuous because it pleases: But in feeling that it pleases after such a particular manner, we, in effect, feel that it is virtuous. The case is the same as in our judgments concerning all kinds of beauty, and tastes, and sensations. Our approbation is implied in the immediate pleasure they convey to us (Hume 1739-40).

After establishing that moral judgments are directly related to pain and pleasure, which cause human actions, Hume divides all virtues into natural and artificial. The natural virtues include such moral actions as benevolence, meekness, charity, and generosity. On the other hand, artificial virtues—which arise from the circumstances and necessity of mankind—produce pleasure and approbation through artifice or contrivance. They include moral actions like justice, keeping promises, allegiance, and chastity. The most interesting point in Hume's philosophy is that the standard object of moral evaluation is the "quality of mind"—a character trait.

It is evident that when we praise any actions, we regard only the motives that produced them, and consider the actions as signs or indications of certain principles in the mind and temper. The external performance has no merit. We must look within to find moral quality. We cannot do this directly; therefore, fix our attention on actions, as on external signs. But these actions are still considered as signs, and the ultimate object of our praise and approbation is the motive that produced them.

Therefore, it appears that all virtuous actions derive their merit only from virtuous motives and are considered merely as signs of those motives. From this principle, I conclude that the first virtuous motive, which bestows a merit on any action, can never be a regard to the virtue of that action, but must be some other natural motive or principle. To suppose, that the mere regard to the virtue of the action may be the first motive, which produced the action, and rendered it virtuous, is to reason in a circle. Before we can have such a regard, the action must be really virtuous; and this virtue must be derived from some virtuous motive: And consequently the virtuous motive must be different from the regard to the virtue of the action. A virtuous motive is requisite to render an action virtuous. An action must be virtuous, before we can have regard for its virtue. Some virtuous motives, therefore, must be antecedent to that regard (Hume 1739-40).

The fundamental difference between natural and artificial virtues is found in the good that results from a single act. In natural virtue, this single act always produces the same good as it is the object of natural passion. In the case of artificial virtue, the single act may produce different outcomes demanding different moral judgments. For example, a court judgment will be considered unjust if it frees a criminal due to a lack of evidence. However, the same verdict will be appreciated if it frees an innocent accused because the prosecution failed to prove its accusations.

All intellectual outputs fall to the province of artificial virtues, which suggests that our morality dictates our moral judgments, which, in turn, persuade the will to execute the conclusions made by the faculty of understanding. Jeremy Bentham's memorable maxim seems very relevant here:

> Nature has placed mankind under the governance of two sovereign masters, pain and pleasure. They alone point out what we ought to do and determine what we shall do; the standard of right and wrong, and the chain of causes and effects, are both fastened to their throne. They govern us in all we do, all we say, all we think; every effort we can make to throw off our subjection to pain and pleasure will only serve to demonstrate and confirm it. A man may claim to reject their rule, but in reality, he will remain subject to it. The principle of utility recognizes this subjection and makes it the basis of a system that aims to have the edifice of happiness built by the hands of reason and law. Systems that try to question it deal in sounds instead of sense, in caprice instead of reason, in darkness instead of light (Bentham 2000, 1).

Thus, Adam Smith's morality made him believe in the virtues of individual freedom and political equality, which are most consistent with human nature that selfishly tries to accumulate wealth. Accordingly, he showed how this selfish human nature could further the economic welfare of individuals and society. On the contrary, Karl Marx saw all evils in the institution of private property and sought to destroy the system through the proletarian revolution. Both used the principles of logic to make their cases and succeeded abundantly. From epistemological perspectives, we cannot judge their theories as true or false and right or wrong because they understand the future effects of private property on human society in the opposite way. Thus, all the academic debates being fought since the 19th century concerning socialism and capitalism rest on an illogical platform.

2.4 Conclusion

The book begins with three promises. The first two include an analysis of its subject matters from the perspectives of "why economists disagree"—a general debate in the discipline—by employing the empiricist philosophy of John Locke and David Hume. These promises are attempted in this chapter.

After presenting the concerned disagreements as an integral part of the discipline's general problem, the chapter summarizes Locke and Hume's empiricism. This philosophical theory is founded on the belief that the raw materials of all speculative enterprises are simple ideas obtained from experience. Based on this basic agreement, Locke and Hume enunciate two theories that are of enormous importance to the intellectual industry. Locke argues that human knowledge is produced in two steps. The first step is entirely internal because it takes place within the mind by the faculty of human understanding concerned with all cognitive activities. The reasoning process, which generates human knowledge, takes place in this first step. Since this process is entirely internal, conclusions arrived here are called "private knowledge." Here, principles of logic play a critical role. The second step involves communicating this knowledge through language, where grammar plays a pivotal role. The published or spoken propositions are called public knowledge. Since this knowledge is subject to interpretation, disagreements naturally arise as different individuals understand it differently.

Hume reinterprets Locke's empiricism to determine the ultimate nature of human knowledge and the causes of disagreements. He established that our morals ultimately control all reasoning. In other words, morality supplies the motives for human reasoning, which, in turn, guides the faculty of understanding. However, custom, the great guide of human understanding, only serves our passions. Finally, intellectual passions are primarily determined by human morality as reasoning can only discover the truth or falsity of our proposition. However, to excite our passions, we need the perceptions of right or wrong, good or bad, which are moral concepts, not logical ones.

The next chapter will apply these theories to examine the motives and morals of our five authors.

Guelph Public Library

CHAPTER III
MARSHALL, JNK, ROBBINS, JMK, AND SAMUELSON: MOTIVES AND MORALS

We all agree that economists study human behaviour that is distinguished by the adjective "economic." We also know they are deeply divided over the issue concerning the types of behaviour qualifying this category. The preceding chapter has promised to examine this situation with the help of Locke and Hume's empiricism. The following paragraphs fulfill this promise by briefly describing our five distinguished economists' educational and professional profiles to guesstimate their motives and morals.

3.1 Alfred Marshall

Alfred Marshall (1842-1924) was born in Bermondsey, South East London, and grew up in London's suburb Clapham. He was sent to Merchant Taylor's School at the age of nine, where he showed significant academic promise, particularly an aptitude for mathematics. In 1862, at the age of 20, Marshall entered St John's College, Cambridge, on an open exhibition and studied the Mathematical Tripos, Cambridge University's most prestigious degree competition. He first studied ethics for a year in Germany, and then psychology and economics, and completed the degree in 1865, securing the Second Wrangler position. This success helped him get elected to a Fellowship at St John's, where he became a Lecturer in Moral Sciences in 1868, specializing in political economy. By 1870, he committed his career to developing political economy into a new social science. He persistently laboured to develop and refine his economic ideas by deepening his understanding and grasp of both the existing economic literature and the reality of the world of economics. In 1875, Marshall visited the United States for four months. He toured the whole of the East and travelled as far as San Francisco, engaging in talks with the economics scholars of both Yale and Harvard. The principal purpose of his tour was to study the economics of protectionism that the new world had been pursuing.

In 1877, he married Mary Paley, who was a part of the first group of students he taught at Newnham Hall (later Newnham College). His marriage to Mary Paley cost him his job because Cambridge University strictly enforced the celibacy principle at that time. As a result, Marshall moved to University College, Bristol, and worked as its first Principal and Professor of Political Economy. He completed and published his first book, the *Economics of Industry*, with his wife in 1879. This book made Marshall a rising star in the rapidly expanding horizon of the political economy. With the death of W.S. Jevons in 1881, he appeared as the British leader of the new scientific school of economics both in continental Europe and North America.

In 1881, Marshall resigned from his job at Bristol due to health reasons and spent the next year mainly travelling, with a lengthy stopover in Palermo. At this time, he conceived the idea of composing his most famous book, *Principles of Economics*. He returned to Bristol in 1882 but moved to Oxford the following year when a Balliol lectureship became available due to the unexpected death of Arnold Toynbee, Professor of Political Economy. However, his association with Oxford was cut short due to the sudden death of Henry Fawcett, who had been Professor of Political Economy at Cambridge since 1863. Marshall returned to Cambridge as the Chair and Professor of Political Economy—a post he held till 1908. At the age of 66, he resigned from his Cambridge job to devote himself entirely to writing.

Our concern is with the *Principles of Economics*, not with Marshall's complete scholarship. The *Principles* went through eight editions, with the last one completed in 1920. As Marshall notes in the preface of the 8th edition, it was a reprint of the seventh, making it a sixth reprint. Therefore, we might better appreciate Marshall's morals and motives in composing the treatise if we focus on his associations since his entry to Cambridge in 1868.

Marshall was a mathematical genius, but he turned to political economy, which was then taught as a moral science. Thus, philosophical issues, including moral and political aspects, constituted a necessary background for studying political economy established by the pioneer political economists, including Adam Smith and J.S. Mills. Marshall's decision to disown his natural advantage—mathematics—and to commit to political economy suggests that he was intellectually inclined to moral issues and social welfare.

This truth is testified by his association with Henry Sidgwick in Cambridge's moral sciences discussion group called the Grote Club. His association with Sidgwick was particularly critical in forming his philosophical aptitudes to developing economics as a social science. Marshall spoke the following words during Sidgwick's memorial:

> Though not his pupil in name, I was in substance his pupil in Moral Science, and I am the oldest of them in residence. I was fashioned by him. He was, so to speak, my spiritual father and mother: for I went to him for aid when perplexed, and for comfort when troubled, and I never returned empty away. The minutes that I spent with him were not ordinary minutes; they helped me to live. I had to pass through troubles and doubts somewhat similar to those with which he, with broader knowledge and greater strength, had fought his way, and perhaps of all the people who have cause to be grateful to him, none has more than I (Keynes 1924).

In his obituary for Alfred Marshall, Keynes describes the great economist with the following words:

> The study of economics does not seem to require any specialized gifts of an unusually high order. Is it not,

intellectually regarded, a very easy subject compared with the higher branches of philosophy and pure science? Yet good, or even competent, economists are the rarest of birds. An easy subject, at which very few excel! The paradox finds its explanation, perhaps, in that the master-economist must possess a rare combination of gifts. He must reach a high standard in several different directions and must combine talents not often found together. He must be a mathematician, historian, statesman, philosopher—to some degree. He must understand symbols and speak in words. He must contemplate the particular in terms of the general and touch abstract and concrete in the same flight of thought. He must study the present in the light of the past for the purposes of the future. No part of man's nature or his institutions must lie entirely outside his regard. He must be purposeful and disinterested in a simultaneous mood, as aloof and incorruptible as an artist, yet sometimes as near the earth as a politician (DeLong 2017).

3.2 John Neville Keynes

John Neville Keynes (henceforth JNK) was born on August 31, 1852, to a very wealthy and educated non-conformist (Congregationalist) family in Salisbury, Wiltshire, England. His father, Dr. John Keynes, spent his entire career on horticulture. As a Congregationalist family member, his education began at a local school at the Amersham Hall, a dissenting academy, where he showed great promise for classics and mathematics. In 1869, he won the Gilchrist Scholarship to study at University College, London (UCL), the school that specialized in teaching non-conformist students, who were excluded by the Religious Test Acts from Cambridge and Oxford universities. After receiving his B.A. with honours in 1870, JNK somehow managed to enroll at the University of Cambridge on his third attempt. He was awarded a mathematical scholarship to Pembroke College. However, he did not stay with the mathematics core and soon switched to the Moral Science Tripos, showing a unique affinity for logic. It was around this time that he came under the influence of Alfred Marshall.

Unlike other brilliant students, JNK was not quite sure about the career he should pursue. Therefore, he completed degrees at both University College, London, and Cambridge in 1876 and succeeded in getting elected simultaneously to a Fellow of both Pembroke College and UCL. Due to Marshall's influence, JNK became interested in economics but remained focused primarily on logic. However, after Marshall left Cambridge in 1877, JNK gave up the political economy and concentrated exclusively on logic.

JNK got engaged to Florence Ada Brown in 1880, which endangered his Pembroke fellowship (Cambridge fellowships were then reserved for bachelors). To retain his association with Cambridge, he took up an administrative job in 1882 with Cambridge's Local Examinations Syndicate as an Assistant Secretary and married Florence. His first son, John Maynard, was born a year later. He was appointed Secretary in 1892, a position that he held until 1910. In 1884, he was appointed University Lecturer in Moral Sciences, which he held until 1911. He was also appointed Cambridge University Lecturer in Moral Sciences in 1884, the year his first book, *Studies and Exercises in Formal Logic,* was published. He also served as Chairman of the Special Board for Moral Sciences (1906-1912) and as Chairman of the Special Board for Economics and Politics (1908-1920). However, his Oxford experience persuaded him to re-encounter economics and produce his famous classic *The Scope and Method of Political Economy* in 1891. In this masterpiece, JNK synthesizes the historical and theoretical approaches of the Classical and Neoclassical schools and facilitated the method for formalizing the methodological approach of the Marshallian school. This book earned him a Doctor of Science degree from the University of Cambridge.

JNK was a master applied logician who is often erroneously described as a philosopher. In *Studies and Exercises in Formal Logic*, he defended pure formal logic against the influences of philosophical logic of Kant or Hegel and empirical logic of John Stuart Mill. Another significant contribution to logic is the refinement of the concept, non-categorical syllogism, a logical inference that uses all propositions as its units. The categorical syllogisms conclude from their premises. On the other hand, non-categorical syllogisms study the proposition values concerning other propositions. Propositions are viewed as single, non-decomposable units with their true internal value. This syllogistic system can be traced from the Stoic logicians. However, it was not fully appreciated as a separate branch until the work of JNK.

In the *Scope and Method of Political Economy*, JNK attempts to close the gap between the two schools of thought, famously known as the Methodenstreit or battle of methods. These two schools include the Austrian school of economics led by Carl Menger and the German historical school of economics led by Gustav Schmoller. The Austrians insisted on a deductive approach and stressed the importance of pure theory, while Schmoller's German group emphasized the importance of inductive studies. JNK believed that both schools hold extreme views about the roles of inductive and deductive logic in economic research because methods are required to understand the way an economy functions. Inductive reasoning supplies general premises required for applying deductive logic, while deduction is required for developing general laws that are to be tested by inductive procedures. Thus, JNK suggested a syncretistic methodical approach to economic research.

3.3 Lionel Robbins

Lionel Charles Robbins was born in Sipson, west of London, on November 22, 1898. His father, Rowland Richard (1872–1960), was a farmer. Robbins's university education began at University College, London, which was interrupted by the First World War. He served in the Royal Field Artillery between 1916 and 1918 as an officer when he was wounded and returned home. After the war, he resumed his studies at the London School of Economics (LSE). He graduated with first-class honours in 1923 and began his graduate studies in economics in January 1924 with a research assistantship from William Beveridge, a famous British economist and liberal politician, then the Director of the London School of Economics and Political Science. He was an LSE lecturer from 1925 to 1927 and was promoted to political economics in 1929.

Robbins claims that the origins of his *Essay* went back to his early years at the LSE. Therefore, a review of his undergraduate education at the LSE and then his attempts at teaching introductory economics at Oxford and the LSE are critical to understanding the *Essay's* morals and motivation. He was puzzled about the nature and subject matter of economics in his undergraduate classes. This overwhelmed him during 1929-31 when he lectured on the subject at the introductory courses both in Oxford and the LSE. According to his lecture notes, he consolidated his famous definition of economics by the end of 1928, which also indicates the evolution of his views on the methodology of economics.

3.4 John Maynard Keynes

John Maynard Keynes (henceforth JMK) was born in Cambridge, Cambridgeshire, England, on June 5, 1883. He came from a middle-class family, and his father, John Neville Keynes, was a famous economist at University of Cambridge. Because of poor health, JMK was tutored at home by his mother and a governess. In January 1892, at the age of eight and a half, he began his regular studies at St Faith's preparatory school and soon became top of his class, excelling in mathematics. JMK won a scholarship to enroll at the Eton College in 1897, where he displayed remarkable intellectual abilities in a wide range of subjects, including mathematics, classics, and history. He left Eton for King's College, Cambridge, in 1902 to study mathematics. There JMK turned to economics under the influence of Alfred Marshall, leaving philosophy. He was very active in extra-curriculum activities. JMK was elected to the University Pitt Club and was an active member of the semi-secretive Cambridge Apostles society, a debating club primarily reserved for extraordinary undergraduate students. He was also elected President of the Cambridge Union Society and Cambridge University Liberal Club. Concerning religious views, he was known to be an atheist.

In May 1904, Keynes received a first-class B.A. in mathematics. Without enrolling in the graduate program, he remained at the university for the next two years, taking part in debates, studying philosophy, and informally attending graduate economics lectures for one term. This was his only formal education in the subject.

In 1906, he took civil service exams and began his career as a clerk in the India Office in October 1908. However, he soon got bored with his work and returned to Cambridge to work on probability theory in a project privately funded by his father and Professor Pigou. His debut in professional article writing began next with the publication of an article in *The Economic Journal*. He founded the Political Economy Club, a weekly discussion group and accepted a lectureship in economics that Alfred Marshall personally funded. In 1911, JMK was appointed the editor of *The Economic Journal* and published his first book, *Indian Currency and Finance*, in 1913. This publication got him appointed to the Royal Commission on Indian Currency and Finance.

In 1914, JMK went to London to serve the British Government at its request and took up an official position at the Treasury in January 1915, where his performance proved to be legendary. In 1917, he was appointed Companion of the Order of the Bath for his wartime work, which led to his appointment as the Treasury's financial representative to the Versailles Peace Conference in 1919. He attended the Versailles Peace Conference in Paris as an economic adviser to the British Prime Minister David Lloyd George. However, his experience at the conference was so disappointing that he resigned from his job and planned to begin an activist's role.

There were three principal players at Versailles—Prime Minister Lloyd George (Britain), Prime Minister Clemenceau (France), and President Woodrow Wilson (America)—who wanted to punish Germany for starting the war for different reasons. Accordingly, they imposed a war-compensation package, which virtually crippled Germany financially.

JMK published his book *The Economic Consequences of the Peace* in 1919, in which he analyzed the conditions of the war-ravaged German economy and predicted the draconian effects, which ordinary Germans have to suffer. This work demonstrated JMK's ability to utilize all his rare gifts—his passion and skill as an economist. In addition to economic analysis, the book contained pleas to the reader's sense of compassion:

> I cannot leave this subject as though it is just treatment wholly depended either on our pledges or on economic facts. The policy of reducing Germany to servitude for a generation, of degrading the lives of millions of human beings, and of depriving a whole nation of happiness should be abhorrent and detestable—abhorrent and detestable, even if it were possible, even if it enriched ourselves, even if it did not sow the decay of the whole civilized life of Europe (Cullinane 2012)

In 1921, JMK published *A Treatise on Probability*, which was an outstanding contribution to the philosophical and mathematical underpinnings of probability theory. Here, he defends the critical view that probabilities were no more or less than truth values intermediate between simple truth and falsity.

In 1922, JMK continued his campaign to reduce German reparations by publishing *A Revision of the Treaty*, and in 1923, he published *A Tract on Monetary Reform,* wherein he attacked the post-World War I deflation policies in Europe and America.

In the 1920s, JMK planned a theoretical work to examine the relationship between unemployment, money, and prices, which was published in two volumes as *Treatise on Money* in 1930. A central idea of the work is that the level of unemployment will rise if the quantity of money saved exceeds the quantity of money invested. The book's other key theme is the unreliability of financial indices for representing an accurate—or indeed meaningful—indication of general shifts in purchasing power of currencies over time.

However, JMK's most outstanding contribution to economics, his magnum opus, is *The General Theory of Employment, Interest and Money*, published in 1936. This book, written in the Great Depression (1929-1939), demonstrated the fundamental flaws in classical economics. The paradigm on which this conventional wisdom is founded is Say's law "supply creates its demand." In the long run, without any government intervention, all markets will be cleared as prices will adjust as required. The Great Depression unmasked this myth. JMK argued that the long-lasting downfall in the economic activities around the world is not a market problem; it is a problem of the economy. He introduced the concept of price stickiness, which argues that workers might refuse to reduce their wage demands, which the classical economists believe is rational. Because of this price stickiness, the interaction of "aggregate demand" and "aggregate supply" might create a stable unemployment equilibrium. Since this is a phenomenon of the economy, not a market one, the government, not the market, is responsible for unlocking the disequilibrium in the labour market. Therefore, the government needs to boost aggregate demand through its spending programs. Participating directly in economic activities by financing expended public programs is the main policy instrument in this regard.

Thus, *The General Theory* is nowadays considered the foundation of modern macroeconomics and JMK is credited for dividing economics into micro and macro compartments. The book revolutionized economic debates and discourses in the western world. Unfortunately, JMK could not participate in these intellectual activities as he suffered a massive heart attack in 1937. He began to recover in 1939. However, his professional energies were directed primarily toward public policy issues, the practical side of economics: allocating resources for the war efforts, post-war negotiations with America, and developing a new international financial order for the global economy. In particular, he was instrumental in creating the Bretton Woods monetary system, which included establishing two supra-national institutions—the International Monetary Fund and the World Bank—and later the General Agreement on Tariffs and Trade, which has eventually converted into the World Trade Organization.

JMK was decorated with many awards and offices for his extraordinary public services. In June 1942, he was rewarded with a hereditary peerage in the King's Birthday Honours; his title was gazetted as Baron Keynes of Tilton in the County of Sussex on July 7 that same year and participated in the House of Lords' session on the Liberal Party benches. This great economist died on April 21, 1946, at the age of 62.

3.5 Paul Anthony Samuelson

Paul Anthony Samuelson was born in Gary, Indiana, on May 15, 1915. His father, Frank Samuelson, was a pharmacist, and Ella née Lipton was his mother. Samuelson described his family as made up of upwardly mobile Polish immigrants who settled in Gary but moved to Chicago in 1923 due to financial reasons.

Samuelson graduated from the then Hyde Park High School and completed his Bachelor of Arts and Master of Arts degrees from Chicago University in 1935 and 1936. For his Ph.D. degree, he moved to Harvard, where he worked with Joseph Schumpeter, Wassily Leontief, Gottfried Haberler, and Alvin Hansen. After completing his Ph.D. from Harvard, Samuelson went to MIT in 1941 and worked as an assistant professor. Six years later, he became a full-time professor. He devoted his entire life to the service of MIT and remained there until his death.

His contributions to economics are enormous, recognized with various awards, including the second Nobel Prize in economic sciences. This great economist died on December 13, 2009, at the age of 94. Samuelson has left a legacy; on his shoulders stands the modern science of economics. Fortunately, before his death, he wrote the Centrist Proclamation for the 19th edition of his textbook *Economics*, demonstrating his motives and morals as an economist.

Samuelson was a mathematical hulk who became fascinated with economics in early 1932 when attending a lecture on the British economist Thomas Malthus. Henry Simons and Frank Knight also significantly influenced him to become an economist.

In the post-WWI period, British economists were engaged in two types of debates. The first includes the nature and scope of neoclassical economics, highlighted by the publications of three books discussed above. This debate mainly centres on equity and efficiency, dividing economists into two camps—Marshallian and Robbinsian/Paretian. The other debate was initiated by the prolonged depression on both sides of the Atlantic, which exposed the paucity of long-run equilibrium theory under the laisse-faire policy. In his *General Theory*, Keynes argued that the government has a role in streamlining the economy built on the institution of private property.

Samuelson, a mathematical genius, opened the door to controversy within the discipline by attempting to remedy the unnecessary objections among economists by mathematizing the language of economics, which he believed would reduce the potentials of disagreements or multi-interpretations. With this objective, he titled his Ph.D. thesis *Foundations of Analytical Economics,* completed in 1941, which came out as a book in 1946 with the title *Foundations of Economic Analysis*. Two years later, he summarized his revolutionary thoughts in an introductory textbook titled *Economics*. In this book, Keynes's General Theory was reinterpreted as macroeconomics. As a result, the study of economics was eventually divided into two compartments—microeconomics and macroeconomics.

Since the publication of the two books, economics as a branch of social science changed forever. First, his magnum opus, *Foundations of Economic Analysis*, spread the mathematical revolution in economics. Second, his introductory text dramatically changed the way economics was taught during the pre-WWII period.

3.5.1 The 19th Edition of Economics: A Centrist Proclamation

All introductory textbooks in economics lost their vitality and relevance by the end of World War II. To fill up the vacuum, the first edition of *Economics* appeared in 1948, which introduced macroeconomics into the post-secondary level economics courses. However, both the world and rigorous economic thinking at the frontier of the discipline changed dramatically over the years. To document these changes, the book became known as Samuelson-Nordhaus ECONOMICS, and every three years, the authors published a new edition. In his opinion, this 19th edition is the most remarkable, which is described as "the centrist edition." It proclaims that the mixed economy—which moderates the harsh principles of the market economy with fair-minded governmental oversight—is the right target for a country whose economy is founded on the institution of private property. In other words, centrism or the idea of a mixed economy model is the paradigm, which has guided the authors to compose different parts and chapters of the book. Accordingly the centrist proclamation is below in toto.

> Sciences advance. But they can also recede. That is true of economics as well. By the end of World War II, the leading introductory textbooks in economics had lost their vitality and relevance. Nature abhors a vacuum. The first edition of this textbook appeared as the 1948 edition of Samuelson's ECONOMICS. It introduced macroeconomics into our colleges and served as the gold standard for teaching economics in an increasingly globalized world.
>
> Both the economy and economics have changed greatly over the years. Successive editions of this textbook, which became Samuelson-Nordhaus ECONOMICS, have documented the evolutionary changes in the world economy and have provided the latest rigorous economic thinking at the frontier of the discipline.
>
> To our surprise, this nineteenth edition may be one of the most significant of all revisions. We call this the centrist edition. It proclaims the value of the mixed economy — an economy that combines the tough discipline of the market with fair-minded governmental oversight.
>
> Centrism is of vital importance today because the global economy is in a terrible meltdown — perhaps worse than any cyclical slump since the Great Depression of the 1930s. Alas, many textbooks have strayed too far toward over-complacent libertarianism. They joined the celebration of free-market finance and supported dismantling regulations and abolishing oversight. The bitter harvest of this celebration was seen in the irrationally exuberant housing and stock markets that collapsed and led to the current financial crisis.

The centrism we describe is not a prescription that is intended to persuade readers away from their beliefs. We are analysts and not cult prescribers. It is not ideology that breeds centrism as our theme. We sift facts and theories to determine the consequences of Hayek-Friedman libertarianism or Marx-Lenin bureaucratic communism. All readers are free to make up their own minds about best ethics and value judgments.

Having surveyed the terrain, this is our reading: Economic history confirms that neither unregulated capitalism nor overregulated central planning can organize a modern society effectively.

The follies of the left and right both mandate centrism. Tightly controlled central planning, which was widely advocated in the middle decades of the last century, was abandoned after it produced stagnation and unhappy consumers in communist countries.

What exactly was the road to serfdom that Hayek and Friedman warned us against? They were arguing against social security, a minimum wage, national parks, progressive taxation, and government rules to clean up the environment or slow global warming. People who live in high-income societies support these programs with great majorities. Such mixed economies involve both the rule of law and the limited liberty to compete.

We survey the centrist approach to economics in the pages that follow. Millions of students in China, India, Latin America, and emerging societies have sought economic wisdom from these pages. Our task is to make sure that the latest and best thinking of economists is contained here, describing the logic of the modern mixed economy, but always presenting in a fair manner the views of those who criticize it from the left and the right.

But we go a step further in our proclamation. We hold that there must be a limited centrism. Our knowledge is imperfect, and society's resources are limited.

We are also mindful of our current predicament. We see that unfettered capitalism has generated painful inequalities of income and wealth, and that supply-side fiscal doctrines have produced large government deficits. We observe that the major innovations of modern finance, when operating in an unregulated system, have produced trillions of dollars of losses and led to the ruin of many venerable financial institutions.

Only by steering our societies back to the limited center can we ensure that the global economy returns to full employment where the fruits of progress are more equally shared (Samuelson and Nordhaus 2010, xvi-xvii).

3.6 Concluding Commentary

The preceding paragraphs briefly describe the personal and professional profiles of five renowned economists selected for the purpose of this study. Let's now discuss their similarities and differences.

All our authors, except Robbins, were gifted mathematicians who chose to pursue economics in their professional lives. However, a significant difference is found in the way they applied their mathematical skills in their works. Marshall and JNK renounced their natural advantage, favouring a subject that was then considered a component of moral sciences. Both enriched their experience in philosophy through reading and association. Marshall, who made utmost efforts to dissociate political economy from moral sciences by establishing it as a branch of social science, discouraged any effort for mathematizing the economics language. JNK did the same by interpreting his logic in plain English. JMK did not enroll in the economics graduate program. Instead, he chose a career in public service, working for both the British government and the international community during the two world wars; however, he did not stick to it. Public service is a laboratory for economists to experiment with their theories. Here, they apply their theoretical knowledge to allocate scarce government revenues to the competing policy targets and assess their impacts on individual and social welfare. In public service, the two compartments of economics—positive and normative—find their true tests. Hence, instead of theorizing the definition, methodology, and scope of economics, JMK explained how the science is applied in a democratic political system.

From this perspective, Samuelson was completely different. He believed that the main source of disagreements in economics is its loose language, where he could make landmark contributions. Accordingly, he directed all his mathematical gifts to make the language of economics more rigorous by using advanced methods of calculus and matrix algebra. It was not his moral zeal for public welfare that inspired him to teach and research economics. On the contrary, he was motivated by the prospects of professional success in the discipline. In this regard, he differed from Marshall and the two Keynes.

Marshall, JNK, and JMK meet the requirements of able economists. They were social scientists who improved their natural capabilities through self-training and associations with relevant people. More specifically, their motives were more philosophical than scientific, which has been proven in their writing. To them, the *homo economicus* is not a selfish mechanical creature, solely motivated to earn and accumulate wealth without regard to what happens to others. HE is a caring person who pursues economic actions to maximize its interest—utility or profit—consistent with the laws of the land. A similar judgment cannot be awarded to Robbins. His personal and professional profiles do not suggest that he had significant interests in studying economics from social perspectives—whether welfare or enforcement of the law. To him, HE is a mechanically selfish creature who is solely motivated to earn and accumulate wealth without regard to what happens to others.

Robbins seems to be a poor choice in the company of such master economists. Intellectually, he did not show much promise, although he did complete his undergraduate from the LSE at the top of his class. However, he was a prolific writer and outstanding public speaker.

Vilfredo Pareto was the author of *Manual of Political Economy*. He had degrees in mathematical, physical, and engineering sciences from University of Turin and began his career as an engineer at the Joint Stock Railway Company of Florence in April 1870. He served the company for more than twenty years. In April 1892, Pareto joined University of Lausanne, Italy, as the chair of Political Economy and began his new career in economics and sociology. His educational and professional experience and his passion for classical Greek, Roman, and Renaissance humanistic literature influenced his academic interests. He was an ardent advocate of laissez-faire policies and later leaned toward fascism.

Pareto eloquently expresses his political passion in his famous book, the *Manual of Political Economy*, which begins with the three main objectives for studying political economy. The first objective is to gather useful prescriptions for private individuals and public authorities. Here the interest lies in private and social usefulness in the study of political economics. Second, the writer might have the right doctrine that shows all kinds of benefits to the nation and humanity. Once again, the purpose here is usefulness. The objectives differ in their practical and normative implications—the former is a collection of precepts, while the latter is a treatise on morality. Finally, the author might only search for uniformities among the concerned variables without worrying about giving recipes or precepts and without seeking happiness, benefits, or humanity's well-being or a part of it. Here, the writer's purpose is purely scientific; he/she wants to know and understand political economy, nothing more. Pareto's purpose in writing the *Manual* is the third one:

> I ought to warn the reader that in this Manual, I have in mind this third objective exclusively. It is not that I deprecate the other two; I sincerely intend to distinguish and separate the methods and to point out the one that will be adopted in this book (quoted in Elahi 2005, 25-26).

Robbins and Pareto agree with the objective of studying economics in a political system, which protects and promotes the institution of private property as a fundamental individual right. They believe in the general premise that science is free from value judgments, meaning economics cannot have a welfare objective. The overwhelming majority of economists seem to agree with them. However, if we look at the conditions created by COVID-19, we might want to re-examine our belief. All economists, including health economists, expect the government to rescue the economy and society from natural disasters.

In the following five chapters, we will examine the arguments and opinions of our five authors in light of professional and moral revelations.

CHAPTER IV
ALFRED MARSHALL: DEFINITION AND SUBSTANCE OF ECONOMICS

4.1 Introduction

This chapter reviews Marshall's arguments and opinions regarding the definition and scope (substance) of economics articulated in his *Principles of Economics* (1890). The review process is completed in three steps. First, Marshall's arguments and opinions are summarized section by section without interpretation. Second, these arguments and opinions are criticized under the heading—A Critical Commentary. Finally, the chapter ends with a conclusion. This three-step procedure will be followed in the subsequent four chapters.

Alfred Marshall was a leading figure in developing economics as a social science. He influenced the discipline intellectually as well as professionally. His most significant intellectual contribution is the development of the partial equilibrium model, articulated in the *Principles*. This model, on which the entire edifice of modern economics rests, has become the basic methodology of microeconomics. Marshall's professional contributions lie in his service as a leader and mentor whose two most famous pupils were John Maynard Keynes and Arthur Cecil Pigou.

Nevertheless, the influence of Marshall's contributions declined dramatically after WWII; today, he is regarded as a historical figure—a subject for the historians of economic thoughts. One reason he lost professional respect was due to his position on mathematics' role in the study of economic science. He was against mathematizing economics because mathematics is a deductive science while economics is fundamentally an inductive discipline. Therefore, the practical purpose for studying economics might be significantly lost if our conclusions are driven by mathematical logic rather than facts and experience.

State-of-the-art suggests that modern economists' preferences for abstract reasoning is critically responsible for the decay in the soundness and value of their research. For long, economists have been demonstrating more interest in fiction and pseudoscience than in facts and knowledge. In their eagerness to prove their mathematical genius, they have overlooked the critical teachings of the *Principles*, which may be found in four appendices added to Book I: (i) the growth of free industry and enterprise, (ii) the growth of economic science, (iii) scope and methodology of economics, and (iv) abstract reasoning. These appendices constitute the background information from which Marshall deduced the ideas and principles articulated in Book I. Accordingly, the following paragraphs summarize the main points of these appendices before presenting the ideas of Chapters I and II.

4.2 The Growth of Free Industry and Enterprise (Appendix A)

This appendix narrates the evolution of economic activities in the western hemisphere as "free industry and enterprise." In the vocabulary of modern economics, "free industry" is equivalent to "market economy," while "free enterprise" is synonymous with the firm. However, modern reviewers might not appreciate Marshall's discussions in Appendix A because they appear more imaginative than historical.

Marshall begins by describing the birth and evolution of agriculture in human civilizations and how it spread in the West. Agriculture, originally practiced in warm climates, was the first industry that initiated the evolution of human civilization. It involved cultivating crops by cleaning lands and domesticating animals. The evolution of *homo sapiens* in Africa testifies this truth. The development of agriculture was also the most critical element in the evolution of modern civilization because it introduced the idea, ownership, political conception, and the practice of private property. In those days, physical labour was the primary means of production as the stage of technology was very primitive. Farming, which was guided and regulated by the customs of inherited institutions and race qualities, was a self-sufficient family venture. Custom was "a crystallized form of oppression and suppression. The ruling tribes gave their energies to war and politics, not to industry." Therefore, there were few scopes for technological development during this period.

The unique feature of the social life of the time was that most villages were like extended families. These villages were ordinarily located near river basins, where lands were fertile and well-watered. These rivers also offered easy means of communication, suitable for simple forms of trade and division of labour.

However, the farming situation was completely different in ancient Greece, the birthplace of western civilizations. The country was composed of numerous mountainous islands, separated by the sea, whose soil was less suitable for crop production. Accordingly, the city-states of Greece were heavily dependent on food imports. Because of the country's unique position in the Mediterranean, it could control crucial trade routes and seaports in the region and collect revenues both through trade and piracy. Being culturally advanced, the Greeks thought themselves superior to all known races, whom they called barbarians, i.e., uncivilized or primitive. Therefore, for the Greeks, slavery was a natural institution, and enslaving members of other races was morally just.

In ancient Athens, the slave population was significantly higher than the Greek origins. This allowed the wealthy Greeks to put slaves in charge of agricultural and other economic activities, while focusing on politics and other cultural activities. For this reason, modern generations can learn very little from the Greeks about the economics of industry and enterprise. However, ancient Greece was the cradle of modern civilizations, not only in the western hemisphere but also throughout the world, because it achieved progress in arts, education, philosophy, and politics—critical elements for understanding modern economics. The Greeks were socially and intellectually free. Their male offspring spent time on military training, learning philosophy, and the art of rhetoric and demagogy. All this eventually helped the development of science—the true source of economic progress in human society.

With the decline in Greek power, civilization moved westwards to Rome. The Romans were a military power, not a great nation involved in economic and cultural developments. Ancient Rome was an agrarian and slave-based economy whose main concern was feeding the vast number of citizens and legionaries. However, its industry and commerce lacked public attention and investment because the Romans imported their necessities through military might, not bought the products of skilled workers in which the citizens took pride.

> Traffic and industry alike were pursued almost with a sole eye to the money gains to be derived from them; and the tone of business life was degraded by the public disdain which showed itself in the 'legal and practically effective restriction' of the Senators from all forms of business except those connected with the land (Marshall 1890, 420).

Despite economic defects, ancient Rome made tremendous contributions to jurisprudence and defining property rights that exerted a profound influence on the development of the economy and economic science. The Roman Law steadily enlarged the sphere of contract; gave it greater precision, elasticity, and strength. Eventually,

> social arrangements had come under its dominion; the property of the individual was clearly marked out, and

he could deal with it as he pleased. From the breadth and nobility of the Stoic character, modern lawyers have inherited a high standard of duty: and from its austere self-determination, they have derived a tendency to define sharply individual rights in property (Marshall 1890, 421).

The next European power was the Teutons, a Germanic tribe, which conquered Rome in the 2nd century B.C. The bonds of custom and ignorance also blinded them. They were overly attached to affections for their institutions and customs of their families and tribe. They prided themselves on their strength and energy and cared little for knowledge and arts, which eventually allowed the Saracens, the Muslims from the middle east, to overpower them. They learned the best lessons of the conquered people and nurtured arts and sciences. However, the climate and sensuality of their religion rapidly reduced their vigour, which made them incapable of exercising any significant influence on the problems of modern civilization.

Complete and direct self-government is a prerequisite for developing "free industry and enterprise," which did not begin until the end of the 18th century when America emerged as an independent state on the world map. During previous periods, the government was only controlled by a select few, who belonged to the privileged upper class, and treated ordinary workers as lower class. Accordingly, despite enjoying the freedom of managing their local affairs, these people lacked the courage, confidence, and an ambitious mind required for success in business ventures. Then both the central government and the local magnates curtailed the freedom of industry by prohibiting migration and levying taxes.

> Even those of the lower classes who were nominally free were plundered by arbitrary fines and dues levied under all manner of excuses, by the partial administration of justice, and often by direct violence and open pillage. These burdens fell chiefly on just those people who were

more industrious and thriftier than their neighbours—those among whom, if the country had been free, the spirit of bold enterprise would gradually have arisen to shake off the bonds of tradition and custom (Marshall 1890, 422).

Feudalism, which originated in the Teutonic race, played a critical role in the development of free industry and enterprise as it helped to develop the political habits of discipline and order among the dominant class and educated the common people. However, under the cover of outward "beauty," the system was ruthless and unclean, both physically and morally. In this situation, the Church, which helped the weak and diminished their suffering, was the only refuge. More importantly, however,

> the monasteries were the homes of industry, and in particular of the scientific treatment of agriculture: they were secure colleges for the learned, and they were hospitals and alms-houses for the suffering. The Church acted as a peace-maker in great matters and in small: the festivals and the markets held under its authority gave freedom and safety to trade (Marshall 1890, 424).

Nevertheless, the Church helped little to develop faculties of self-confidence and self-determination among the poor and oppressed. It helped many individuals endowed with exceptional natural talents to rise through the Church's own offices to the highest posts. Instead, the Church encouraged the forces of feudalism to keep the working classes ignorant, devoid of enterprise, and in every way dependent on those above them.

In this circumstance, the military force of feudalism would have weakened so much as to create chaos in society. This situation was prevented by the

> invention of printing, the Revival of Learning, the Reformation, and the discovery of the ocean routes to the New World and to India. Any one of these events alone would have been sufficient to make an epoch in history, but coming together as they did and working all

in the same direction, they effected a complete revolution (Marshall 1890, 425).

Although the Spanish Peninsula took the lead in the new maritime adventure, it moved northward to Holland and then to France and England, which eventually became the chief contenders of the ocean. In the race between the two superpowers, France ultimately gave in to the British monarchy.

The British empire, where the Sun never set, flourished rapidly. Economic, political, and cultural miracles happened in Europe due to two principal reasons—philosophical revival and the Industrial Revolution. The Middle Ages in Western Europe ended with the rise of the Renaissance, an enlightened period of cultural, artistic, political, and economic movements in Europe that took place from the 14th century to the 17th century. It helped rediscover classical philosophy, literature, and art. The second critical element in the development of free industry and enterprise was Scientific Revolution, the emergence of modern science in Europe toward the end of the Renaissance period and continued through the late 18th century. During this period, mathematics, physics, astronomy, biology (including human anatomy), and chemistry transformed society's views about nature. All these culminated in what made the western hemisphere truly the master of the universe—the industrial revolution. This phase of European history (1760 to 1840) reflects the transition of agrarian and artisan economic structures to new manufacturing processes in Europe and the United States. This transition included extensive use of machines in production, new chemical manufacturing and iron production processes, the increasing use of steam and water power, the development of machine tools, and the rise of the mechanized factory system. Therefore, the Industrial Revolution transformed the feudalist mode of production into the capitalist one in which the ownership of capital dominated both social and political lives in the state.

Marshall believes that the custom of primogeniture was also a reason for the rapid transformation of a feudalist society to a capitalist one in England because the younger sons of noble families sought their fortunes among ordinary people.

This fusion of different ranks tended to make politics business-like, while it warmed the veins of business adventure with the generous daring and romantic aspirations of noble blood (Marshall 1890, 427).

The freedom of industry and enterprise inspired smart individuals to train in special skills and trades and seek the best employment of their labour and capital. These chained activities produced a complex industrial organization, small and big, with the division of labour. The most vital aspect of the Industrial Revolution was the emergence of the class of "business undertakers." This process had originated in England's agriculture. Farmers, who were willing to take risks, rented land from the landlords for cultivation with hired labour. In the same way, entrepreneurs or business undertakers borrowed capital from financial institutions and developed their own businesses.

In the new system of business undertaking, the critical issue was labour value. Until the 18th century, the undertakers of manufacturing industries could hire labour both as retail and wholesale inputs. However, beginning in the 19th century, the rule changed, and the value of labour, an industrial input, began to be determined by the forces of market demand and supply. This new organization of industry, it was claimed, significantly improved production efficiency because under competitive market structure, labour is supposed to be employed in its best job. This argument, however, ignores the fact that the labour market, in general, is imperfectly competitive. In many cases, the structure of the labour market is entirely monopsonist. Oligopoly is certainly the standard labour market structure. All countries in which the "free industry and enterprise" has given birth to a class of business undertakers suffer from this evil nature of economic freedom. Now first are we getting to understand the extent to which the capitalist employer, untrained to his new duties, was tempted to subordinate the well-being of his workpeople to his own desire for gain; now first are we learning the importance of insisting that the rich have duties as well as rights in their individual and in their collective capacity; now first is the economic problem of the new age showing itself to us as it really is. This is partly due to a wider knowledge and a growing earnestness. But however wise and virtuous our grandfathers had been, they could not have seen things as we do, for they were hurried along by urgent necessities and terrible disasters (Marshall 1890, 434).

The most important job of an economist is to suggest necessary policy instruments to protect the ordinary people from the economic exploitation of the "capitalist class."

4.2.1 Critical Commentary

This appendix narrates the evolution of economic activities in the western hemisphere as the "free industry and enterprise." Nowadays, this phrase is interpreted by two terms—"market economy" and "the firm." Although Marshall's discussion is substantial, it is not necessarily substantive because he ignores the contributions of two original authors—John Locke and Karl Marx—whose writings are at the centre of all controversies about politics and economics. A modern nation-state is founded on two social systems—one political and another economic. The political system, which defines and determines law and order in society, regulates the behaviour of its residents while the economic system engages individuals to produce the means of subsistence and comforts.

The fundamental methods of livelihood revolve around a single economic institution— property—which a nation-state can control under two different political philosophies. The first, practiced from time immemorial, is called the institution of private property. John Locke, the author of the theory of democratic nation-state, was the first philosopher who argued that owning and accumulating private property is an inviolable individual right, which no legitimate government can violate. Therefore, the institution of private property becomes the fundamental pillar of the economy of a democratic political system. On the other hand, Karl Marx thought this institution fundamentally exploitative, meaning political and economic justice cannot be served in a civilized society without abolishing it in principle.

Economics is a social science that studies how an economy is supposed to be regulated once the nation-state has adopted its economic philosophy concerning the institution of private property. The economics we study investigates the cause-and-effect relations among variables of an economy founded on this institution. This kind of nation-state considers the possession of private property as an inviolable individual right. This theory, as mentioned above, comes directly from John Locke. Marshall overlooked this history when discussing the growth of industry and enterprise, meaning Appendix A weakens the quality of discussion on the definition and substance of economic science. Accordingly, modern readers might find it difficult to see how his notions of "material welfare in the ordinary business of life" are related to the study of economics, which is primarily concerned with developing theories through generalizations.

4.3 The Growth of Economic Science (Appendix B)

Appendix A traced the roots of economic freedom (free industry) in the western world; Appendix B is intended to trace the parallel growth in economic science. The present-day social conditions might have origins in early Aryan and Semitic institutions, but they little influenced the modern economic speculations. Similarly, although modern economics developed together with other sciences during the periods of Reformations and Renaissance, the industrial system, founded on slavery and philosophy, which disdained manufacturing and commerce, had little in common with the brave citizens. They were proud of their trade and shares in governing the State.

In the middle of the 18th century, Quesnay, a French economist and intellectual leader of the physiocrats, made the first systematic approach to develop the political economy as a branch of social science. The physiocrats, who believed in the principle of obedience to Nature, first proclaimed the doctrine of "free trade" as a broad principle of action. However, they failed to advance their theory because

> they confused the ethical principle of conformity to Nature, which is expressed in the imperative mood, and prescribes certain laws of action, with those causal laws which science discovers by interrogating Nature, and which are expressed in the indicative mood (Marshall 1890, 438).

Adam Smith, who was aided by the excellent works of his friend David Hume, rescued the science from this dilemma by publishing his Magna Carter, *The Wealth of Nations,* in 1776.

> He resided a long time in France in personal converse with the Physiocrats; he made a careful study of the English and French philosophy of his time, and he got to know the world practically by wide travel and by intimate association with Scotch men of business. To these advantages, he added unsurpassed powers of observation, judgment, and reasoning. The result is that wherever he differs from his predecessors, he is more nearly right than they; there is scarcely any economic truth now known of which he did not get some glimpse. And since he was the first to write a treatise on wealth in all its chief social respects, he might on this ground alone have a claim to be regarded as the founder of modern economics (Marshall 1890, 439).

He developed the physiocratic doctrine of free trade with so much practical wisdom, and with so much knowledge of the actual conditions of business, as to make it a great force in real life, and he is most widely known both here and abroad for his argument that Government generally harms by interfering in trade. While giving many instances of how self-interest may lead the individual trader to act injuriously to the community, he contended that even when the Government acted with the best intentions, it nearly always served the public worse than the enterprise of the individual trader however selfish he might happen to be. So great an impression did he make on the world by his defence of this doctrine that most German writers have it chiefly in view when they speak of Smithianismus (Marshall 1890, 439).

Nevertheless, the *Inquiry* was not his critical contribution to economic science. His chief critical contribution was "to combine and develop the speculations of his French and English contemporaries and predecessors as to value." His ingenious merits lie in making an epoch in economic thought. He first made a careful and scientific inquiry into how value measures human motive both on the consumption and production sides—consumers reveal their motives through their demand to purchase wealth, while efforts and sacrifices (real cost of production) undergone by the producers reflect their motives to earn profits.

Adam Smith introduced political economy as a branch of social science, which his contemporaries and immediate successors pushed forward speedily but in the wrong direction.

> There is then some justice in the charges frequently brought against the English economists of the beginning of the last century that they neglected to inquire with sufficient care whether a greater range might not be given to collective as opposed to individual action in social and economic affairs and that they exaggerated the strength

of competition and its rapidity of action: and there is some ground, though a very slight one, for the charge that their work is marred by a certain hardness of outline and even harshness of temper. These faults were partly due to Bentham's direct influence, partly to the spirit of the age of which he was an exponent. But they were partly also due to the fact that economic study had again got a good deal into the hands of men whose strength lay in vigorous action rather than in philosophical thought (Marshall 1890, 440-41).

In this regard, the theory of currency could be considered an exception because human motives, except the desire for wealth, are of little consequence. Accordingly, Ricardo, who led the brilliant school of deductive reasoning, was on safe ground. Finally, the economists dealt with the theory of foreign trade and corrected Smith's flaws. However, in economics, pure deductive reasoning is suitable for the theory of money, meaning the critical considerations in the economic analysis involve inductive reasoning, i.e., economic inquiries should be guided by facts and observations than deductive logic.

The English economists were not negligent about economic facts in their studies. Tooke, McCulloch, and Porter ably continued the statistical studies of Petty, Young, Eden, and others. In this regard, the parliamentary inquiries into the working classes' condition, in which economists contributed significantly, are outstanding examples of using inductive reasoning in economics.

Nevertheless, a certain degree of narrowness characterized the works of Hume, Smith, Young, and others. This narrowness concerned their failure to study history on a systematic plan.

In consequence, the writers of that time, able and earnest as they were in their search for the actual facts of life, worked rather at haphazard. They overlooked whole groups of facts that we now see to be of vital importance, and they often failed to make the best use of those they collected. And this narrowness was intensified when they passed from the collection of facts to general reasoning about them (Marshall 1890, 441-42).

The primary flaw of these classical economists was that they did not "allow enough for the dependence of man's character on his circumstances." For example, Ricardo and his followers regarded the economic agent as "a constant quantity" who had no variations. To them, all Englishmen were city dwellers whom they knew intimately. This conceptual infirmity was particularly harmful in studies that concern different cultures and countries. They were aware of the peculiarities of people living in different countries but seemed to regard those peculiarities as superficial, which were removable as soon as they realized that Englishmen could teach them better techniques.

> The same bent of mind that led our lawyers to impose English civil law on the Hindus led our economists to work out their theories on the tacit supposition that the world was made up of city men. And though this did little harm so long as they were treating money and foreign trade, it led them astray as to the relations between the different industrial classes (Marshall 1890, 442).

However, these economists' most harmful flaw was that they failed to realize how much the habits and institutions of the industry are liable to change. More specifically, they "did not see that the poverty of the poor is the chief cause of that weakness and inefficiency which are the causes of their poverty." The socialists underlined the possibility of perfecting human nature but failed to make progress because they offered little historical and scientific evidence to back up their views.

> The socialists did not study the doctrines they attacked, and there was no difficulty in showing that they had not understood the nature and efficiency of the existing economic organization of society. The economists, therefore, did not trouble themselves to examine carefully any of their doctrines, and least of all their speculations as to human nature (Marshall 1890, 442).

During the progress in economic thought, a fundamental change took place in treating man's character and efficiency, which became particularly noticeable in the study of wealth distribution. While the earlier economists regarded this natural and social variable as a fixed quantity, the modern economists treated it as a product of the circumstances. This change in viewpoint was caused by three factors: (i) changes in human nature during the last fifty years, (ii) the direct influence of individual writers, socialists, and others, and (iii) the indirect influence of a similar change in some branches of natural science.

As noted before, natural sciences made extraordinary progress at the beginning of the 18th century under a universal premise—the subject matter of each branch of science is "constant and unchanged in all countries and all ages." The developments in the "mathematico-physical group of sciences" were gradually caught up by the biological group of sciences by the end of the century.

> They were learning that if the subject matter of science passes through different stages of development, the laws that apply to one stage will seldom apply without modification to others; the laws of the science must have a development corresponding to that of which they treat. The influence of this new notion gradually spread to the sciences, which relate to man and showed itself in the works of Goethe, Hegel, Comte, and others (Marshall 1890, 443).

The speculations and discoveries of biology now had the world's attention, as had physics years earlier, which introduced marked changes "in the tone of the moral and historical sciences."

> Economics has shared in the general movement and is getting to pay every year greater attention to the pliability of human nature and how the character of man affects and is affected by the prevalent methods of the production, distribution, and consumption of wealth (Marshall 1890, 443).

J. S. Mill introduced this approach in his remarkable *Principles of Political Economy*, which distinguished humans from the mechanical element.

Simultaneously, "a higher notion of social duty" had been spreading in the political and social podiums—the Parliament, the press, and the pulpit. These mediums began to speak the spirit of humanity with distinction and earnestness.

> Mill and the economists who have followed him have helped this general movement onwards, and they, in their turn, have been helped onwards by it. Partly for this reason, partly in consequence of the modern growth of historical science, their study of facts has been broader and more philosophic.
>
> Thus, in every way, economic reasoning is now more exact than it was: the premises assumed in any inquiry are stated with more rigid precision than formerly. However, this greater exactness of thought is partly destructive in its action; it is showing that many of the older applications of general reasoning were invalid because no care had been taken to think out all the assumptions that were implied and to see whether they could fairly be made in the special cases under discussion. As a result, many dogmas have been destroyed, which appeared to be simple only because they were loosely expressed; but which, for that very reason, served as an armoury with which partisan disputants (chiefly of the capitalist class) have equipped themselves for the fray (Marshall 1890, 444).

The lead in the modern science of economics undoubtedly came from the English economists, but the reception of their ideas varied from one country to another. The "French school" pursued the path laid out by its great thinkers of the 18th century and avoided many errors and confusion, specifically concerning wages, which were "common among the second rank of English economists."

From the time of Say downwards, it has done a great deal of useful work. In Cournot, it has had a constructive thinker of the highest genius, while Fourier, St Simon, Proudhon, and Louis Blanc have made many of the most valuable, as well as many of the wildest suggestions of Socialism (Marshall 1890, 445).

The "American school," which was protectionists, began to underline the importance of free industry, enterprise, and free trade under the influence of some new thinkers. Economic science also showed signs of renewed vigour in two of its old homes—Holland and Italy. However, it was the "German school" that made the most significant contributions in modern economics. It acknowledged Adam Smith's leadership but was "irritated more than any others" by the insular narrowness and self-confidence of the Ricardian school. More specifically, it protested English advocates' theory of transporting the free trade model of a manufacturing country to an agricultural country without modification. The "German school" insisted that "physiocrats and Adam Smith's school downplayed the importance of national life by underlining selfish individualism and a limp philanthropic cosmopolitanism."

The "German school" took the lead in the comparative study of both economics and general history.

They have brought side by side the social and industrial phenomena of different countries and different ages; have so arranged them that they throw light upon and interpret one another, and have studied them all in connection with the suggestive history of jurisprudence. They have given their chief attention to the historical treatment of the science and its application to the conditions of German social and political life, especially to the economic duties of the German bureaucracy. But led by the brilliant genius of Hermann, they have made careful and profound analyses that add much to our knowledge, and they have greatly extended the boundaries of economic theory (Marshall 1890, 446).

German thought also inspired the study of socialism and the functions of the State.

It is from German writers, some of whom have been of Jewish origin, that the world has received the greater part of the most thoroughgoing of recent propositions for utilizing the property of the world for the benefit of the community with but little reference to the existing incidents of ownership. It is true that on closer investigation, their work turns out to be less original as well as less profound than at first sight appears: but it derives great power from its dialectic ingenuity, its brilliant style, and in some cases, from its wide-reaching though distorted historical learning (Marshall 1890, 446).

4.3.1 Critical Commentary

The origin of modern economics is often traced to the writings of the great Greek philosopher Aristotle. Marshall followed this tradition in initiating his discussions about the growth of the industry and of economic science. Accordingly, this part of the commentary reviews Marshall's arguments in light of Aristotle's political and economic philosophies.

Aristotle divided his philosophy about the freemen and their existence into two parts—moral and political. The *Nicomachean Ethics* presents his moral philosophy, while *Politics* presents his political philosophy. The two books together describe how the freemen could achieve the ultimate end of life—to be happy, i.e., to live a good life.

Aristotle begins the Nicomachean Ethics with these words: *"Every art and every inquiry, and similarly every action and pursuit, is thought to aim at some good; and for this reason, the good has rightly been declared to be that at which all things aim."* However, their ends are not always the same. Sometimes, the activities they carry out are themselves the ends; sometimes, the ends are products of their activities. For example, food is eaten to satisfy hunger, while a house is built for both protection and comfort, meaning these activities and their ends are different.

This is the nature of human behaviour; we ordinarily do things for the sake of achieving something else. Therefore, the best thing in life, Aristotle says, is the one which is done for its own sake. The best thing in a freeman's life is "living a good life" or "living well." Thus, achieving happiness in life is the ultimate end of human life. Freemen can achieve happiness only by living in the state, a political community or association. So, Aristotle concludes that man is, by nature, a *political animal* and the state before man's creation.

The objective of ancient Greek philosophy was to explain why a freeman ought to obey laws if he does not have to (Lee 1987). In other words, the Greek philosophers attempted to explain why freemen must obey laws if they have enough power to ignore the government. However, the economic and political situations of 17th century Europe were dramatically different. The authority of the monarchy—the divine institution that ruled the nation-states—came under challenge from the propertied class. In this situation, Locke articulated his theory of politics and governance, which argued that all men, not just the propertied, are naturally free. They inherit certain natural rights, which no government can violate. One of these inviolable entitlements includes the right to own and accumulate property. The sole purpose of establishing a government in human society is to protect and promote these rights. By this declaration, Locke made the institution of private property the fundamental pillar of the economy of a democratic state. Accordingly, as a social science discipline, economics is supposed to study those issues of the economy that are directly related to achieving the fundamental end of democracy.

4.3.1.1 Controversial Issues

When Marshall's description of the growth of economic science is closely examined, the modern generations of economists might not be satisfied. First, he made the same mistake that classical and other neoclassical economists had made—he ignored Locke's theory about how property is created in a civilized society, meaning he did not analyze private property institutions from their political context. As mentioned before, Locke philosophized that the application of human labour is the only way property can be created in a civilized society. If properties are distributed based on Locke's principle, then the question of exploitation can never come up for debate, meaning that wealth has been accumulated in human societies by violating Locke's principle from time immemorial. If we stick to professional virtue and read Marx's surplus-value theory carefully, we will see the reasons for present-day economic inequality. Marshall also ignored Marx.

Second, Adam Smith wrote two treatises—*Theory of Moral Sentiments* (TMS) and *The Nature and Causes of the Wealth of Nations* (WN). During the 1840s and 1850s, some German economists argued that Smith's view on human psychology expressed in the two books is not consistent. While the TMS underlines that sympathy is a fundamental feature of human nature, the WN is written on the premise that selfishness is the primary factor that drives individuals in economic undertakings. This controversial observation by the German intellectuals helped create the *Das Adam Smith Problem*, which still attracts some economists' attention.

The following two stanzas from the WN are responsible for creating this controversy:

> Every individual… neither intends to promote the public interest, nor knows how much he is promoting it… he intends only his own security; and by directing that industry in such a manner as its produce may be of the greatest value, he intends only his own gain, and he is in

this, as in many other cases, led by an invisible hand to promote an end which was no part of his intention. ... It is not from the benevolence of the butcher, the brewer, or the baker, that we expect our dinner but from their regard to their own interest. We address ourselves, not to their humanity but their self-love, and never talk to them of our necessities but of their advantages (Smith 1776).

These messages are destined to create confusion and controversy when taken out of context. Adam Smith did not detail the philosophy of human nature because analyzing the subject is of little interest to the economic profession. The subject is a philosophical issue and, therefore, deserves to be investigated in philosophical discourses. However, economic activities are guided by human nature because it controls our passions and emotions, which are directly related to economic actions and activities. Hence, economists must construct their discipline based on the premise, which explains the nature of human behaviour under the institution of private property. Adam Smith, a master moral philosopher, made human selfishness a foundational premise of his political economy without spending any effort to explain it. Latter economists, intentionally or out of ignorance, introduced philosophical debates in economic discourses.

Whether individuals behave selfishly or not is a subject of philosophical discussion, not economic analysis. This being an ethical issue should be discussed in that forum, perhaps as a special topic. However, the science of economics is concerned with deriving theories and principles concerning relations among economic variables that are consequences of human nature related to wealth. Thus, assuming motives behind economic actions is critical to deriving any economic theory or law. JNK details this point, which will be discussed later. Moreover, this motive must be selfish if we are to study the operation of a private commodity market where the forces of demand and supply determine the price. Has any altruistic economist argued that these supply and demand functions can be derived with an altruistic motive?

4.3.1.2 Constructive Issues

Marshall must be praised for underlining the methodological truth that Adam Smith's most critical contribution in economics lies in connecting empirical measurement of value with human motives. His observation seems consistent with Aristotle's ethical theory of end, which differentiates between motives for undertaking specific activities and those activities' outcomes. This is possibly the most fundamental reason for disagreements among economists about the nature and scope of economics. For example, according to Robbins, a producer's primary motive is to accumulate wealth. However, by Aristotle's philosophy, wealth creation is not the primary motive. Individuals create wealth because it enables them to enjoy what they desire—comforts and conveniences, power and social recognition, etc. Since these desires vary from one individual to another, the motives behind economic undertakings must also vary.

4.4 The Scope and Method of Economics (Appendix C)

4.4.1 Scope

Some writers, following Comte, argue that "the scope of any profitable study of man's action in society must be coextensive with the whole of social science." According to these authors, attempts to create a separate social science to study a specific aspect of humanity will be futile because this particular feature of human behaviour might not be satisfactorily isolated from all others. Therefore, they advise economists to abandon their efforts for creating distinct social science and direct them toward establishing a unified and all-embracing social science.

However, this opinion is unsustainable because human actions and activities in modern society are "too wide and too various to be analyzed and explained by a single intellectual effort." Comte and Spencer, although gifted with "unsurpassed knowledge and great genius," wrote little about how to construct a unified social science. Instead, they only left behind ideas about this so-called unified social science through broad surveys and suggestive hints.

> The physical sciences made slow progress so long as the brilliant but impatient Greek genius insisted on searching after a single basis for the explanation of all physical phenomena, and their rapid progress in the modern age is due to a breaking up of broad problems into their component parts. Doubtless, there is a unity underlying all the forces of nature, but whatever progress has been made toward discovering it has depended on knowledge obtained by persistent specialized study, no less than on occasional broad surveys of the field of nature as a whole. And similar patient detailed work is required to supply the materials that may enable future ages to understand better than we can the forces that govern the development of the social organism (Marshall 1890, 448).

However, Comte must be commended for his insistence that even the natural scientists specializing in each field have a duty to keep close and constant correspondence with their colleagues engaged in neighbouring areas.

> Specialists who never look beyond their own domain are apt to see things out of true proportion; much of the knowledge they get together is of comparatively little use; they work away at the details of old problems which have lost most of their significance and have been supplanted by new questions arising out of new points of view, and they fail to gain that large illumination which the progress of every science throws by comparison and analogy on those around it. Comte did good service, therefore, by

insisting that the solidarity of social phenomena must render the work of exclusive specialists even more futile in social than in physical science.

But, as Mill urges, Comte only proves what no thoughtful person would deny, that a person is not likely to be a good economist who is nothing else. Social phenomena acting and reacting on one another, they cannot rightly be understood apart; but this by no means proves that the material and industrial phenomena of society are not themselves susceptible of useful generalizations, but only that these generalizations must necessarily be relative to a given form of civilization and a given stage of social advancement (Marshall 1890, 448).

4.4.2 Methodology: Deductive vs. Inductive

All social sciences, including economics, employ deductive as well as inductive reasoning methods. However, in economics, the basic research methodology is induction, not deduction. In this regard, the economists have one advantage compared to their colleagues engaged in other social sciences, which lies in the clarity of the cause-effect relations. For example, if the price of an ordinary commodity rises, our mind, without any support from our faculty of understanding, will predict that its demand is likely to be negatively affected. Such precision is not possible in the case of sociology or political science. However, this deductive advantage does not suggest that economists can forge chains of reasoning. This feature of economic relations helps to forge many "short chains and single connecting links." Marshall defends his argument by citing Gustav Friedrich Schmoller (1838-1917), a reputed German economist:

> To obtain a knowledge of individual causes, we need induction; the conclusion of which is indeed nothing but the inversion of the syllogism which is employed in

deduction... Induction and deduction rest on the same tendencies, the same beliefs, the same needs of our reason (Marshall 1890, 450).

This feature of economic relations tasks the economists with a critical job that determines the quality of conclusions and predictions of their research.

> If the economist reasons rapidly and with a light heart, he is apt to make bad connections at every turn of his work. He needs to make careful use of analysis and deduction, because only by their aid can he select the right facts, group them rightly, and make them serviceable for suggestions in thought and guidance in practice; and because, as surely as every deduction must rest based on inductions, so surely does every inductive process involve and include analysis and deduction. *Or to put the same thing in another way, the explanation of the past and the prediction of the future are not different operations, but the same worked in opposite directions, the one from effect to cause, the other from cause to effect* [emphasis added] (Marshall 1890, 450).

No economic event can be explained soundly without identifying the factors that affected it and discovering how they had done so individually. Accordingly, our explanation is always susceptible to error if our knowledge of these factors is imperfect. When

> our knowledge and analysis are complete, we are able by merely inverting our mental process to deduce and predict the future almost as certainly as we could have explained the past on a similar basis of knowledge. It is only when we go beyond a first step that a great difference arises between the certainty of prediction and the certainty of explanation: for any error made in the first step of prediction will be accumulated and intensified in the second; while in interpreting the past, the error is not so likely to be accumulated; for observation or recorded

history will probably bring a new check at each step. The same processes, both inductive and deductive, are used in nearly the same way in the explanation of a known fact in the history of the tides and in the prediction of an unknown fact (Marshall 1890, 450).

It is true our observation or history might tell us whether two events happened at the same time or one before the other. However, this information cannot tell us whether the first was the cause of the second.

That can be done only by reason acting on the facts. When it is said that a certain event in history teaches this or that, a formal reckoning is never made for all the conditions which were present when the event happened; some are tacitly, if not unconsciously, assumed to be irrelevant. This assumption may be justifiable in any particular case, but it may not. Wider experience, more careful inquiry, may show that the causes to which the event is attributed could not have produced it unaided; perhaps even that they hindered the event, which was brought about in spite of them by other causes that have escaped notice (Marshall 1890, 451).

This reasoning controversy is rampant in the intellectual world. Whenever an argument is met with opposition, it is considered to be a sort of trial. Critics offer challenging explanations with new facts; "the old facts are tested and rearranged, and in some cases shown to support the opposite conclusion from that on behalf of which they were at first invoked." This is done by ignoring the truth that two economic events cannot be alike in all respects.

And if we are dealing with the facts of remote times, we must allow for the changes that have meanwhile come over the whole character of economic life: however closely a problem of today may resemble in its outward incidents another recorded in history, it is probable that a closer examination will detect a fundamental difference between their real characters. Till this has been made, no valid argument can be drawn from one case to the other (Marshall 1890, 451).

This difficulty in interpreting past events in current economic research makes it important to examine the relationship between economic theory and economic history critically. As a part of general history, economic history informs us about the nature of past social institutions and the consequences of their policies. For this type of work, little intensive analysis is needed; an active and inquiring mind can easily do the job.

Saturated with a knowledge of the religious and moral, the intellectual and aesthetic, the political and social environment, the economic historian may extend the boundaries of our knowledge and may suggest new and valuable ideas, even though he may have contended himself with observing those affinities and those causal relations which lie near the surface (Marshall 1890, 451).

Much of this work needs little more than common sense and wit, a sound sense of proportion, and extensive life experience, not detailed scientific inquiry. However, this intuitive methodology cannot conduct all types of economic research.

Natural instinct will select rapidly and combine justly considerations that are relevant to the issue at hand, but it will select chiefly from those which are familiar; it will seldom lead a man far below the surface or far beyond the limits of his personal experience. And it happens that in economics, neither those effects of known causes nor those causes of known effects that are most patent are generally the most important. 'That which is not seen' is often better worth studying than that 'which is seen' (Marshall 1890, 555).

This is particularly true if the purpose of the research is not to deal with current or temporary interests; the purpose is "seeking guidance in the construction of a far-reaching policy for the public good; or if, for any other reason, we are concerned less with immediate causes, than with causes of causes."

Economics has advanced more rapidly and aggressively than its neighbouring fields because it is more definite and exact than any other. However, widening its scope will invariably involve some loss of its scientific precision. In this regard, there is no hard and fast rule to determine whether this loss of precision is worth more or less gain resulting from its greater breadth of outlook.

> There is a large debatable ground in which economic considerations are of considerable but not dominant importance, and each economist may reasonably decide for himself how far he will extend his labours over that ground. He will be able to speak with less and less confidence the further he gets away from his central stronghold, and the more he concerns himself with conditions of life and with motives of action which cannot be brought to some extent at least within the grasp of the scientific method. Whenever he occupies himself largely with conditions and motives, the manifestations of which are not reducible to any definite standard, he must forego nearly all aid and support from the observations and the thought of others at home and abroad, in this and earlier generations; he must depend mainly on his own instincts and conjectures; he must speak with all the diffidence that belongs to an individual judgment. But if, when straying far into less known and less knowable regions of social study, he does his work carefully, and with full consciousness of its limitations, he will have done excellent service (Marshall 1890, 556).

4.4.3 Critical Commentary

Unlike the preceding two appendices, the present and the following ones make lasting contributions to studying the science of economics. Marshall's arguments about the scope and the subject matter of economics are again consistent with Aristotle's theory of "Golden Mean." According to this theory, virtue is the mean between two extremes—excess and deficiency—both of which are vices. For example, courage constitutes the middle point between cowardice—extreme deficiency, and recklessness—extreme excess.

Marshall's criticisms of Comte and Spencer concerning a unified social science are most logical. His commendations about Comte's insistence about keeping our eyes open at the neighbouring fields of study are equally crucial for developing economics as a social science. However, Robbins's unqualified emphasis on the meaning of the word "economic" and using opportunity cost as the barometer to determine whether an "economic action" is eligible to be included in the subject matter of economics does not widen the scope of economic investigations. Instead, this suggestion makes the study of economics less useful to society.

Marshall's observations concerning the methodology of economic investigations are perhaps more critical today than when he highlighted them. Economics is an empirical science, meaning its basic methodology is supposed to be inductive. As such, its theories and laws are deduced through observation, analysis, and continuous verification. Through this scientific process, economists first explain the cause-and-effect relations among economic variables, which, in turn, become predictions for a future time. Thus, explanations and predictions are just two sides of the same coin. In this whole process, deductive reasoning has but a small role.

4.5 Uses of Abstract Reasoning in Economics (Appendix D)

The principal methodology of economic research is induction, which assembles facts, arranges and analyzes them, and infers general statements or principles through analysis and deduction.

> Then for a while, deduction plays the chief role: it brings some of these generalizations into association with one another, works from them tentatively to new and broader generalizations or laws, and then calls on induction again to do the main share of the work in collecting, sifting, and arranging these facts to test and 'verify' the new law (Marshall 1890, 557).

Therefore, there is no room for long trains of deductive reasoning in economics. Even the frequent use of mathematical formulas in economic studies does not violate this principle. The contrary only occurs when "a pure mathematician uses economic hypotheses for the purpose of mathematical diversions; for then his concern is to show the potentialities of mathematical methods on the supposition that material appropriate to their use had been supplied by economic study." Nevertheless, an economist needs to learn mathematical sciences because their "terse and exact languages" help concisely and clearly express specific economic laws and relations.

> If we shut our eyes to realities, we may construct an edifice of pure crystal by imaginations that will throw sidelights on real problems and might conceivably be of interest to beings who had no economic problems at all like our own. Such playful excursions are often suggestive in unexpected ways: they afford good training to the mind: and seem to be productive only of good, so long as their purpose is clearly understood (Marshall 1890, 557).

Deductive logic or abstract reasoning serves the logical function of studying economics when its purpose is fully understood. Disagreements over understanding this purpose seem to be a problem in economic research. For example, money is the medium of exchange through which modern economies function. Most economists understand that money-earning is the object of human motive. To them, money and wealth are synonymous. However, the function of money in economics should be seen from a wholly different angle. It is a measure of motive.

> When we want to induce a man to do anything for us, we generally offer him money. It is true that we might appeal to his generosity or sense of duty, but this would be calling into action latent motives that are already in existence rather than supplying new motives. If we have to supply a new motive, we generally consider how much money will just make it worth his while to do it (Marshall 1890, 557-58).

Nevertheless, from a theoretical perspective, this function of money is a mere "accident."

> It is quite possible that there may be worlds in which no one ever heard of private property in material things or wealth as it is generally understood, but public honours are meted out by graduated tables as rewards for every action that is done for others' good. If these honours can be transferred from one to another without the intervention of any external authority, they may serve to measure the strength of motives just as conveniently and exactly as money does with us. In such a world, there may be a treatise on economic theory very similar to the present, even though there might be little mention in it of material things and no mention at all of money (Marshall 1890, 558).

This point would have meant little if people's minds had not been misled by the perception that money is "an exclusive regard for material wealth to the neglect of other and higher objects of desire." People unequivocally neglect money's role in economics as an economic motive.

The only conditions required in a measure for economic purposes are that it should be something definite and transferable. Its taking of a material form is practically convenient but is not essential.

The pursuit of abstractions is a good thing when confined to its proper place. But the breadth of those strains of human character with which economics is concerned has been underrated by some writers on economics in England and other countries, and German economists have done good service by emphasizing it. They seem, however, to be mistaken in supposing that it was overlooked by the founders of British economics. It is a British habit to leave much to be supplied by the common sense of the reader; in this case, reticence has been carried too far and has led to frequent misunderstanding at home as well as abroad. It has led people to suppose the foundations of economics to be narrower and less closely in touch with the actual conditions of life than they really are (Marshall 1890, 558).

Adolph Wagner (1835 –1917), a German economist and politician, divided economic motives into egoistic and altruistic categories. The egoistic motives are divisible into four classes. The first includes striving for one's economic advantage and fearing their economic need. The second concerns the fear of punishment and the hope of reward. The third consists of honour and the striving for recognition, including the desire for others' moral approbation and the fear of shame and contempt. The last is the craving for occupation, the pleasure of activity, and the pleasure of the work itself and its surroundings, including the pleasures of the chase.

The altruistic motive is wholly concerned with "the impelling force" of the inward command to moral action, the pressure of the feeling of duty, and the fear of one's inward blame, that is, of the gnawing of conscience.

In its pure form, this motive appears as the 'Categorical Imperative,' which one follows because one feels in one's soul the command to act in this or that manner and feels the command to be right... The following of the command is no doubt regularly bound up with feelings of pleasure and the not following it with feelings of pain. Now it may be and often is that these feelings act as strongly as the Categorical Imperative, or even more strongly, in driving us, or in taking part in driving us on to do or to leave undone. And in so far as this is the case, this motive also has an egoistic element, or at least it merges into one (Marshall 1890, 559).

4.5.1 Critical Commentary

The purpose of this appendix is to clarify Marshall's view on the role and importance of deductive logic. The two points developed above are of critical importance today. First, the principal methodology of economic research is induction, suggesting that a long train of deductive reasoning has little room in economics. If someone does this, the research will involve testing the potentials for analyzing economic issues in mathematical sciences. This is a wholly different concept of exposing economic theories and laws clearly and concisely. Here the objective is about making economics an applied branch of mathematics. The economic literature that has developed after WWII contains plenty of examples of this kind of research.

The second point concerns Marshall's observations on the economic man's motive in pursuing their pecuniary activities. It appears that the clear majority of modern economists believe that money-making is the native force that propels individuals to pursue production or production-related activities. Therefore, the economic reward is the only factor that can accelerate economic growth. Moreover, this is the dogma that forms the foundation of economic policy in modern democracies, whose effects have manifested in massive economic inequality, which is economic injustice.

Nevertheless, Marshall's reasoning in Appendix D does not appear entirely free from ambiguity. First, the title of the appendix, *Uses of Abstract Reasoning in Economics*, is not very clear. We can refer to Locke's teachings about the use of general and abstract terms. There are abstract terms or words because abstract ideas are perceptions that have no physical referents. However, the sense in which Marshall uses the concept is an activity, not an idea. Since activity cannot be abstract, the meaning of "abstract reasoning" is unclear.

Second, Marshall again brings up the moral issues concerning human motive in pursuing economic actions, for which he uses the German economist and politician Adolph Wagner. However, this subject is outside the purview of economic research, meaning any attempt by economists to judge the efficacy of a motive is supposed to be futile. Therefore, any assumption concerning economic motive should be taken as received information, without any comparison. Humans are born with both selfish and altruistic motives, meaning economic agents are always under the influence of both motives. However, which motive a particular individual will prefer depends on both their moral character and available social opportunities. Therefore, comparing the two types of motives or choosing one kind instead of the other seems arbitrary.

4.6 Introduction (Chapter I)

Chapter I begins with a summary statement about the nature and the substance of economics: *Political Economy or Economics is a study of mankind in the ordinary business of life; it examines that part of individual and social action that is most closely connected with the attainment and with the use of the material requisites of well-being. Thus, it is on the one side a study of wealth, and on the other, and more important side, a part of the study of man.*

This opening statement is the most significant point in this chapter. Other points Marshall illustrates here are interesting but subject to criticism. For example, poverty is the subject matter of Section 2, which examines "the question of whether poverty is necessary gives its highest interest to economists."

> Now, at last, we are setting ourselves seriously to inquire whether it is necessary that there should be any so-called 'lower classes' at all: that is, whether there need be large numbers of people doomed from their birth to hard work in order to provide for others the requisites of a refined and cultured life while they themselves are prevented by their poverty and toil from having any share or part in that life (Marshall 1890, 7).

Marshall acknowledges that economics, being a science, cannot answer this question because "the answer depends partly on the moral and political capabilities of human nature, and on these matters, the economist has no special means of information." However, he adds that the answer also depends upon facts and inferences that are within the economics domain, which makes poverty relevant for economic research.

Few modern economists would agree with Marshall because this is evidently a political question. Today's development economics does not deal with this type of question. Instead, it analyzes the causes of poverty under the non-socialist political system, which is founded on the institution of private property and suggests policy measures to reduce its severity.

Section 4 seems to make the most exciting but controversial points of this chapter. Here Marshall challenges the conventional wisdom that competition is the principal economic force that distinguishes the modern forms of industrial life from earlier ones.

> But this account is not quite satisfactory. The strict meaning of competition seems to be the racing of one person against another, with special reference to bidding for the sale or purchase of anything. This kind of racing

is no doubt both more intense and more widely extended than it used to be: but it is only a secondary, and one might almost say, an accidental consequence from the fundamental characteristics of modern industrial life (Marshall 1890, 8).

These characteristics include, among others, self-reliance and independence in choosing one's course of actions, deliberate and prompt choices and judgments, the habit of forecasting the future, and shaping one's course regarding distant aims. They might coax people to compete with one another. Nevertheless, "they may tend, and just now indeed they are tending, in the direction of co-operation and combination of all kinds good and evil."

These are "tendencies toward collective ownership and collective action" that are very different from earlier times. In earlier times, these tendencies were the outcomes of custom, not of any passive drifting into association with one's neighbours; nowadays, they are the results of individual free choice made after the careful, deliberate judgment of one's best interest—selfish or unselfish.

> The term 'competition' has gathered about it evil savour and has come to imply a certain selfishness and indifference to the well-being of others. Now it is true that there is less deliberate selfishness in early than in modern forms of industry, but there is also less deliberate unselfishness. It is deliberateness, and not selfishness, that is the characteristic of the modern age. For instance, while custom in a primitive society extends the limits of the family and prescribes specific duties to one's neighbours that fall into disuse in a later civilization, it also prescribes an attitude of hostility to strangers.

> In modern society, the obligations of family kindness become more intense, though they are concentrated on a narrower area, and neighbours are put more nearly on the

same footing with strangers. In ordinary dealings with both, the standard of fairness and honesty is lower than in some of the dealings of a primitive people with their neighbours: but it is much higher than in their dealings with strangers. Thus, it is the ties of neighbourhood alone that have been relaxed: the ties of family are in many ways stronger than before, family affection leads to much more self-sacrifice and devotion than it used to do, and sympathy with those who are strangers to us is a growing source of a kind of deliberate unselfishness that never existed before the modern age. That country, which is the birthplace of modern competition, devotes a larger part of its income than any other to charitable uses and spent twenty million on purchasing the freedom of the slaves in the West Indies.

If competition is contrasted with energetic co-operation in unselfish work for the public good, then even the best forms of competition are relatively evil, while its harsher and meaner forms are hateful. And in a world in which all men were perfectly virtuous, competition would be out of place, but so also would be private property and every form of private right. Men would think only of their duties, and no one would desire to have a larger share of the comforts and luxuries of life than his neighbours. Strong producers could easily bear a touch of hardship, so they would wish that their weaker neighbours while producing less, should consume more. Happy in this thought, they would work for the general good with all the energy, the inventiveness, and the eager initiative that belonged to them, and mankind would be victorious in contests with nature at every turn. Such is the Golden Age to which poets and dreamers may look forward. But in the responsible conduct of affairs, it is worse than folly to ignore the imperfections that still cling to human nature.

We may conclude then that the term 'competition' is not well suited to describe the special characteristics of industrial life in the modern age. We need a term that does not imply any moral qualities, whether good or evil, but which indicates the undisputed fact that modern business and industry are characterized by more self-reliant habits, more forethought, more deliberate and free choice. There is not one term adequate for this purpose: but Freedom of Industry and Enterprise, or more shortly, Economic Freedom, points in the right direction, and it may be used in the absence of a better. Of course, this deliberate and free choice may lead to a certain departure from individual freedom when co-operation or combination seems to offer the best route to the desired end. The questions how far these deliberate forms of association are likely to destroy the freedom in which they had their origin and how far they are likely to be conducive to the public weal lie beyond the scope of the present volume (Marshall 1890, 9-11).

4.6.1 Critical Commentary

The introductory chapter of the *Principles* launches an epoch-making definition of economics. At the same time, Marshall seems to initiate a rather confusing idea about the motives behind economic undertaking. First, this epoch-making definition is reproduced here for ready reference: *Political Economy or Economics is a study of mankind in the ordinary business of life; it examines that part of individual and social action that is most closely connected with the attainment and with the use of the material requisites of well-being. Thus, it is on the one side a study of wealth, and on the other, and more important side, a part of the study of man.*

Marshall treats political economy and economics synonymously in this definition, which is probably why he never talked about them in the rest of the book. To the modern generations of economists, the two terms represent two different topics. Economics means mainstream economics, which embraces several sub-fields, while political economy, which focuses on the interrelationships among individuals, governments, and public policy, is an interdisciplinary branch of the social sciences. Marshall did not see political economy in this way.

Second, Marshall considers economics a study of humankind in the ordinary business of life, which is associated with "the attainment and use of the material requisites of well-being." Thus, all aspects of ordinary business do not fall under the jurisdiction of economic research. For example, smuggling and human trafficking are not deemed eligible for economic investigation because they are illegal. Similarly, selling sex is an ordinary business of life for some women; yet it is not considered a topic for economic investigation because it does not contribute to a society's welfare. Economics is concerned with only those ordinary businesses of life that society approves because they contribute to its general welfare.

Since discovering moral truths is the end of our intellectual inquiry, attaining material welfare may sound like a partial truth but is not undoubtedly wrong. However, Marshall's conception of the "ordinary businesses of life" does not seem very clear, which is evident in his treatment of the role of "competition" in the production of "material requisites of well-being." In section 4, Marshall challenges the conventional wisdom concerning its view about the role of competition in the capitalistic economy of his time. He argues that modern industrial life, although intensely competitive, transforms traditional economic agents into self-reliant and independent, who can make deliberate and prompt choices and judgments and forecast the future and shape their course concerning distant aims. These reformed characteristics of modern industrial life would drive individuals "toward collective ownership and collective action."

Thus, Marshall concludes that "competition" is an ill-suited term to describe the unique characteristics of industrial life in the modern age.

We may conclude then that the term "competition" is not well suited to describe the special characteristics of industrial life in the modern age. We need a term that does not imply any moral qualities, whether good or evil, but which indicates the undisputed fact that modern business and industry are characterized by more self-reliant habits, more forethought, more deliberate and free choice. There is not one term adequate for this purpose: but Freedom of Industry and Enterprise, or more shortly, Economic Freedom, points in the right direction; and it may be used in the absence of a better (Marshall 1890, 11).

Unfortunately, Marshall did not explain what he meant by the term "economic freedom," for which we do not know its meaning. However, several civil society organizations have developed across the world that use Marshall's idea. The Heritage Foundation in the US is one such organization whose mission is to "formulate and promote conservative public policies based on the principles of free enterprise, limited government, individual freedom, traditional American values, and a strong national defence." For this purpose, it has developed an index to estimate the degree of economic freedom prevailing in the global village and publishes its report annually. It includes four primary criteria: (i) the rule of law (property rights, judicial effectiveness, and government integrity); (ii) government size (tax burden, government spending, and fiscal health); (iii) regulatory efficiency (business freedom and labour freedom); and (iv) market openness (trade freedom, investment freedom, and financial freedom). All these criteria are imprecise, meaning their estimated values mean little for the theoretical idea Marshall wanted us to share.

Marshall's opinion about the role of competition in the free-market economy and the motive of the economic agents raises many questions. First, the entirety of humankind is not involved in economic activities that come under the jurisdiction of economic research. The dependent class of the population—children and senior citizens—are consumers, but they do not ordinarily participate in production activities, meaning they are to be excluded from our microeconomic model. Second, the adult population, which takes part in the market, plays a dual role. They are simultaneously producers and consumers but of different commodities. It is a fact that the market demand includes all individuals who have purchasing power, but a small number of individuals generally controls the market supply. Although selfishness is not a condition for constructing the market demand curve, it is undoubtedly a condition for constructing the market supply curve. Marshall seems to have failed to see the differential motive of the same individual playing dual roles in the market. Third, Marshall's interpretation of human nature is unsatisfactory. Since altruism or sympathy for fellow human beings is a fundamental feature of human nature, competition versus cooperation became a hot topic for some deductive economists. This debate is fundamentally flawed because the ends of the two activities, to borrow Aristotle's maxim, are fundamentally different. Individuals intentionally compete for personal or private gain while they voluntarily cooperate for community gain. In both cases, the primary human motive is self-interest. No matter how selfless a human action might appear, self-interest, self-love, in Rousseau's terminology, always supply the necessary passions for undertaking the action. Hume beautifully explains in his *Treatise* that there must be a passion behind all human actions.

The whole purpose of economic science, or microeconomics, to be more specific, is to develop demand and supply theories and suggest appropriate policy measures to regulate the behaviour of economic agents in the interest of the political community to which they belong. Without the downward demand curves and upward sloping supply curves, there is no science of economics.

Is it possible to derive these curves under the assumption that consumers and producers cooperate in the market to determine the exchange value of the commodity they are concerned about? The words competition and cooperation need to be explained from the empiricist perspective.

4.7 The Substance of Economics (Chapter II)

This chapter, divided into seven sections, presents Marshall's full understanding of economics as a branch of social science. The first section summarizes his thoughts about the nature and substance of economics, while the 7th section concludes the chapter. Both sections are reproduced below verbatim to avoid the risk of misinterpretation and offer readers an opportunity to form their own opinions. However, the chapter's main points will be synthesized at the end of this discussion, together with other arguments illustrated in the preceding paragraphs.

4.7.1 Nature and Substance of Economic Reasoning (Section 1)

> Economics is a study of men as they live, move, and think in the ordinary business of life. But it concerns itself chiefly with those motives which affect, most powerfully and most steadily, man's conduct in the business part of his life. Everyone worth anything carries his higher nature with him into business, and, there as elsewhere, he is influenced by his personal affections, by his conceptions of duty, and his reverence for high ideals. And it is true that the best energies of the ablest inventors and organizers of improved methods and appliances are stimulated by a noble emulation more than by any love of wealth for its own sake. But, for all that, the steadiest motive to ordinary business work is the desire for the pay that is the material reward of work. The pay may be

on its way to be spent selfishly or unselfishly, for noble or base ends, and here the variety of human nature comes into play. But the motive is supplied by a definite amount of money: and it is this definite and exact money measurement of the steadiest motives in business life, which has enabled economics far to outrun every other branch of the study of man. Just as the chemist's fine balance has made chemistry more exact than most other physical sciences, so this economist's balance, rough and imperfect as it is, has made economics more exact than any other branch of social science. But, of course, economics cannot be compared with the exact physical sciences: for it deals with the ever-changing and subtle forces of human nature.

It concerns itself chiefly with those desires, aspirations, and other affections of human nature, the outward manifestations of which appear as incentives to action in such a form that the force or quantity of the incentives can be estimated and measured with some approach to accuracy, and which therefore are in some degree amenable to treatment by scientific machinery. *An opening is made for the methods and the tests of science as soon as the force of a person's motives—not the motives themselves—can be approximately measured by the sum of money* [emphasis added], which he will just give up in order to secure a desired satisfaction, or again by the sum which is just required to induce him to undergo a certain fatigue.

It is essential to note that the economist does not claim to measure any affection of the mind in itself, or directly, but only indirectly through its effect. No one can compare and measure accurately against one another, even his own mental states at different times: and no one can measure the mental states of another at all except indirectly and conjecturally by their effects. Of course, various affections belong to man's higher nature and others to his lower and are thus different in kind. But, even if we confine our attention to mere physical pleasures and pains of the same kind, we find that they can only be compared indirectly by their effects. In fact, even this comparison is necessarily, to some extent, conjectural unless they occur to the same person at the same time.

For instance, the pleasures which two persons derive from smoking cannot be directly compared: nor can even those which the same person derives from it at different times. But if we find a man in doubt whether to spend a few pence on a cigar, a cup of tea, on riding home instead of walking home, we may follow ordinary usage and say that he expects from them equal pleasures.

If then we wish to compare even physical gratifications, we must do it not directly but indirectly by the incentives they afford to action. If the desires to secure either of two pleasures will induce people in similar circumstances each to do just an hour's extra work or will induce men in the same rank of life and with the same means each to pay a shilling for it, we then may say that those pleasures are equal for our purposes because the desires for them are equally strong incentives to action for persons under similar conditions.

Thus, measuring a mental state, as men do in ordinary life, by its motor-force or the incentive which it affords to action, no new difficulty is introduced by the fact that some of the motives of which we have to take account belong to man's higher nature and others to his lower.

For suppose that the person, whom we saw doubting between several little gratifications for himself, had thought after a while of a poor invalid whom he would pass on his way home, and had spent some time in making up his mind whether he would choose a physical gratification for himself, or would do a kindly act and rejoice in another's joy. As his desires turned now toward the one, now the other, there would be a change in the quality of his mental states, and the philosopher is bound to study the nature of the change.

But the economist studies mental states rather through their manifestations than in themselves, and if he finds they afford evenly balanced incentives to action, he treats them *prima facie* as for his purpose equal. He follows indeed in a more patient and thoughtful way, and with greater precautions, what everybody is always doing every day in ordinary life. He does not attempt to weigh the real value of the higher affections of our nature against those of our lower: he does not balance the love for virtue against the desire for agreeable food. He estimates the incentives to action by their effects just in the same way as people do in common life. He follows the course of ordinary conversation, differing from it only in taking more precautions to make clear the limits of his knowledge as he goes. He reaches his provisional conclusions by observations of men in general under given conditions without attempting to fathom the mental and spiritual characteristics of individuals. But he does not ignore the mental and spiritual side of life. On the contrary, even for the narrower uses of economic studies, it is important to know whether the desires which prevail are such as will help to build up a strong and righteous character. And in the broader uses of those studies, when they are being applied to practical problems, the economist, like everyone else, must concern himself with the ultimate aims of man and take account of differences in real value between gratifications that are equally powerful incentives to action and have therefore equal economic measures. A study of these measures is only the starting point of economics: but it is the starting point (Marshall 1890, 14-16)

4.7.1.1 Critical Commentary

In this introductory section, Marshall argues more like a philosopher than a social scientist. Economics is a social science. Therefore, it cannot study "men as they live and move and think in the ordinary business of life." This is because every individual lives differently, moves differently, and thinks differently, suggesting that the economists must find some regularities in their behaviours and actions to formulate theories and principles. Then, these theories and principles must be useful to the government to regulate the economy because we live in a political society.

Nevertheless, he rightly argues that economics studies "the force of a person's motives, not the motives themselves that can be reasonably measured in terms of money." Economists cannot directly measure the affections of the mind, but they can reasonably approximate their effects in monetary terms. In other words, economists study the individual's mental states through their manifestations, not the actual mental states.

4.7.2 Limitations of Money as the Measure of Motive (Section 2)

However, measuring human motives with money has two critical limitations. First, the same sum of money may represent different levels of pleasure or satisfaction to different people under different circumstances. Even a shilling might measure greater or lesser pleasure to the same person at different times due to a change in income or tastes. Therefore, it is not logical to argue that two people of the same income will "derive equal benefit from its use or that they would suffer equal pain from the same diminution of it." Nevertheless, these individual variations may average out in a large sample, meaning income could be considered a good proxy for measuring total pleasure.

Second, economic motives are directly affected by the level of earned income. A shilling is more valuable to a poor person than to the rich.

> But this source of error also is lessened when we are able to consider the actions and the motives of large groups of people. If we know, for instance, that a bank failure has taken £200,000 from the people of Leeds and £100,000 from those of Sheffield, we may fairly assume that the suffering caused in Leeds has been about twice as great as in Sheffield, unless indeed we have some special reason for believing that the shareholders of the bank in the one town were a richer class than those in the other, or that the loss of employment caused by it pressed in uneven proportions on the working classes in the two towns.

> By far, the greater number of the events with which economics deals affect in about equal proportions all the different classes of society so that if the money measures of the happiness caused by two events are equal, it is reasonable and in accordance with common usage to regard the amounts of the happiness in the two cases as equivalent. And, further, as money is likely to be turned to the higher uses of life in about equal proportions, by any two large groups of people taken without special bias from any two parts of the western world, there is even some *prima facie* probability that equal additions to their material resources will make about equal additions to the

fullness of life and the true progress of the human race (Marshall 1890, 17).

4.7.2.1 Critical Commentary

Marshall mentions two defects of money as a measure of utility or pleasure consumers obtain from buying a commodity, which today is described as two demand shifters—tastes and incomes. Due to changes in these factors, the same sum of money might measure different degrees of pleasure to the same person at different times or to different persons at the same time. He then argues that these variations in the level of pleasure obtained from consumption are supposed to average out in a large sample.

However, this inference is subject to criticism because it does not consider the nature of the commodity in question. Marshall overlooks what he has been persistently pressing—economics is an inductive, not deductive, science. Consider, for example, red meat. If its price doubled overnight, the low-income consumers might immediately shift to poultry or other protein substitutes. However, this price change may mean nothing to a person earning a million dollars a month. Take away his million-dollar job and pay him the salary of an ordinary worker, and his reaction to the red meat price adjustment will dramatically change. All this suggests is that in studying consumer demand, we ignore the fact that there is a *system of natural choice*, which we all obey. This system is the chronological significance of different commodities in human life. Under all circumstances, we will first meet our basic needs—food, drink, clothing, and accommodation. If we are sick, taking medical care is an utmost priority. Once we meet these basic needs, we will look for convenience and entertainment if surplus income is available. "Value of money" and "marginal utility of money" are deductive concepts, which need to be understood as "value of income" and "marginal utility of income." Only then we may use them in the context of a particular commodity study and examine their implications as the price changes.

4.7.3 Habits and Customs Reflect Deliberate Choice (Section 3)

The preceding section discussed issues related to the monetary measurement of the economic agent's motives through their actions or manifestations. These motives are deliberate and calculative because the concerned actions are taken after careful consideration of their advantages and disadvantages. In other words, all the economic actions, which do not satisfy this condition, remain excluded from economic analysis. In general, the economic agent does not formally calculate two sides of a balance sheet as indicated above. However, all adult human beings regularly experience flashbacks after making a decision: "It does answer this question" or "the choice was poorly made." In these thoughts lies the deliberateness of economic choice. However, it should be noted that habits or customs under one circumstance may not influence the same set of actions under different circumstances.

Given this situation, the most systematic part of people's lives constitutes earning their livelihoods.

> The work of all those engaged in any one occupation can be carefully observed; general statements can be made about it and tested by comparison with the results of other observations, and numerical estimates can be framed as to the amount of money or general purchasing power that is required to supply a sufficient motive for them. The unwillingness to postpone enjoyment, and thus to save for future use, is measured by the interest on accumulated wealth that affords a sufficient incentive to save for the future. However, this measurement presents some special difficulties, the study of which must be postponed (Marshall 1890, 19).

4.7.3.1 Critical Commentary

This section seems ambiguous. In Appendix B, Marshall argues that the chief characteristic of modern industrial life is "deliberateness," not conventional "selfishness," which he reaffirms in the above section. However, he defines economics as a study of humankind in its ordinary business of life, where "people do not weigh beforehand the results of every action." These two statements are contradictory. Second, David Hume was the first epistemologist to demonstrate the influence of habits and customs in the development of scientific theories:

> Custom, then, is the great guide of human life. It is that principle alone which renders our experience useful to us, and makes us expect, for the future, a similar train of events with those which have appeared in the past. Without the influence of custom, we should be entirely ignorant of every matter of fact beyond what is immediately present to the memory and senses. We should never know how to adjust means to ends, or to employ our natural powers in the production of any effect. There would be an end at once of all action, as well as of the chief part of speculation (Hume 1748).

Marshall uses this theory in the specific context of economics without crediting the original author. However, his efforts in applying Hume's theory is susceptible to criticism.

Third, there is little connection between the action and the end when these habits or customs are formed under different conditions. Thus, Marshall argues that the only activity in which the effects of customs remain uniform involves "earning a living." In making this conclusion, Marshall overlooks that the economic agents are simultaneously involved in two kinds of activity—production and consumption. Earning a livelihood is related to production but not to consumption. This contradiction, familiar in economic literature, has been created by overlooking the significance of the dual roles that individuals play in modern industrial society. Without the simultaneous consideration of both demand and supply sides, the conception of the private market carries little meaning, which, in turn, makes the definition of economics hollow.

4.7.4 Section 4: Nature of Economic Motives

The conventional wisdom maintains that economic motives are primarily selfish; individuals pursue their economic objectives without considering what happens to others. This proposition, however, is not entirely true. Money is a means toward ends, which may be noble or ignoble. Thus, it is true that economic science pivots around "money" or "general purchasing power" or "command over material wealth." This is not because "money or material wealth is regarded as the main aim of human effort, nor even as affording the main subject matter for the economist's study." The fundamental reason is that "in this world of ours, it is the one convenient means of measuring human motive on a large scale."

Moreover, man's mind is not closed to all other considerations, save his selfish gain, even if money-making supplies the primary motive for economic activities.

> For even the most purely business relations of life assume honesty and good faith, while many of them take for granted, if not generosity, yet at least the absence of meanness, and the pride which every honest man takes in acquitting himself well (Marshall 1890, 18).

4.7.4.1 Critical Commentary

This section again examines the nature of economic motives, which the conventional wisdom regards as selfish. Marshall tries to argue that this premise is not entirely true. However, this topic should be better left for the moral philosophers as economists are not well-qualified to deal with this subject. Neither is it necessary for them to resolve the issue. We need to assume that the motives behind all economic activities—production, exchange, and consumption—are selfish by nature. Marshall's efforts here are simplistic and unnecessary.

4.7.5 Section 5: Preference for Occupation

The individual's preference for occupation renders another challenge to the selfish-motive proposition because they ordinarily try to avoid manual jobs for two main reasons—they are laborious and are of lower social rank. In other words,

> the desire to earn the approval, to avoid the contempt of those around one is a stimulus to action which often works with some uniformity in any class of persons at a given time and place, though local and temporary conditions influence greatly not only the intensity of the desire for approval but also the range of persons whose approval is desired.
>
> As there may be a taint of selfishness in a man's desire to do what seems likely to benefit his fellow workers, so there may be an element of personal pride in his desire that his family should prosper during his life and after it. But still, the family affections generally are so pure a form of altruism that their action might have shown little semblance of regularity had it not been for the uniformity in the family relations themselves (Marshall 1890, 19).

4.7.5.1 Critical Commentary

Marshall challenges the orthodox selfish-motive proposition by arguing that individuals prefer non-manual jobs because they are both less-laborious and socially more honourable. This argument is not sustainable from either an economic or philosophical viewpoint. From the economic viewpoint, one of the main reasons why individuals prefer non-manual or white-collar jobs is because they get both higher compensations and greater psychological satisfaction or utility from them. From the philosophical point of view, what we call "selfless" is one kind of self-interest or self-love. What could be the possible reason behind Socrates's voluntary acceptance of capital punishment if he did not believe that dying is superior to the compromised life? This example is not economic, but it does demonstrate the difficulty in Marshall's argumentation.

4.7.6 Section 6: Cooperation and Collective Action

This section discusses the importance of the motive for collective action in the study of economics. English economists have been excessively preoccupied with the motives of an individual action, which have blurred their vision about the fact that individuals are both social and political animals, and as students of social science, they ought to highlight this feature during the investigation of an individual's private behaviour.

> As a cathedral is something more than the stones of which it is made, as a person is something more than a series of thoughts and feelings, so the life of society is something more than the sum of the lives of its individual members. It is true that the action of the whole is made up of that of its constituent parts and that in most economic problems, the best starting point is to be found in the motives that affect the individual, regarded not indeed as an isolated atom but as a member of some particular trade or industrial group, but it is also true, as German writers have well urged, that economics has a great and an increasing concern in motives connected with the collective ownership of property and the collective pursuit of important aims (Marshall 1890, 20).

Thus, "the chief subjects" of economic science are to overcome the difficulties offered by the variety of motives and the consequent difficulties of measuring them.

Almost every point touched in the present chapter will need to be discussed in fuller detail with reference to one or more of the leading problems of economics (Marshall 1890, 20).

4.7.6.1 Critical Commentary

Here Marshall reiterates his objection to the conventional wisdom's postulation of selfish competition. His objection is not entirely meritless, given the fact that it treats economic agents as mechanical selfish creatures. Individuals are social and political animals—a fact that needs to be considered in all economic studies. However, this point does not imply that individuals have to be cooperative in every aspect of their lives, and they are not. There are some areas of social life where cooperative actions are indispensable, and there are others where their actions have to be competitive. Economics is one of the areas where competition, not cooperation, raises the right passion for maximizing utility or profits. Arguing otherwise is inconsistent with the principles of the basic model in which forces of demand and supply determine exchange value.

4.7.7 Section 7: Conclusion

Economists study the actions of individuals but study them in relation to social rather than individual life and therefore concern themselves but little with personal peculiarities of temper and character. They watch carefully the conduct of a whole class of people, sometimes the whole of a nation, sometimes only those living in a certain district, more often those engaged in some particular trade at some time and place: and by the aid of statistics, or in other ways, they ascertain how much money on the average members of the particular group they are watching are just willing to pay as the price of a certain thing they desire, or how much must be offered to them to induce them to undergo a certain effort or abstinence they dislike. The measurement of motive thus obtained is not indeed perfectly accurate, for if it were, economics would rank with the most advanced of the physical sciences and not, as it actually does, with the least advanced.

Yet the measurement is accurate enough to enable experienced persons to forecast fairly well the extent of the results that will follow from changes in which motives of this kind are chiefly concerned. Thus, for instance, they can estimate very closely the payment that will be required to produce an adequate supply of labour of any grade, from the lowest to the highest, for a new trade which it is proposed to start in any place. When they visit a factory of a kind that they have never seen before, they can tell within a shilling or two a week what any particular worker is earning by merely observing how far his is a skilled occupation and what strain it involves on his physical, mental, and moral faculties. And they can predict with tolerable certainty what rise of price will result from a given diminution of the supply of a certain thing and how that increased price will react on the supply.

And, starting from simple considerations of this kind, economists go on to analyze the causes which govern the local distribution of different kinds of industry, the terms on which people living in distant places exchange their goods with one another, and so on: and they can explain and predict the ways in which fluctuations of credit will affect foreign trade, or again, the extent to which the burden of a tax will be shifted from those on whom it is levied and onto those for whose wants they cater, and so on.

In all this, they deal with man as he is: not with an abstract or "economic" man, but a man of flesh and blood. They deal with a man who is largely influenced by egoistic motives in his business life to a great extent with reference to them, but who is also neither above vanity and recklessness, nor below delight in doing his work well for its own sake, or in sacrificing himself for the good of his family, neighbours, or country; a man who is not below the love of a virtuous life for its own sake. They deal with man as he is: but being concerned chiefly with those aspects of life in which the action of motive is so regular that it can be predicted, and the estimate of the motor forces can be verified by results, they have established their work on a scientific basis.

For in the first place, they deal with facts that can be observed and quantities that can be measured and recorded so that when differences of opinion arise with regard to them, the differences can be brought to the test of public and well-established records, and thus, science obtains a solid basis on which to work. In the second place, the problems, which are grouped as economical because they relate especially to man's conduct under the influence of motives that are measurable by a money price, are found to make a fairly homogeneous group. Of course, they have a great deal of subject matter in common: that is obvious from the nature of the case. But, though not so obvious *a priori*, it will also be found to be true that there is a fundamental unity of form underlying all the chief of them, and that in consequence, by studying them together, the same kind of economy is gained, as by sending a single postman to deliver all the letters in a certain street, instead of each one entrusting his letters to a separate messenger. For the analyses and organized processes of reasoning that are wanted for any one group of them will generally be found useful for other groups.

The less then we trouble ourselves with scholastic inquiries as to whether a certain consideration comes within the scope of economics, the better. If the matter is important, let us take account of it as far as we can. If it is one as to which there exist divergent opinions, such as cannot be brought to the test of exact and well-ascertained knowledge, if it is one on which the general machinery of economic analysis and reasoning cannot get any grip, then let us leave it aside in our purely economic studies. But let us do so simply because the attempt to include it would lessen the certainty and the exactness of our economic knowledge without any commensurate gain, and always remembering that some sort of account of it must be taken by our ethical instincts and our common sense when they as ultimate arbiters come to apply to practical issues the knowledge obtained and arranged by economics and other sciences (Marshall 1890, 20-22).

4.7.7.1 Critical Commentary

Like the first section, this last section, which describes Marshall's provisional conclusions about the definition and the substance of economics, is a reproduction in toto. These conclusions appear more controversial than those of Robbins. Robbins was wrong in defining economics as a social science and its subject matter, as shown in Chapter VII. However, Marshall's conclusions are controversial because they challenge both Adam Smith and J.S. Mill.

First, Marshall argues that economists study individuals' actions within society, not individual life. Accordingly, personal peculiarities of temper and character are of little concern to the study of economics. It examines "man as he is: not with an abstract or 'economic' man, but a man of flesh and blood." This premise directly clashes with Smith's characterization of economic agents busy managing the ordinary businesses of life. It is true that all classical economists, including Adam Smith, focused their attention on the production side of the commodity market because they were concerned with the prevailing issues of the day: production of an adequate supply of necessaries and conveniences and generation of necessary public revenues. Therefore, their conception of political economy was appropriate for the society in which they lived.

Nevertheless, bringing consumption into the basic model of economics does not resolve the issue in our time. Instead, Marshall's maxim merely complicates the matter because, in modern economies, the production sector is a complex system dominated by knowledge and experience. Therefore, Marshall's idea of a "flesh and blood producer" seems far removed from the real world. Here, we see the relevance of empiricist theory in understanding economic literature. We do not know what Adam Smith meant by the phrase: *Every individual... neither intends to promote the public interest, nor knows how much he is promoting it... he intends only his own security; and by directing that industry in such a manner as its produce may be of the greatest value, he intends only his own gain, and he is in this, as in many other cases, led by an invisible hand to promote an end which was no part of his intention.* We read his statement and interpret it in line with our moral motive.

Second, J.S. Mill is credited for conceiving the idea of economic man. He did not attribute the features, which characterize this critical idea in modern time. Mill's exact statement is the following:

> [Political economy] does not treat the whole of man's nature as modified by the social state, nor of the whole conduct of man in society. It is concerned with him solely as a being who desires to possess wealth and who is capable of judging the comparative efficacy of means for obtaining that end (Mill 1874).

By economic man, Mill meant an economic agent engaged in production activities with the primary objective of creating wealth. Since Marshall's time, neoclassical economists have turned this necessary and straightforward idea into a sort of mythical creature who has little connection with reality. Being annoyed by the popularity of this neoclassical movement, Marshall directly challenged the empirical foundation of this idea.

Both Marshall and the neoclassical admirers of *homo economicus* seem equally responsible for denigrating one of the most critical concepts required for economic model-building. We can pick any textbook on introductory economics or microeconomics, which shows us how we apply this concept. We derive market demand and supply curves respectively from the individual demand curve and the firm's marginal cost curve.

4.8 Conclusion

The preceding chapter described Marshall as a moral or ethical person, a socially concerned person in the modern language. His opinions, summarized and criticized above, are to be judged from this perspective. For quick reference, his definition is reproduced below:

> Political Economy or Economics is a study of mankind in the ordinary business of life; it examines that part of individual and social action that is most closely connected with the attainment and with the use of the material requisites of well-being. Thus, it is on the one side a study

of wealth, and on the other, and more important side, a part of the study of man.

Several aspects of this statement are worth mentioning. First, Marshall limits the study of economics to the consumption and production of material wealth. This delimitation is quite consistent with his predecessors Adam Smith, David Hume, and J.S. Mill. Being a socially concerned person, he also added social welfare to define the boundary of economics as a social science discipline. However, there is indeed a question about the word "material" in our time. For "material production," which implies the production of food and other necessities, is no longer an issue in industrially advanced democracies, meaning the economic environment has dramatically changed since his predecessors dealt with the subject.

Second, the "ordinary business" of life itself is a very confusing vocabulary, and Marshall has made it more confusing. This phrase refers to "the attainment and use of the material requisites of well-being," which might have been true during Adam Smith's time, but certainly not today. In modern days, the tourism industry depends on aircraft and luxury ships. The production of aircraft and luxury ships is not an ordinary business of life, which usually means the production of necessities and conveniences, as Adam Smith suggested.

Third, his claim that economics is a study of human nature related to acquiring and disposing of wealth is logically incorrect, which Neville shows plainly in the next chapter. The study of human nature, in its entirety, is a job for the philosophers. Moreover, this study has proved to be the most contentious and controversial in philosophy. Therefore, finding common ground about the fundamental nature of our economic agent, the *homo economicus*, is virtually impossible. Economists would do much better by leaving the topic to its proper place—philosophy—and taking their conclusions as data as Smith did.

Fourth, Marshall's claim that economics studies human behaviour from the social perspective, not the individual commonly believed, is most controversial.

> They watch carefully the conduct of a whole class of people, sometimes the whole of a nation, sometimes only those living in a certain district, more often those engaged in some particular trade at some time and place: and by the aid of statistics, or in other ways, they ascertain how much money on the average the members of the particular group they are watching are willing to pay as the price of a certain thing they desire, or how much must be offered to them to induce them to undergo a certain effort or abstinence they dislike. The measurement of motive thus obtained is not indeed perfectly accurate, for if it were, economics would rank with the most advanced of the physical sciences and not, as it actually does, with the least advanced (Marshall 1890, 20).

This statement appears more subjective than scientific. It describes what the economists do; they do not explain how the economic agents behave in their real lives. The human behaviour economists study concerns the ownership of private property. Thus, the same economic agent will behave very differently depending upon the political system that governs the state, viz. democracy and socialism. Then, in democracy, the economic agent behaves differently depending upon its role in the market. As a producer, its behaviour will be guided by the prospects of making profits, while as a consumer, it will maximize utility under budget constraints. If we do not make these assumptions, we will never be able to derive well-behaved supply and demand curves. In economics, the economic agent has no scope to be magnanimous.

Fifth, Marshall is wrong in interpreting the role of *homo economics* in the development of the economics discipline. Mill introduced the concept in the 1830s to facilitate analyzing the economic behaviour of the selfish being Smith pictured in the

WN and demonstrating how the "invisible hand" operates in the best interest of society. Marshall criticized the concept in the following manner:

> In all this, they deal with man as he is: not with an abstract or "economic" man, but a man of flesh and blood. They deal with a man who is largely influenced by egoistic motives in his business life to a great extent with reference to them, but who is also neither above vanity and recklessness, nor below delight in doing his work well for its own sake, or in sacrificing himself for the good of his family, neighbours, or country; a man who is not below the love of a virtuous life for its own sake. They deal with man as he is: but being concerned chiefly with those aspects of life in which the action of motive is so regular that it can be predicted, and the estimate of the motor forces can be verified by results, they have established their work on a scientific basis (Marshall 1890, 21).

This statement cannot be used in a scientific inquiry because it is plainly judgmental. The reasons for which Marshall makes this subjective statement hardly explain the rationale for which Mill introduced this concept. Firstly, the fundamental issue of economics, which Adam Smith introduced, was to study individuals' exchange behaviour in the context of the institution of private property. In this system, the fundamental unit of analysis is the commodity market. To construct a general model for this kind of economy, we must make simplifying assumptions, which involves assuming a single consumer and a single producer representing the entire community of consumers and producers. The commodity in question is homogeneous, meaning consumers cannot discriminate between producers for any economic reason. The individual producers cannot charge different prices because the commodity is homogeneous. The consumer chooses the consumption level by maximizing total utility subject to the budget constraint, while the producer maximizes profits by minimizing costs. No such thing can happen if we take Marshall's description of "a man of flesh and blood." This is because all these characteristics signify the economic agent's deliberateness both as a consumer and producer, not an individual of flesh and blood. Finally, no two men of flesh and blood react precisely the same way to any price change.

If we believe in John Locke's system of governance, we must agree with Marshall that pursuing social welfare should be the primary premise of studying economics. It is a moral law that can prevent economic injustice in an economy founded on private property institutions. Aristotle showed us this academic truth about two and a half thousand years ago. Locke reminded us of the same principle under the social environment created by the Age of Enlightenment in Europe. Adam Smith elaborated the idea in the context of the Industrial Revolution; he argued very persuasively that liberal trade and domestic policies would help achieve both private and public welfare.

CHAPTER V

JOHN NEVILLE KEYNES: SCOPE AND METHOD OF ECONOMICS

John Neville Keynes (JNK) concludes Chapter I, stating that a single phrase is inadequate to describe political economy methods. By this statement, he highlights differing opinions of the old English and the new German schools. However, this difference is one of degree, not of kind, because it becomes indistinguishable when the actual works of the two schools are compared. Nevertheless, JNK devotes Chapters II and III to illustrate his doctrines concerning the definition and scope of economics, succinctly summarized below, with two objectives. First, the book argues that the post-WWII economists have been indulging a gross mistake by neglecting JNK's contributions to the methodological discussion in economics. Second, his ideas will better help understand Robbins's Chapter II to be examined in the next chapter.

5.1 On the Relation of Political Economy to Morality and Practice (Chapter II)

5.1.1 The Distinction Between Economic Uniformities, Economic Ideals, and Economic Precepts

When JNK was learning and practicing economics in the 19th century, the debate over the nature and scope of the political economy centred around its relation with practical issues concerning ideals and precepts. Although these areas—economic uniformities, ideals and precepts—are tangled together, they belong to different departments in the classification of knowledge, which are respectively called positive science, normative science, and art.

As the terms are here used, a positive science may be defined as a body of systematized knowledge concerning what is; a normative or regulative science as a body of systematized knowledge relating to criteria of what ought to be, and concerned therefore with the ideal as distinguished from the actual; art as a system of rules for the attainment of a given end. The object of a positive science is the establishment of uniformities, of a normative science the determination of ideals, of art the formulation of precepts (Keynes 1904, 34-35).

Thus, calling the political economy by any of these names is merely a matter of nomenclature and classification. However, to avoid all confusion emanating from this nomenclature, each department needs to be defined unambiguously.

5.1.2 The possibility of studying economic laws or uniformities without passing ethical judgments or formulating economic precepts

A positive branch of economics is free from all moral judgments and the complexities of actual economic activities. It describes and explains pure economic phenomena. This proposition is a truism because studying economic uniformities without passing ethical judgments or formulating economic precepts does not require any proof. However, the misapprehension caused by this misconception needs to be dispelled. This misconception concerns the suggestion that economic laws, formulated without moral judgments, are tantamount to denying the truth that moral considerations have little bearing on economic phenomena. Interestingly, this charge cannot be substantiated by "the actual writings of English economists of the first rank at any period." Nevertheless, this tone and attitude may be observed in the writings of some famous interpreters of economic science.

We may conclude the argument contained in this section by the remark that, just as the science of psychology recognizes the existence and operation of moral motives, yet does not pass ethical judgments, so political economy may recognize the operation of moral motives in the economic world, and yet not become an ethical science (Keynes 1904, 46).

5.1.3 Grounds for Recognizing a Distinct Positive Science of Political Economy, the Sole Province of Which Is to Establish Economic Uniformities

The methodological question in economics does not concern whether a positive inquiry should form the foundation of its research. The real question is "whether it shall be systematically combined with ethical and practical enquiries, or pursued in the first instance independently." Here JNK offers three grounds for independently pursuing positive inquiry in the political economy.

First, amalgamating "what is" and "what ought to be" inquiries will prevent obtaining transparent, clear, and unbiased answers to both sets of questions. For example, if wage rates appear unfair, we cannot correct them unless we know the laws determining wage rates in a competitive labour market. The value of a positive theory can be measured only in terms of its bearing on practical questions. Economists are supposed to aim at developing positive theories keeping in view its practical implication.

> It may be added that since purely economic data rarely by themselves suffice for the complete solution of practical problems, either our solution of the latter will be incomplete, or else the discussion that belongs to the positive science of economics will not improbably be overlaid by the introduction of considerations, which, so far as it is concerned, are extraneous (Keynes 1904, 49).

Second, combining theoretical and practical inquiries is equivalent to confirming the prevalent confusion concerning the nature of many economic truths, which interprets theorems of pure science as maxims for practical guidance. The public seems to be disposed to the misconception that the principles of political economy are essentially rules of conduct.

> Thus, because in economic theory, men's action in buying and selling is commonly assumed to be governed by self-interest, political economy is supposed to inculcate selfishness; because many economic truths are based on the postulate of competition, trades-unions are spoken of as violating economic laws, and because it is laid down that, in a perfect market, price is determined by supply and demand, the science is represented as teaching that price ought so to be determined. This kind of confusion is perhaps particularly common in England, where, for reasons that are to be found in the historical development of the science, political economy has, to a large extent, become identified in the public mind with the policy of laisse faire (Keynes 1904, 51-52).

Third, the positive inquiry should be recognized as a distinct and independent political economy branch for another good reason. To form an agreement on positive theories, we only need uniformities among facts. However, in normative theories, the disputants may never agree because they foster different subjective views. Consider the problem of socialism versus capitalism. This debate can never reach a conclusion because proponents of socialism consider private property a machine of exploitation and injustice, while those of capitalism consider the institution an inviolable individual right.

In the rest of the book, the term political economy will mean positive science if used without qualification. However, this demarcation does not suggest that the economists pursuing these theoretical investigations would consider them entirely out of the bound of ethical judgment or practical significance of their theorems.

5.1.4 Applied Economics

Concluding that positive inquiry is an independent department of political economy, JNK argues that there ought to be another department called "applied economics." In making this statement, he did not add any new idea but merely reiterated the long history. In his 1803 classic, *A Treatise on Political Economy; Or the Production, Distribution and Consumption of Wealth*, Say first hinted at the idea of applied economics. He argued for applying the general principles of political economy to derive the rule of action of any combination of circumstances under study (Backhouse and Biddle 2000). Mill directly used the phrase "Applications to Social Philosophy" in the title of his book. JNK noted that the "English school," consisting of J.S. Mill, John Elliott Cairnes, and Nassau Senior, believed in the existence of a positive, abstract, and deductive political economy and argued for maintaining "a sharp line of distinction between political economy itself and its applications to practice."

5.1.5 Political Economy and Ethics

This section explains the nature of the political economy as a normative science, i.e., "what ought to be" inquiry. In logical order, it stands in between positive economics, i.e., "what is" inquiry and the practical application of economic principles—the art of economics. It may be described as a branch of applied economics and, for that reason, may be called the ethics of political economy. Here, the functions of economists and moralists are combined as "the general principles of social morality being considered in their special bearing on economic activities."

> In pursuing this enquiry, our object is scientifically to define men's duties in their economic relations one

with another, and, above all, the duties of society, in so far as it can by its action control or modify economic conditions. In other words, we seek to determine standards whereby judgment may be passed on those economic activities whose character and consequences have been established by our previous investigation of economic facts. We seek, moreover, to determine ideals in regard to the production and distribution of wealth so as to best satisfy the demands of justice and morality. It is subsequently the function of applied economics, or of the so-called art of political economy, to enquire how nearly the ideal is capable of being attained, and by what means, and to determine how, subject to the above condition, the greatest aggregate happiness may be made to result from the least expenditure of efforts (Keynes 1904, 61-62).

For example, the question that the medieval moralists raised about what constitutes a "just price" belongs to the ethics of political economy.

The relative value to be attached to different methods of investigation is very different, whether we take the ethical and practical standpoint or the purely scientific standpoint. Thus, it would be generally agreed that, in dealing with practical questions, an abstract method of treatment avails less and carries us much less further than when we are dealing with theoretical questions. In other words, in dealing with the former class of questions, we are, to a greater extent, dependent upon history and inductive generalization (Keynes 1904, 63).

5.1.6 Methodological Importance of the Distinctions Indicated in This Chapter

This section concludes the chapter by succinctly summarizing the two main points of methodological importance underlined above. First, the tendency to merge the two questions, "what is" and "what ought to be," confuses discussions about economics and economical methods.

The relative value to be attached to different methods of investigation is very different, whether we take the ethical and practical standpoint or the purely scientific standpoint. Thus, it would be generally agreed that, in dealing with practical questions, an abstract method of treatment avails less and carries us much less far than when we are dealing with theoretical questions. In other words, in dealing with the former class of questions, we are, to a greater extent, dependent upon history and inductive generalization (Keynes 1904, 63).

Second, economic uniformities and economic precepts are often relative to particular states of society, meaning the latter's general relativity may be affirmed with less qualification than the former's. The art of political economy necessarily differs between countries because of the difference in practical questions. The practical questions usually involve arguments from both theoretical and practical perspectives, meaning all decisions need to be made based on the relative importance of the issue concerned.

Hence, in general, a given economic policy can be definitely formulated only for nations having particular economic surroundings and having reached a certain stage of economic development. Applied to nations not similarly situated, the policy is likely at least to require modification. It is even possible that what is excellent for a given nation at a given time may be actively mischievous and injurious for another nation or for the same nation at a different period of its economic history. It follows, similarly, that the value of the economic institutions of the past cannot adequately be judged by reference to existing conditions alone. We are not here denying the relativity of economic theorems but merely affirming the greater relativity of economic precepts. Unless the distinction between theorems and precepts is carefully borne in mind, the relativity of the former is likely to be overstated (Keynes 1904, 64-65).

5.2 On the Character and Definition of Political Economy Regarded as a Positive Science (Chapter III)

This chapter describes and discusses the scope of political economy conceived as a positive science and the methods by which its theorems are derived. The chapter is divided into five sections summarized below.

5.2.1 Political Economy and Physical Science

There is always an issue about the relation between political economy and physical sciences because wealth production is one of the main objects of the former study. This relation is indirect even though political economy depends on the information supplied by the natural sciences. Physical sciences develop the laws of their fields, which political economy takes as data, not subject matter, for developing its theories concerning how economic agents react to changes in economic variables. One way to see this relationship is to revive our memories about the role that resource limitation plays in consumer and producer theories.

> The relation of political economy to the physical sciences is then simply that it presupposes them; it is sometimes concerned with physical laws as premises but never as conclusions. Accordingly, when the production of wealth is said to be one of the great departments of economic science, reference is made primarily to what may be called the social laws of the production of wealth (i.e., to the 'various influences exerted on production by division of labour, foreign trade, methods of distribution, and so forth'), rather than to the physical processes by whose

aid production is carried on. The physical requisites of the production of wealth need to be summarized in their broadest outlines, but the science is not directly concerned with the technique of different trades and occupations. Again, whilst economists recognize the physical conditions affecting men's economic efficiency, the immediate effects of these conditions are accepted as facts from physiology and other sciences; it is only in so far as they indirectly affect or are affected by the social facts of wealth that economic science itself investigates them (Keynes 1904, 85-86).

5.2.2 Political economy and psychology

The sciences dealing with humans are divisible into two categories. One group considers the individual or the private nature of human activities, while the other considers them members of society. Political economy belongs to the second group.

> It is true that some of the problems discussed by the science—those relating, for example, to the functions of capital—would arise in a more or less rudimentary form in relation to an isolated individual, and it is accordingly possible: to illustrate certain elementary economic principles by reference to the conduct of a Robinson Crusoe. As soon, however, as we advance beyond the threshold of the science, it becomes necessary to regard human beings not in isolation but as members of associated communities, including others besides themselves. The most prominent characteristic of actual economic life is the relation of mutual dependence that subsists between different individuals, and political economy may be said to be essentially concerned with economic life as a special aspect of social life (Keynes 1904, 87-88).

Therefore, the political economy should be treated as a social rather than moral or psychological science.

It presupposes psychology just as it presupposes the physical sciences, and the natural starting point for the economist in his more abstract enquiries is a consideration of the motives by which individuals are usually influenced in their economic relations, but the science is not, therefore, a branch of psychology. The bare facts that other things being equal, men prefer a greater to a smaller gain, that under certain conditions they will forego present for the sake of future gratifications and the like, are psychological facts of great economic importance. But they are assumed by the economist, not established by him. He does not seek to explain or analyze them, nor does he investigate all the consequences to which they lead. Economic laws, in the strict sense, are different from the above. They are not simple laws of human nature but laws of complex social facts resulting from simple laws of human nature (Keynes 1904, 88-89).

Furthermore, it will be argued in the following chapter that the phenomena of the industrial world cannot be satisfactorily explained by deductive reasoning from a few elementary laws of human nature.

5.2.3 Political Economy: A Social Science as Distinguished from a Political Science

JNK's conception of social and political sciences seems different from our modern conceptions. For this reason, this section is reproduced verbatim.

From whatever point of view we look at it, political economy is best described as a social science, and if a distinction is drawn between social and political sciences, it must, notwithstanding its name, be regarded as belonging to the former and not the latter category.

While science sometimes takes account of political and legal conditions, it is essentially concerned with man in his social as distinguished from his political relations. In other words, it is only in certain departments of political economy that we are concerned with men in their special character as members of a State. As remarked by Knies, 'a large preliminary division of political economy has to investigate only the social-economic life of man independently of all political influences.' The laws of distribution and exchange under conditions of free contract may be taken as an example. These laws do not exhaust the political economy, but at any rate, they fill a large and fundamentally important place in science. Again, while economic doctrines may be in some cases relative to particular political conditions, they are more frequently relative to particular stages of industrial organization that are, to a considerable extent if not altogether, independent of political influences.

The above remarks relate primarily to the positive science of economics. Regarding the political economy in its practical aspect, the connexion with politics is more intimate. Applied economics may indeed be said to be mainly concerned with the economic activities of the State in its corporate capacity or of individuals as controlled by the State. Still, as we have already had occasion to show, economic maxims—having for their object the interests of society as a whole—may also be formulated for the guidance of individuals acting independently of external constraints (Keynes 1904, 92-93).

5.2.4 Definitions of Wealth and Economic Activity

Before formally defining the political economy as a positive science, this section examines two terms—wealth and economic activities. One of the critical characteristics of wealth is that it imparts utility, which signifies the power of satisfying human needs and desires both directly and indirectly. There are many means that can satisfy human needs and desires, meaning characteristics aside from the possession of utility need to be added to distinguish wealth from other means. Just because something isn't bought or sold doesn't mean it doesn't have exchange value, for many things have exchange value that never enter the market.

With this introduction, JNK defines wealth as anything that has the power to satisfy human needs through potential exchangeability, which brings four things within its dominion. First, it includes all desirable material commodities capable of appropriation, such as food, books, buildings, and machines. Second, it embraces rights and opportunities for using, receiving, or deriving benefit from material commodities, such as mortgages and other debts, shares in public and private companies, patents, and copyrights. Third, personal services, which are not involved in any material production, such as those rendered by entertainment providers, lawyers, and physicians, are also included in the category of wealth. Finally, wealth includes the right to command or control a person's services over a given period.

> In regard to services, it is to be observed that although the benefits they confer may be more or less permanent, they are in themselves merely transient phenomena. They are, however, the produce of labour; they admit to being made the subject of exchange, and they may possess exchange value. They give rise, therefore, to problems analogous to those which present themselves in connexion with material wealth, and they are accordingly rightly included under wealth from our present standpoint (Keynes 1904, 96-97).

JNK defines economic activity analogously as a human activity that directs itself toward the production and appropriation of such means of satisfying human needs capable of being made the subject of exchanges.

The economic life of a community is constituted by the economic activities of the members of which it is composed, acting either in their individual or in their corporate capacity. The term economy is sometimes used as equivalent to economic life, and by national economy is meant as the economic life of a nation. It is to be observed that as civilization advances, each individual becomes more and more dependent on others for the satisfaction of his needs, and hence, economic life increases in complexity. In other words, with the progress of society, the organization of industry and the distribution of industrial functions grow increasingly complicated, and the phenomena resulting from men's economic activities become more and more varied in character (Keynes 1904, 100).

5.2.5 Definition of Political Economy

JNK concludes the chapter by formally defining the political economy as a positive science concerned with the phenomena of wealth. This definition, he argues, has the merit of being straightforward. It is not concerned with physical, psychological, or political phenomena directly; it deals with the phenomena, which originate from human activities in a social setting. *Accordingly, political economy may be defined as the science that treats the phenomena arising out of humankind's economic activities in society.*

5.3 Conclusion

This chapter does not comment on JNK's discourses as they did not appear confusing except for two points. First, he treats psychology as a branch of natural sciences. This conception is not consistent with the modern definition, which considers psychology to be a branch of social sciences. Modern psychology, which studies individuals' mental health both from personal and social perspectives, has been established by separating it from ethics or moral philosophy, which studies human behaviour from its moral perspective—right or wrong; good or evil, etc. Second, JNK's conception of political science is also different from its current status. This point is important because political science is a very important branch of social sciences today.

Nevertheless, JNK's conclusion about the definition and scope of economics is of lasting importance to the present and coming generations of economists: As a positive science, political economy is concerned with the phenomena of wealth, i.e., the phenomena arising out of humankind's economic activities in society. This definition is simple and straightforward, which makes it uncontroversial. No objections can be raised about this statement. However, the current generation of economists must ask itself: Why did the generations of economists neglect JNK given the fact that his articulations are most scientific? The significance of this question will be clear when we finish reviewing Robbins's *Essay*.

CHAPTER VI
ROBBINS: ENDS, MEANS, AND SCARCITY

Robbins's *Essay* has two objectives. First, it attempts to determine the "precise notions" of the subject matter of economics and its generalizations. Second, it explains "limitations and the significance of these generalizations, both as a guide to the interpretation of reality and as a basis for political practice." This book is concerned with the first objective. Accordingly, the following pages critically examine the first three chapters of the *Essay*.

6.1 The Subject Matter of Economics (Chapter I)

6.1.1 Introduction (Section 1)

> The object of this *Essay* is to exhibit the nature and significance of Economic Science. Its first task, therefore, is to delimit the subject matter of Economics—to provide a working definition of what Economics is about (Robbins 1945, 1).

This, however, is no simple job. Over the last hundred and fifty years, economists have established a body of well-accepted generalizations, yet they have failed to reach a shared position concerning the ultimate nature of the common subject matter of these generalizations. The central chapters of the standard works on Economics retail, with only minor variations, the main principles of the Science. But the chapters in which the object of the work is explained still present wide divergences. We all talk about the same things, but we have not yet agreed upon what it is we are talking about (Robbins 1945, 1).

This disagreement, however, is not unexpected. About a century ago, Mill pointed out that science was defined long after it was practiced. "Like the wall of a city, it has usually been erected, not to be a receptacle for such edifices as might afterwards spring up, but to circumscribe an aggregate already in existence." Therefore, defining the scope of any science will not be satisfactory until it has reached a particular stage of development.

> For the unity of a science only shows itself in the unity of the problems it is able to solve, and such unity is not discovered until the interconnection of its explanatory principles has been established. Modern Economics takes its rise from various separate spheres of practical and philosophical enquiry—from investigations of the Balance of Trade—from discussions of the legitimacy of the taking of interest. It was not until quite recent times that it had become sufficiently unified for the identity of the problems underlying these different enquiries to be detected. At an earlier stage, any attempt to discover the ultimate nature of the science was necessarily doomed to disaster. It would have been a waste of time to have attempted it (Robbins 1945, 2-3).

Once a discipline reaches this unification stage, it is most appropriate and urgent to delimit its scope of study because further progress will be hindered if its objective is not clearly indicated.

> The problems are no longer suggested by naïve reflection. They are indicated by gaps in the unity of theory, by insufficiencies in its explanatory principles. Unless one has grasped what this unity is, one is apt to go off on false scents. There can be little doubt that one of the greatest dangers that beset the modern economist is the preoccupation with the irrelevant—the multiplication of

activities having little or no connection with the solution of problems strictly germane to his subject (Robbins 1945, 3).

6.1.1.1 Critical Commentary

This section states the objective of this chapter, which is to provide "a working definition" of economics. More specifically, this chapter intends to outline the subject matter of economics by proposing a new definition. The objective, therefore, is both revolutionary and novel. It is revolutionary in the sense that, unlike Marshall, Robbins proposes to break away from the conventional definition. It is also novel because he wants to accomplish this objective from the body of well-agreed generalizations reached over the past hundred and fifty years: "We all talk about the same things, but we have not yet agreed what it is we are talking about."

Robbins's reasoning in this section suffers from two critical difficulties. First, from the empiricist perspective, the quoted statement does not appear clear. How could we talk about the same thing when we cannot agree on its meaning or definition? By this statement, he seems to be confirming Hume's theory that different authors imply different ideas about the definition of discipline. If so, then we are not talking about the same thing. For example, if the word "economics" bore the same idea to both Marshall and Robbins, they could not write two treatises with entirely different messages. Marshall argues that augmenting "material welfare" is precisely the reason why economic investigations are carried out in a civilized society. On the contrary, Robbins argues that human welfare is no business of economics because it is a science.

Second, Robbins's reference to Mill concerning the definition of science raises some questions, which may be explained by underlining the professional connections among three great philosophers—David Hume (1711-1776), Jeremy Bentham

(1748-1832), and J.S. Mill (1806-1873). Hume influenced Bentham with his empiricist philosophy, while Bentham directly influenced Mill as a family friend. Thus, it is more likely that Mill referred to Locke and Hume's empiricist theory, not the way Robbins used him.

6.1.2 The "Materialist" Definition of Economics (Section 2)

The orthodox authorities, including Cannan, Marshall, Pareto, and Clark, describe economics as the study of the causes of material welfare. This definition makes good sense in everyday vocabulary because the words "economic" and "material" are more or less synonymous. However, economics is a science, not an ordinary language. Therefore, the test of the soundness of its definition rests on its capacity to describe the ultimate subject matter of the science's main generalizations.

> And when we submit the definition in question to this test, it is seen to possess deficiencies which, so far from being marginal and subsidiary, amount to nothing less than a complete failure to exhibit either the scope or significance of the most central generalizations of all (Robbins 1945, 5).

The theory of wages can be used to exhibit the logical gaps in conventional wisdom. In a strict sense, wages are the sum of money earned by the work performed at stipulated rates under an employer's supervision. In economics, the term is used to imply "labour income" to distinguish it from profits.

> Now it is entirely right that some wages are the price of work that may be described as conducive to material welfare—a sewage collector's wages, for instance. However, it is equally true that some wages, the wages of the orchestra members, for instance, are paid for work, which has not the remotest bearing on material welfare. However, the one set of services, equally with the other,

commands a price and enters into the exchange circle. The Theory of Wages is as applicable to the explanation of the latter as it explains the former. Its elucidations are not limited to wages that are paid for work ministering to the 'more material' side of human well-being—whatever that may be (Robbins 1945, 5-6).

No serious economist is likely to delimit the body of economic generalizations that contains the wage theory in this manner. However, many eminent economists have questioned the applicability of economic analysis to examine the achievement of ends other than material welfare.

Professor Cannan has urged that the Political Economy of War is 'a contradiction in terms' apparently on the ground that since Economics is concerned with the causes of material welfare, and since war is not a cause of material welfare, war cannot be part of the subject matter of Economics. As a moral judgment on the uses to which abstract knowledge should be put, Professor Cannan's strictures may be accepted. But it is abundantly clear, as Professor Cannan's own practice has shown, that, so far from Economics having no light to throw on the successful prosecution of modern warfare, it is highly doubtful whether the organizers of war can possibly do without it. It is a curious paradox that Professor Cannan's pronouncement on this matter should occur in a work which, more than any other published in our language, uses the apparatus of economic analysis to illuminate many of the most urgent and the most intricate problems of a community organized for war (Robbins 1945, 7).

This habit on the part of modern English economists of describing Economics as concerned with the causes of material welfare is all the more curious when we reflect upon the unanimity with which they have adopted a non-material definition of 'productivity.' Adam Smith, it will be remembered, distinguished between Productive and Unproductive Labour, according to as the efforts in question did or did not result in the production of a tangible material object. The labour of some of the most respectable orders in the society is, like that of menial servants, unproductive of any value and does not fix or realize itself in any permanent subject or vendible commodity which endures after that labour is past… The sovereign, for example, with all the officers both of justice and war who serve under him are unproductive labourers… In the same class must be ranked some of both the gravest and most important and some of the most frivolous professions: churchmen, lawyers, physicians, men of letters of all kinds; players, buffoons, musicians, opera singers, opera dancers, etc. (Robbins 1945, 7-8).

Modern economists, including Cannan, have rejected this conception of productivity as inadequate. *The opera singers and dancers' labour should be treated as "productive" so long as it is the demand object.* The materialist proponents argue that this labour is productive because it entertains the people involved in producing goods that yield material welfare.

But, if this is so, is it not misleading to go on describing Economics as the study of the causes of material welfare? The services of the opera dancer are also wealth. Economics deals with the pricing of these services equally with the pricing of the services of a cook. Whatever Economics is concerned with, it is not concerned with the causes of material welfare as such (Robbins 1945, 9).

The reason why this definition of economics persists is mainly historical.

It is the last vestige of physiocratic influence. English economists are not usually interested in questions of scope and method. In nine cases out of ten, where this definition occurs, it has probably been taken over quite uncritically from some earlier work. But, in the case of Professor Carman, its retention is due to more positive causes, and it is instructive to attempt to trace the processes of reasoning that seem to have rendered it plausible to so penetrating and so acute an intellect (Robbins 1945, 9).

Cannan's conception of "what is economic and what is not" comes directly from his book *Wealth of Nations*. Chapter II titled *Fundamental Conditions of Wealth for Isolated Man and for Society* distinguishes between economic and non-economic issues. The materialist definition makes good sense from this perspective, for which it "deserves vindication in some detail." Under Robinson Crusoe's living conditions, which Cannan investigates, digging potatoes is an economic activity that directly contributes to material welfare, while talking to a parrot is a non-economic activity that contributes to non-material welfare. This distinction is crystal-clear.

However, suppose that after being rescued, Crusoe takes up parrot-talking as an occupation. It does not seem very logical to argue that his activity is non-economic because his material welfare depends on the profession.

Professor Cannan does not pause to ask whether his distinction is very helpful in the analysis of an exchange economy—though, after all, it is here that economic generalizations have the greatest practical utility. Instead, he proceeds forthwith to consider the 'fundamental conditions of wealth' for society considered as a whole. And here again, his definition becomes plausible: once more, the aggregate of social activities can be sorted out into the twofold classification it implies. Some activities are devoted to the pursuit of material welfare: some are not. We think, for instance, of the executive of a communist society, deciding to spend so much labour-time on the provision of bread, so much on the provision of circuses (Robbins 1945, 10-11).

Even then, Cannan's argument is subject to critical challenge. His distinction between economic and non-economic activities based on their contributions to material or non-material welfare suggests that society will accumulate more wealth by spending a greater proportion of time on material ends than in immaterial ends. However,

> we must also admit that using the word 'economic' in a perfectly normal sense, there still remains an economic problem, both for society and for the individual, of choosing between these two kinds of activity—a problem of how, given the relative valuations of product and leisure and the opportunities of production, the fixed supply of twenty-four hours in the day is to be divided between them. There is still an economic problem of deciding between the 'economic' and the 'non-economic.' One of the main problems of the Theory of Production lies half outside Professor Cannan's definition. Is not this in itself a sufficient argument for its abandonment? (Robbins 1945, 11).

6.1.2.1 Critical Commentary

Robbins argues that the conventional conception of economics does not adequately explain the scope and the significance of its most central generalizations. He substantiates his conclusion with the help of the wage theory, which shows that the wage-determination process both in the manufacturing and entertainment industries is alike.

This analogy seems erroneous. Economists are concerned only with the economic behaviour of income-earning adults, although they are affected by innumerable social forces. Then, among the economic behaviour, we primarily focus on the exchange behaviour manifested in commodity markets. Thus, the commodity market is the universal unit of all economic research. Finally, the market analysis involves only three endogenous variables—supply, demand, and price—although a host of economic and non-economic factors affect the exchange mechanism.

All this suggests that, like other social sciences, we need to identify and isolate the human behaviour that is innate or natural. The degree of this naturalness may vary from one individual to another, but the feature must be present in some form in every economic agent. From this perspective, restricting the theory of wages to labour income does not diminish any virtue related to the study of economics. The similarity between the above two industries' labour markets suggests that the entertainment business is supposed to be a critical subject matter of economic research. Nevertheless, the word "material" may be confusing in modern times.

On the contrary, it helps us concentrate on the fundamental economic problems that a democratic society is supposed to resolve—producing adequate material goods and services to meet the demand for necessities and conveniences of civilized humankind. If we do not have enough food to satisfy our hunger or a comfortable room to sleep, it is obvious that we would not go to the opera for psychological entertainment. Thus, the phrase "material welfare" continually reminds us of our jurisdiction of intellectual inquiry. It is not a limitation of the study of economics, as Robbins suggests; it is an excellent moral and scientific guide to develop our discipline for which society permits us to make our livelihood and help us satisfy our curious mind. Robbins's question, "Is it not misleading to go on describing Economics as the study of the causes of material welfare?" is contestable both academically and politically.

Even if we accept Robbins's objection to the word "material," we cannot agree with his view that the study of economics has no welfare objective. First, as Aristotle said, aiming at *the good* must be the objective of all human actions and inquiries. Without this objective, no dispassionate study can be conducted, particularly in social sciences. This is because the absence of social welfare means an anarchic society, not a society governed by law and order.

Second, all intellectual outputs are meant for the consumption of others in society as their producers do not use them. Therefore, it is a legitimate political question of why society should allow us to produce something that is not useful. For example, the government keeps a considerable police force to maintain law and order in the country, whose fundamental purpose is to protect and promote individual rights. No right can be more fundamental than the right to remain alive. Therefore, society must question the economic study of assassination, which considers a "hired killer" a rational person. How could this activity (committing a crime) be a subject of an economic investigation? All these have been possible because we have agreed with Robbins that human welfare is no business of economics. It is a science; it is value-free. By doing this, we have significantly harmed the usefulness and relevance of economics as the master social science.

6.1.3 The "Scarcity" Definition of Economics (Section 3)

This academic situation regarding the definition and subject matter of economics is both undesirable and unacceptable. Nevertheless, the materialist definition can be used as a clue to develop a definition, "which shall be immune from all these strictures." This new perspective can be quickly developed by examining "the case of the isolated man" examined above, whose chief economic problem is to divide his time between producing real income and enjoying leisure.

The economic condition of Robinson Crusoe concerns four economic issues. First, he desires both real income and leisure. Second, he does not have enough time to satisfy both wants suitably. Third, he has a choice; he can increase his real income or real leisure by allocating more time to the one he most wants. Finally, the nature of his wants for real income and leisure are different.

This scenario can be considered a replica of the modern socio-economic environment:

> The ends are various. The time and the means for achieving these ends are at once limited and capable of alternative application. At the same time, the ends have different importance. Here we are, the sentient creatures with bundles of desires and aspirations, with masses of instinctive tendencies all urging us in different ways to action. But the time in which these tendencies can be expressed is limited. The external world does not offer full opportunities for their complete achievement. Life is short. Nature is niggardly. Our fellows have other objectives. Yet, we can use our lives for doing different things, our materials and the services of others for achieving different objectives (Robbins, 1945, pp.12-13).

However, the existence of these fundamental personal problems by *themselves* does not create any economic issue. First, if we only want two things and nothing else, and we have ample time and means to acquire them, then our conduct will assume "none of those forms which are the subject of economic science. Nirvana is not necessarily single bliss. It is merely the complete satisfaction of all requirements." Second, the limited means do not create an economic issue if they cannot be used in alternative opportunities. They can be scarce relative to our desires, but we cannot economize them.

> The Manna, which fell from heaven, may have been scarce, but if it was impossible to exchange it for something else or to postpone its use, it was not the subject of any activity with an economic aspect (Robbins 1945, 13).

Finally, the alternative applicability of scarce means by itself does not constitute an economic aspect. Unless they are of different importance in satisfying the individual's need, this condition will produce little effect on the economic agents. For, they would be merely indifferent to different scarce means capable of alternative uses.

But when time and the means for achieving ends are limited and capable of alternative application, and the ends are capable of being distinguished in order of importance, then behaviour necessarily assumes the form of choice. Every act that involves time and scarce means for the achievement of one end involves the relinquishment of their use for the achievement of another. It has an economic aspect. If I want bread and sleep, and in the time at my disposal, I cannot have all I want of both, then some part of my wants of bread and sleep must go unsatisfied. If in a limited lifetime, I would wish to be both a philosopher and a mathematician, but my rate of acquisition of knowledge is such that I cannot do both completely, then some part of my wish for philosophical or mathematical competence or both must be relinquished (Robbins 1945, 13-14).

However, means are not always limited to satisfy our ends or needs. There are many things which we need for our existence. These things do not raise any economic issues because they are gifts of Nature. Air, water in the river, and wild things are natural gifts. They are not subjects of economic analysis because there is no exchange mechanism involved here.

But, in general, human activity, with its multiplicity of objectives, has not this independence of time or specific resources. The time at our disposal is limited. There are only twenty-four hours in the day. We have to choose between the different uses to which they may be put. The services which others put at our disposal are limited. The material means of achieving ends are limited. We have been turned out of Paradise. We have neither eternal life nor unlimited means of gratification. Everywhere we turn, if we choose one thing, we must relinquish others which, in different circumstances, we would wish not to have relinquished. *Scarcity of means to satisfy given ends is an almost ubiquitous condition of human behaviour* [emphasis added].

Here, then, is the unity of the subject of Economic Science, the forms assumed by human behaviour in disposing of scarce means. The examples we have discussed already harmonize perfectly with this conception. Both the services of cooks and opera dancers are limited in relation to demand and can be put to alternative uses. The theory of wages in its entirety is covered by our present definition. So, too, is the political economy of war. The waging of war necessarily involves the withdrawal of scarce goods and services from other uses if it is to be satisfactorily achieved. Therefore, it has an economic aspect. The economist studies the disposal of scarce means. He is interested in the way different degrees of scarcity of different goods give rise to different ratios of valuation between them, and he is interested in the way in which changes in conditions of scarcity, whether coming from changes in ends or changes in means—from the demand side or the supply side—affect these ratios. *Economics is the science that studies human behaviour as a relationship between ends and scarce means, which have alternative uses* [emphasis added] (Robbins 1945, 14-16).

6.1.3.1 Critical Commentary

This is the most critical section of the *Essay* and contains one of the most controversial ideas ever produced in economics science. Aristotle recognized the role of the limited means relative to the needs and desires of the individual. And the solution to this economic situation was suggested in the general framework of the Golden Mean, which defines virtue as the mean of two extremes. During the Age of Enlightenment, spiritual leaders preached the principles of love and sacrifice, which was a way to address the resource paucity issue in three different manners: rich people were urged to avoid extravagance and help the poor, middle-income people were to practice frugality, and poor people in need could get financial and other help. However, Robbins appears to be the first economist who made the concept of scarcity a unifying force in studying economics and developing its laws. Therefore, his argument demands more than curious scrutiny.

First, we need to examine the foundation of his belief by critically evaluating the primary premises of his doctrines because this discussion is deductive. In other words, the principles of deductive logic are used to analyze the concerned topics. In the deductive syllogistic system, the truths of the conclusions are determined by the truths of the primary premises.

Robbins justifies his doctrine by using Robinson Crusoe as an example, whose life depends on satisfying two kinds of needs—material and mental. He digs potatoes to meet the demands of his body and talks to his parrot-pet for entertainment. Robbins asks us to believe that the 24 hours available to Robinson Crusoe is not enough to meet both needs as he wishes. Successive generations have not questioned that his assumption is not objective, i.e., not empirical. This assumption consists of two subjective judgments. Firstly, a day has 24 hours during which the earth completes one rotation around the sun on its axis. This celestial system divides the day into daytime and nighttime. Daytime is for awareness and actions, while nighttime is for rest and sleep. Accordingly, we are all accustomed to this system and allocate our times based on our needs and desires. Perhaps, there is a sort of natural law, which helps us do that. So, it is not entirely clear how Robbins can build his economics doctrine based on the premise that it has little connection with life. Today, when our lives have become hectic due to an abnormal increase in our demands and desires, the clear majority of people have enough time to meet their needs and entertainments with which Crusoe was concerned. Therefore, our ancestors, who had few demands, were under no constraints in allocating their times among different ends. Robbins constructed his scarcity theory based on a false premise.

Finally, it is critically important to visit Neville's comment regarding the use of Robinson Crusoe in discussing the scope and method of political economy. It is not clear why Robbins excluded him from the discussion on the definition and scope of economics.

Second, Robbins's scarcity conception is founded on the simultaneous occurrence of four issues. Let us examine these issues critically, not in light of Robbins's comparison to Robinson Crusoe, but in light of the economic problem of an average adult US citizen.

Assume that the average adult US citizen is a pure wage-earner. Therefore, she spends the wage income, paid biweekly, according to an annual plan, which is drafted based on the total value of take-home incomes received over the year. The total annual take-home income is the financial limit available to her to allocate in different uses, including savings, meaning her annual wage income determines her spending plans, and the prices of different goods are services she consumes. The US citizen has no other role in the market because the market has no control over the commodity she helped produce. Based on this, the following paragraphs examine Robbins's four unifying conditions.

Unlimited Ends: Ends are limitless. This is a catchphrase used routinely in economic debates and discourses. What does this catchphrase mean? A detailed discussion will be presented in the next chapter as Robbins defines the nature of "ends" there. However, it may be noted that this controversy has been created by ignoring the difference between two ideas—demand and desire—one economic and the other psychological. If the end implies desire, then the conception is valid but has no use in economic analysis. However, if the end signifies demand for a commodity, then the phrase has little meaning. Without purchasing power, no one can get anything from the market, meaning they are not consumers. For example, our US citizen wishes to own and drive a Rolls-Royce that costs about half a million US dollars. This will simply be her desire, not demand, because she lacks the necessary purchasing power. Therefore, the Rolls-Royce company does not make its annual production plan based on the dreams of millions of car drivers like our model US citizen. However, she can certainly afford an American Chevy, meaning she is a potential Chevy customer. All car companies, Like Chevy, develop their annual production plan based on the demand of the consumers like our US citizen. Robbins's first factor seems to have little analytical value in economics.

Limited Time and Means: The implication of limited time has been examined above, and limited means is discussed in the following section. Here, we will discuss some related issues. First, Robbins confuses the concepts of possession and wealth. We can own something, which does not carry any exchange value. In that case, it is just a possession, not a commodity. Commodities have exchange value, meaning they have qualities for alternative use. This feature signifies that "the means" is a commodity in the form of money because it can be exchanged in the market. This point suggests that the following statement is controversial:

> If the means of satisfaction have no alternative use, they may be scarce, but they cannot be economized. The Manna, which fell from heaven, may have been scarce, but if it was impossible to exchange for something else or to postpone its use, it was not the subject of any activity with an economic aspect.

For, an economic means must have an exchange value or else it is not a means in economics.

Alternative Uses and Different Demand Elasticities: The third and the fourth unifying conditions Robbins lists are similar. The third condition says that the means must have exchange value in alternative uses. This is a tautology because anything obtained through the exchange must have an exchange value. However, the fourth condition demands critical consideration because it seems to indicate that Robbins is contradicting himself.

Marshall talks of the elasticity of wants. Robbins states the same thing as the differing importance of various ends. As he says, if two ends are of equal importance and there is only a single means to choose between them, the consumer will be indifferent [the vocabulary "a single means" is not clear].

This phenomenon is described in the modern economic language by three demand elasticities—price, income, and cross. A lower value of price elasticity (less than 1) indicates that the commodity has few substitutes, suggesting a low value of cross elasticity. A low value of income elasticity indicates that the concerned commodity little responds to income variations. Our experience shows that some commodities are both price and income-inelastic. These commodities belong to the group that constitutes the necessities of life, such as food, clothing, and accommodation. On the other hand, both price and income elasticities of commodities, which enhance our physical and mental comforts, are high. Some of these commodities belong to Veblen's conspicuous consumption category.

According to Robbins, the scarcity of means is the fundamental unifying feature of economic study. This statement is undoubtedly true if we agree that economics has little to do with social welfare. Take the case of health economics. It is founded on the basic microeconomics model, which suggests that superb medical services are available to those who can afford them. There are two problems with this non-philosophical view. First, if we live in a democratic political system, we must ask ourselves whether the principles of democracy on which our constitution is founded permit this kind of health policy. Second, if we treat healthcare as a personal responsibility, our health economics is founded on faulty pillars. This is particularly true in Western democracies because most of these countries guarantee universal access to medical care. Even in the US, which does not practice "socialized medicine," the federal government provides health insurance to all senior citizens. Thus, the economics of health taught at our universities is founded on a controversial theoretical framework.

6.1.4 Economics and the Exchange Economy (Section 4)

Robbins does not dismiss the orthodox definition of economics as wrong. Instead, he describes the two definitions, respectively, as classificatory and analytical. The orthodox articulation of economics is classificatory in that

> it marks off certain kinds of human behaviour directed specifically to procuring material welfare and designates these as the subject matter of economics. Other kinds of conduct lie outside the scope of its investigations (Robbins 1945, 16).

On the other hand, the analytical conception proposed in this *Essay*

> does not attempt to pick out certain kinds of behaviour but focuses attention on a particular aspect of behaviour, the form imposed by the influence of scarcity. Therefore, it follows from this that in so far as it offers this aspect, any human behaviour falls within the scope of Economic Generalizations (Robbins, 1945, 16).

The new conception does not argue that the production of potatoes is an economic activity and the production of philosophy is not. It instead submits that a social activity has an "economic aspect" if it involves sacrificing other desired alternatives. *There are no limitations on the subject matter of Economic Science save this.*

However, some writers impose another kind of restriction on the scope of economic research, which rejects the materialist conception but argues that economics is concerned with a specific type of social behaviour, implied by the "individualist exchange economy." By this criterion, human behaviour, which does not satisfy the "social" condition, is excluded from the scope of economic inquiry.

Robbins contests this proposition. Economists are involved in examining the complications of the exchange economy purely because of "interest." Like people living in an exchange economy, the isolated man's activities are well qualified for economic analysis. However, economic analysis is unnecessary from the perspective of an isolated man.

> The elements of the problem are given to unaided reflection. Examination of the behaviour of a Crusoe may be immensely illuminating as an aid to more advanced studies. But, from the point of view of Crusoe, it is obviously extra-marginal. So too, in the case of a "closed" communistic society. Again, from the point of view of the economist, the comparison of the phenomena of such a society with those of the exchange economy may be very illuminating. But from the point of view of the members of the executive, the generalizations of Economics would be uninteresting. Their position would be analogous to Crusoe's. For them, the economic problem would be whether to apply productive power to this or to that (Robbins 1945, 17).

However, the two statements implied above suggest two very different ideas. One contends that "economic analysis has most interest and utility in an exchange economy" while the other contends that "its subject matter is limited to such phenomena." The irrationality of the latter position may be shown "conclusively by two considerations." First, both inside and outside of the exchange economy, human behaviour is "conditioned by the same limitation of means in relation to ends," meaning it is "capable of being subsumed under the same fundamental categories."

> The generalizations of the Theory of Value are as applicable to the behaviour of an isolated man or the executive authority of a communist society as to the behaviour of

man in an exchange economy—even if they are not so illuminating in such contexts. The exchange relationship is a technical incident, a technical incident indeed which gives rise to nearly all the interesting complications, but still, for all that, subsidiary to the main fact of scarcity (Robbins 1945, 19).

Second, the exchange economy phenomenon can be better explained by "going behind such relationships and invoking the operation of those laws of choice that are best seen when contemplating the behaviour of the isolated individual."

6.1.4.1 Critical Commentary

Robbins's analysis in this section appears both funny and faulty. It is funny in the sense that he explains the role of exchange in economics studied in a non-socialist political system whose foundation is exchange. He argues that economists examine the complications of the exchange economy purely out of interest. This summary comment raises several difficulties. Firstly, it questions the rationality of spending time and effort on something that is not indispensable to society. Secondly, this analysis cannot be conducted in a socialist political system because it has abolished the institution of private property. When the private interest is removed from the production of wealth, all entrepreneurial ambitions, which are the engine of economic growth, vanish. Finally, consider Robbins's assertion: "Like people living in an exchange economy, the isolated man's activities are well qualified for economic analysis. However, economic analysis is unnecessary from the perspective of an isolated man."

This point is truly interesting as it raises two other issues: Should economics be studied from the perspective of the economic agent or the political society in which she lives? With whom would Robinson Crusoe conduct exchange activities? In his controversial book *Poverty and Famines*, Sen (1981) tells us that exchange can occur between individuals and Nature. The word exchange implies a give-and-take transaction, which questions how one can exchange anything with Nature that only gives but takes nothing.

These issues are important because they involve deductive reasoning, where the primary premise is the most critical determinant of the conclusion's truth. Robbins does not argue that the orthodox characterization is wrong. Instead, he describes it as classificatory because it isolates a specific set of human actions as the subject matter of economics. On the other hand, his definition is analytical because it focuses on a particular aspect of human behaviour and concludes that the science of economics has no jurisdictional limitation except imposed by the scarcity of means. One can legitimately question the meaning of this statement in light of his suggestion discussed above.

The scarcity of means, a highly unpredictable feature of human conduct, is the product of three kinds of accidents—natural, social, and personal. The difference in possession of means related to physical and mental strengths is due to a natural accident. Abilities or inabilities created through social institutions are social accidents. Finally, individuals themselves are responsible for creating the scarcity of means because they did not correctly employ the natural and social endowments available to them. This is a personal accident. Despite these facts, it is difficult to accept that the scarcity of means is the primary factor that economists should consider in conducting an economic inquiry. Individuals respond, intentionally or unintentionally, to the events affecting them. This does not suggest that the knowledge of science can be created on these passive or active motives. Marshall seems sound in his claim that economics does not measure human motives; it measures the effects and affectations of human action.

Robbins comes off as controversial by rejecting a general view concerning "social behaviour" and "individualist exchange economy." According to this view, economics studies "a specific type of social behaviour," expressed by the "individualist exchange economy." Therefore, any activity that does not satisfy this condition falls outside the jurisdiction of economic research.

The issue has been discussed above. Robbins has rejected this argument. From his perspective, he is entirely right because he has renounced the role of welfare, personal or social, in the study of economics. Nevertheless, there are at least two difficulties, which he needs to address for justifying this position. As Hume argues, academics, like other human beings, are under the control of passions excited by their moral conceptions. Therefore, the economists' contention about their discipline's subject matter is under the direct influence of their subjective judgments—moral or amoral. Second, Robbins assumes that he can do anything he wishes without any regard for society's interest. However, whatever we do or can do depends upon the support and sponsorship of the political society we live in. This issue raises two points. First, do we have the right to seek society's support and sponsorship for intellectual activities disregarding its interests? Second, does the political society we live in have any reason to support and sponsor our intellectual enterprises, fully knowing that they are not meant to enhance its interest, let alone the fact that they might involve analyzing illegal activities?

6.1.5 The "Materialist" and "Scarcity" Definitions Compared (Section 5)

This section is reproduced verbatim below to avoid any unintended distortion.

> Finally, we may return to the definition we rejected and examine how it compares with the definition we have now chosen.
>
> At first sight, it is possible to underestimate the divergence between the two definitions. The one regards the subject matter of economics as human behaviour conceived as a

relationship between ends and means, the other as the causes of material welfare. Scarcity of means and the causes of material welfare—are these not more or less the same thing?

Such a contention, however, would rest upon a misconception. It is true that the scarcity of materials indeed is one of the limitations of conduct. But the scarcity of our own time and the services of others is just as important. The scarcity of the services of the schoolmaster and the sewage man have each their economic aspect. Only by saying that services are material vibrations or the like can one stretch the definition to cover the whole field. But this is not only perverse, but it is also misleading. In this form, the definition may cover the field, but it does not describe it. *For it is not the materiality of even material means of gratification which gives them their status as economic goods; it is their relation to valuations. It is their relationship to given wants rather than their technical substance which is significant* [emphasis added]. The "materialist" definition of Economics, therefore, misrepresents the science as we know it. Even if it does not definitely mislead as to its scope, it necessarily fails to convey an adequate concept of its nature. There seems no valid argument against its rejection.

At the same time, it is important to realize that what is rejected is but a definition. We do not reject the body of knowledge which it was intended to describe. The practice of those who have adopted it fits in perfectly with the alternative definition that has been suggested. There is no important generalization in the whole range of Professor Carman's system, for instance, which is incompatible with the definition of the subject matter of Economics in terms of the disposal of scarce means.

Moreover, the very example which Professor Cannan selects to illustrate his definition fits much better into our framework than it does into his. "Economists," he says, "would agree that 'Did Bacon write Shakespeare?' was not an economic question, and that the satisfaction which believers in the cryptogram would feel if it were universally accepted would not be an economic satisfaction... On the other hand, they would agree that the controversy would have an economic side if copyright were perpetual and the descendants of Bacon and Shakespeare were disputing the ownership of the plays." Exactly. But why? Because the ownership of the copyright involves material welfare? But the proceeds may all go to missionary societies. Surely the question has an economic aspect simply and solely because the copyright laws supposed would make the use of the plays scarce in relation to the demand for their use, and would, in turn, provide their owners with command over scarce means of gratification which otherwise would be differently distributed (Robbins 1945, 21-22).

6.1.5.1 Critical Commentary

In this last section, Robbins summarizes his critical observations on the definition and the subject matter of economics and writes down the critical features of the definition he thought appropriate for the science of economics. He begins the section by noting that the difference between the definition he has proposed and the conventional one is not trivial because the former excludes "the scarcity of our own time and the services of others" for being non-material.

This statement is controversial. First, allocating time to increase material welfare was never an issue in humankind's history. Today, it is an issue in the speculative sense, not in an economic sense. This point has been explained above. Second, none of the four criteria, which creates the condition of scarcity in economics, refers to the services provided by other members of the economy. Economic activities related to the supply of commodities in the market can be grouped into three sectors—production, manufacturing, and services. In terms of the GDP share in a modern economy, the contributions of the first two sectors have dramatically declined while those of the service sector have increased. The principles of economics apply equally to all these sectors. Keynes has made this point very unambiguous. The exclusive focus of orthodox economics on material well-being, which is subject to criticism, in no way suggests the exclusion of the service sector from the purview of economic research. Robbins's criticisms fall out of context and proportion.

Third, one of the fundamental premises of Robbins's discourse is that it is not concerned with the social aspects of economic activity. As noted above, the economics of services is studied in the same way the economics of production and manufacturing are studied. Many sub-disciplines have been developed to study the service sectors, such as the financial market, management sciences, etc. The foundational premise of these sub-disciplines is the time-tested model of economics, which is called microeconomics. Therefore, the insistence of orthodox economics on "material welfare" does not prevent expanding the scope of economics as required by the evolutionary changes in our knowledge and culture. However, it prevents the expansion of economics to activities that are either illegal or undesirable from the social viewpoint. One outstanding example of the Robbinsian proliferation in economics is the economics of crimes.

The concluding point Robbins makes is also worth noting. He says that the new definition does not "reject the body of knowledge" generated by orthodox economists. That body of knowledge better fits in the alternative definition. This is because the orthodox definition is classificatory, while his definition is analytical. The fundamental difference between the two definitions concerns the scope of economic investigations. In the orthodox definition, the scope or subject matter is narrow and well-demarcated, while it is almost borderless in the latter.

Robbins's remark raises two critical questions—one professional and the other political—which include preferring Robbins's definition over conventional wisdom. The professional question involves assessing the scientific virtue of treating economics as a borderless social science discipline. The straightforward answer to this question is that the study of human behaviour would not have been divided into four closely related but distinctly independent social sciences if Robbins's conjectures were correct.

The political question concerns economists pursuing their pleasure-seeking activities in the way Robbins has suggested. According to his scarcity definition, the limit to the economic inquiry is the existence of an "economic aspect" that arises in the exchange process due to unlimited ends and limited means. His economic agent has little regard for the laws and customs on which political society is founded and promoting individual and social welfare—the fundamental purpose of this society. This view supports the doctrine of anarchism, not constitutional governance, which rules the global village today.

6.2 Ends and Means (Chapter II)

After proposing a working definition of economics in Chapter I, Robbins examines its implications in this chapter regarding "the status of ends and means as they figure in economic theory and economic history." The chapter is divided into five sections, excluding a one-paragraph introduction. These five sections are summarized and criticized chronologically below. It will be noticed, as we walk with Robbins, that he criticizes two distinguished Cambridge economists, Alfred Marshall and J.N. Keynes, without mentioning them in his discussion.

6.2.1 Economics and Ends (Section 2)

Economics studies the feature of human behaviour that is activated by the scarcity of means to achieve given ends.

It follows that Economics is entirely neutral between ends; that, in so far as the achievement of any end is dependent on scarce means, it is germane to the preoccupations of the Economist. Economics is not concerned with ends as such. It assumes that human beings have ends in the sense that they have tendencies to conduct which can be defined and understood, and it asks how their progress toward their objectives is conditioned by the scarcity of means—how the disposal of the scarce means is contingent on these ultimate valuations (Robbins 1945, 24).

Accordingly, treating any end as "economic" "is entirely misleading."

The habit, prevalent among certain groups of economists, of discussing "economic satisfactions' is alien to the central intention of economic analysis. A satisfaction is to be conceived as an end-product of activity. It is not itself part of that activity which we study. It would be going too far to urge that it is impossible to conceive of 'economic satisfactions.' For, presumably, we can so describe a satisfaction that is contingent on the availability of scarce means as distinct from a satisfaction that depends entirely on subjective factors—e.g., the satisfaction of having a summer holiday, as compared with the satisfaction of remembering it. But since, as we have seen, the scarcity of means is so wide as to influence to some degree almost all kinds of conduct, this does not seem a useful conception. And since it is manifestly out of harmony with the main implications of our definition, it is probably better avoided altogether (Robbins 1945, 25).

Moreover, it is a "misapprehension" on the part of "more neurotic critics of Economic Science" that it is preoccupied "with a peculiarly low type of conduct."

The Economist is not concerned with ends as such. He is concerned with the way in which the attainment of ends is limited. The ends may be noble, or they may be base. They may be "material" or "immaterial"—if ends can be so described. But if the attainment of one set of ends involves the sacrifice of others, then it has an economic aspect.

All this is quite obvious if only we consider the actual sphere of application of economic analysis, *instead of resting content with the assertions of those who do not know what economic analysis is* [emphasis added]. Suppose, for instance, a community of sybarites, their pleasures gross and sensual, their intellectual activities preoccupied with the 'purely material.' It is clear enough that economic analysis can provide categories for describing the relationships between these ends and the means that are available for achieving them. But it is not true, as Ruskin and Carlyle and suchlike critics have asserted, that it is limited to this sort of thing. Let us suppose this reprehensible community to be visited by a Savonarola. Their former ends become revolting to them. The pleasures of the senses are banished. The sybarites become ascetics. Surely economic analysis is still applicable. There is no need to change the categories of explanation. All that has happened is that the demand schedules have changed. Some things have become relatively less scarce, others more so. The rent of vineyards falls. The rent of quarries for ecclesiastical masonry rises. That is all. The distribution of time between prayer and good works has its economic aspect equally with the distribution of time between orgies and slumber. The 'pig-philosophy'—to use poor Carlyle's name for Economics—turns out to be all-embracing (Robbins 1945, 25-26).

Economists are to be partially blamed for this situation because of their "misleading definitions" and "unnecessarily apologetic attitude in the face of criticism."

It is even said that quite modern Economists who have been convinced both of the importance of Economics and of its preoccupation with the 'more material side of human welfare' have been reduced to prefacing their lectures on general Economic Theory with the rather sheepish apology that, after all, bread and butter are necessary, even to the lives of artists and saints." However, the detractors of economics, notably Carlyle and Buskin, never made any efforts to justify their cynicism. Therefore, there are few excuses to reject the theory of 'low ends of conduct' and 'adopt an attitude of superiority as regards the subjects that they are capable of handling.' Speaking generally, "Professor Cannan is a little apt to follow St. Peter and cry, 'Lord, I have never touched the unclean thing.' In the opening chapter of *Wealth*, he goes out of his way to say that "the criterion of buying and selling brings many things into economics which are not commonly treated there and which it does not seem convenient to treat there. A large trade has existed since history began in supplying certain satisfactions of a sensual character that are never regarded as economic goods. Indulgences to commit what would otherwise be regarded as offences against religion or morality have been sold sometimes openly and at all times under some thin disguise: nobody has regarded these as economic goods.

This is surely very questionable. Economists, equally with other human beings, may regard the services of prostitutes as conducive to no 'good' in the ultimate ethical sense. But to deny that such services are scarce in the sense in which we use the term and that there is, therefore, an economic aspect of hired love, susceptible to treatment in the same categories of general analysis as enabling us to explain fluctuations in the price of hired writing, does not seem to be in accordance with the facts. As for the sale of indulgences, surely the status in Economic History of these agreeable transactions is not seriously open to question. Did the sale of indulgences affect the distribution of income, the magnitude of expenditure on other commodities, the direction of production, or did it not? We must not evade the consequences of the conclusion that all conduct coming under the influence of scarcity has its economic aspect (Robbins 1945, 27-28).

6.2.1.1 Critical Commentary

The first point to be noted here is that Robbins uses the term "the status of ends" instead of the common one, "the meaning of ends." The words "meaning" and "status" do not convey the same idea or notion. Meaning or, more appropriately, denotation of a word or a word-group indicates a definite thing—action, feeling, or idea—such as eating, loving, or God. Therefore, we all understand their denotations when they are spoken or written. On the other hand, in ordinary usage, status signifies an official position of a person or the level of respect, admiration, or importance this person commands in social institutions. However, in a specific context, status also means a piece of information about something, such as one's status on Facebook. In this sense, "status" is an abstract noun. Robbins seems to refer to this sense when he says that "economics is not concerned with ends as such." It neither implies human actions nor the objects on which these actions are performed. Instead, it implies human "tendencies" instigated by "scarcity of means" that can be defined and understood.

Scarcity, Robbins rightly says, is "an aspect of behaviour that arises from the insufficiency of means to achieve given ends." This statement demands careful consideration. First, scarcity is a social phenomenon, not a natural feature, meaning its nature and intensity vary from one individual to another due to social reasons in addition to natural ones. Second, it is a relative concept, meaning its intensity critically depends on the relative valuations of both ends and means.

Keeping these features in mind, the following paragraphs critically assess Robbins's conception of scarcity. First, if ends are not what they are, what then are they? Standard dictionaries define "ends" as goals or objectives of some actions—physical or psychological. Robbins does not mean that. However, Robbins states that "a satisfaction is to be conceived as an end-product of activity. It is not itself part of that activity we study." Here, Robbins seems to imply what is called "utility" in modern economics. In other words, by "ends," he implies "utility" or "satisfaction" that a consumer derives from the consumption of a commodity.

Given this definition, the issue that comes up for critical review is to assess the usefulness of this idea for understanding the nature and subject matter of economics. First, it is the norm in economics to derive the demand and supply curves under two different assumptions—profit maximization and utility maximization. These assumptions reflect diagonally different motives of the two groups of market participants—producers and consumers. By defining ends as a utility, Robbins deals with only one side of the market: consumption. Although there is a tendency among modern economists to treat the profit-maximizing activity as a sort of utility, the amount of profit should not be used as a proxy for a psychological variable. This will imply converting a matter-of-fact variable into a psychological one, which will only dissuade the purpose of studying economics.

Second, Robbins's line of reasoning tends to make economics a study of demand in the same way that the classical economists made the political economy a study of supply. The primary difference between the two approaches is the following: The classical economists were primarily concerned with the production of adequate necessities and conveniences as the economic environment of the day demanded. On the other hand, the neoclassical economists identified the flaws in this approach. They proved that the market price of a private commodity does not depend only on its production costs; the nature of market demand plays a very significant role in the market clearing process. However, in correcting this gap in classical economics, the neoclassical school overemphasized the role of demand in studying the market economy. They have converted the nation-states into affluent societies whose primary problem is to study consumer behaviour as technologies are available to respond to their demands. This unbalanced emphasis on the market demand makes it difficult to understand the true nature of economics. Robbins is the leader of this movement in the neoclassical school.

Third, besides these points, we need to revisit Aristotle's maxim in the *Nicomachean Ethics*, which begins by differentiating between "ends" and actions or activities. All actions and inquiries aim at some good. However, the ends sought by these efforts are sometimes activities and sometimes other products apart from the activities that produce them. For example, we eat food to satisfy the demand of our stomachs. Here, eating is not the end; it is a means to our ultimate end of satisfying our hunger. More specifically, consumers buy different commodities to meet different needs and desires. This situation required the economists to invent the abstract term—utility—to compare the psychological values the consumer derives from different commodities.

This description of ends does not seem significantly different from that of Robbins. His relative valuation idea by which each end is represented in economics is the same as utility or satisfaction. However, his assertions that "treating any end as economic is entirely misleading," and "economic satisfaction is alien to the central intention of economic analysis" raise serious questions. Two truths, which Locke and Hume have established, may explain these questions: (i) the primary methodology of science is induction, meaning the real source of scientific knowledge is "experience," and (ii) this knowledge is deduced through studying the cause-and-effect relations among matters of fact.

The classification of facts based on their shared qualities is a fundamental requirement of induction. For example, all human beings are different in some respects, but they must possess some unique or innate characteristics to be qualified as human beings. Similarly, individuals seek multifarious ends in life, which can only be scientifically studied if they are classified into meaningful groups—economic ends, political ends, social ends, etc. They must also provide different kinds of satisfaction because they reflect different ends. Thus, economic ends provide satisfaction concerning the accusation and disposal of wealth, while political ends are targeted to control government power. Similarly, food consumption satisfies our hunger, while accommodation meets our needs for safety and rest. Thus, it is a scientific requirement to classify ends in terms of their natural and social qualities, meaning the phrases "economic ends" and "economic satisfactions" can never be "misleading."

Fourth, *Economics is entirely neutral between ends; that, in so far as the achievement of any end depends on scarce means, it is germane to the Economist's preoccupations.* This deductive statement seems contradictory. Firstly, it contradicts the methodological foundation of economics. Since it is a branch of social science, its primary research methodology is inductive, not deductive. The proposition that "ends are neutral" cannot be sustained through induction. Consider the satisfaction that an individual derives from eating and watching a movie. If the individual is hungry, she is not supposed to spend her fixed money buying a ticket to the cinema instead of buying food. Secondly, the "end neutrality" assumption directly violates the fourth unifying feature of Robbins's scarcity model, which posits that different commodities in the consumer's basket represent different degrees of "importance." Without this assumption, Robbins says, the consumer will be indifferent in her choice of the consumption bundle. How could the consumers become *entirely end-neutral* if they are not indifferent concerning the utility of commodities they consume? Moreover, if the consumer cannot be end-neutral, how could the economist assume them to be?

Thirdly, the demand curve derives its negative slope property from the principle of diminishing marginal utility. If ends are assumed neutral, then it will be mathematically incorrect to draw an indifference curve because its slope represents ratios of marginal utilities of two commodities.

Fifth, Robbins's comment "neurotic critics of Economic Science who do not know what economic analysis is" demands critical scrutiny. Although he did not mention these "neurotic critics" by name, it is not difficult to assume that he refers to the materialist school, whose key architect was Alfred Marshall. Both Marshall and Robbins claim that they are not proposing any new ideas; they are mainly synthesizing the doctrines of the past and contemporary masters with new data and illustrations. These admissions supply much-needed information to assess their opinions. Marshall synthesized the doctrines of Adam Smith, David Ricardo, and J. S. Mill, while Robbins employed the views of Ludwig von Mises and Philip Wicksteed. Therefore, comparing Robbins with Marshall amounts to comparing the contributions of the economists whose views they substantiated. Hume's philosophy seems critical to judge arguments and opinions of our disputants—Marshall and Robbins.

Sixth, Marshall describes economics as the study of human behaviour in the ordinary business of life. By this phrase, he mimics Adam Smith, who underlined in the first sentence of his book that the supply of all necessities and conveniences of life should be the primary objective of studying political economy. Whether a nation is better or worse supplied with this stock is indicated by the proportion of individuals, who helped its production, consume it. We can make this statement with confidence because Marshall testifies that he primarily synthesizes his predecessors' doctrines. Robbins's interpretation of Marshall seems erroneous. He understood "the ordinary business of life" as "a peculiarly low type of conduct." Indeed, Marshall had been more philosophical than scientific in describing the human behaviour supposed to the subject of economic inquiry. However, this aberration does not give any excuse to describe the definition of economics as "preoccupied with a peculiarly low type of conduct."

Seventh, the adjectives "high and low" carry subjective implications, meaning their use in economics might clash with its scientific nature. Accordingly, Robbins's comment demands critical scrutiny. If human activities associated with the production and consumption of necessities and conveniences are of low categories, what kind of economic activities belong to the high-conduct category? To answer this question, we need to be reminded of two points. Firstly, Robbins describes the difference between materialist and scarcity definitions of economics as classificatory and analytical. Secondly, he believes "economic end" and "economic satisfaction" are misleading conceptions.

Robbins has made economics virtually a borderless social science on the argument that the materialist perception excludes many social activities that can be satisfactorily explained with the established laws of economics. However, making the study of economics borderless challenges the idea of dividing social science into different disciplines. If economists can explain human behaviour related to politics, why should we have political science as a separate discipline?

The preceding point underlines the broader implication of Robbins's definition. However, a more interesting point here is that it makes the study of economics virtually meaningless and anti-social. Consider the last paragraph of the section. The services of prostitutes, Robbins agrees, is unethical.

> However, to deny that such services are scarce in the sense in which we use the term and that there is, therefore, an economic aspect of hired love, susceptible to treatment in the same categories of general analysis as enabling us to explain fluctuations in the price of hired writing, does not seem to be per the facts (Robbins 1945, 28).

Robbins's argument seems inconsistent with the fundamental pillar of modern economics. Selling sex and selling books are both economic activities for all the reasons Robbins has illustrated. However, the social values that these activities represent in a civilized society are judged in moral terms—good or bad, honourable or dishonourable. All societies, political or not, have developed and enforced laws and customs that encourage good and honourable activities and discourage harmful and dishonourable activities. In other words, society determines the types of activities its members can pursue freely for their benefit. All criminal activities, like murder, assassination, and theft, have been declared illegal, and laws have been enacted to publish the perpetrators. How could these activities be included in the study of economics simply because they involve the "disposal of scarce means?" There is another issue that demands critical consideration. Selling books is a voluntary activity. Can we say the same thing about selling sex?

Finally, as human activities need to be distinguished from moral perspectives, so socially-sanctioned economic activities/commodities need to be distinguished based on their importance to human life. Food cannot be compared with non-food items because they are not substitutable in any sense. We must eat food every day to survive. If we must spend all our money on food, we will do so to survive. Similarly, medical services and medicines are not ordinary commodities. Nevertheless, modern economists have orchestrated health economics based on the market model of microeconomics. Health economics is an example, which shows how Robbins's misconception has captivated the minds of modern economists.

6.2.3 Economics and the Aesthetic (Section 3)

English industrialist and economist Baron Stamp (1880–1941)—an ardent advocate for preserving the countryside and safeguarding ancient monuments—describes "aesthetics as an economic factor." Stamp, a staunch materialist messenger, argues that indifference to the aesthetic negatively affects national output in the long run:

> That is to say that if we seek first the Kingdom of the Beautiful, all material welfare will be added unto us. And he brings all the solid weight of his authority to the task of stampeding the business world into believing that this is true (Robbins 1945, 29).

> Although the intention of this argument is creditable, it is "difficult to believe that its logic is very convincing." For, there are few *a priori* reasons to assume that the study of ancient monuments and the contemplation of beautiful objects may be both stimulating to the intelligence and restful to our nervous system, and the community offering opportunities for such interests may gain in other, "more material," ways.

> It is surely a fact which we must all recognize that rejection of material comfort in favour of aesthetic or ethical values does not necessarily bring material compensation.

What has happened, of course, is that adherence to the "materialist" definition has prevented Sir Josiah from recognizing the truth that Economics and Aesthetics are not in *pari materia*. Aesthetics is concerned with certain kinds of ends. The Aesthetic is an end that offers itself for choice in competition, so to speak, with others. Economics is not concerned at all with any ends as such. It is concerned with ends in so far as they affect the disposition of means. It takes the ends as given in scales of relative valuation and enquires what consequences follow in regard to certain aspects of behaviour (Robbins 1945, 29-30).

6.2.3.1 Critical Commentary

To explain the difference between the three compartments of economic science—positive, normative, and art—Neville examined the relationship between political economy and the related branches of both social and natural sciences, including ethics, as discussed above. He argued that normative economics combines the functions of both the economist and the moralist to investigate practical public policy issues. Nevertheless, the study of ethics is entirely independent of the study of economics. In analyzing the public policy issues, economists take the principles of ethics as data, not the subject matter of economics.

In this section, Robbins counters Neville under the heading *Economics and the Aesthetic*, where he treats aesthetic and ethics as synonymous. However, Robbins's reasoning in this section appears fallacious for two reasons. First, he defines "ends" in terms of satisfaction or utility, which is a psychological phenomenon. This assumption is necessary to compare "ends" obtained from consuming different commodities. However, readers get confused because, for example, Robbins argues that "ends" obtained from watching a movie are "economic" but not from visiting a monument. Alternatively, he seems to argue that producing a movie is economic but activities involved in preserving a monument are not.

Second, Robbins fails to distinguish between what we today call endogenous and exogenous variables. Price, demand, and supply are all endogenous variables whose values are determined within the model. However, factors that affect these variables may not be all endogenous. For example, the price of an imported commodity may be affected due to changes in the exchange rate, which is treated as an exogenous variable in the model.

However, the most outstanding example of an exogenous variable in modern economics is "good governance." It is now a general belief among economists and public policymakers that good governance directly affects the aid performance of a developing economy. Aid is an injection in an economy in the same way a foreign loan is an injection. The fundamental difference between the two is that the loan needs to be repaid with interest but not aid. To determine the aid policy, the donor governments collect information about the nature of governance in the recipient country. This donor policy does not suggest that economists involved in this policy research must study its entire governance mechanism; this job belongs to political scientists. In the same way, aesthetics, a branch of philosophy that investigates this phenomenon, is concerned with studying human behaviour concerning beauty and taste, and economists can use this information as a datum in choosing different development projects. Describing aesthetics as an economic factor is undoubtedly incorrect, but Robbins's explanation of why this factor should not be accounted for in project analysis is equally flawed.

6.2.4 Economics and Technology (Section 4)

> Economics, then, is in no way to be conceived as we may conceive Ethics or Aesthetics as being concerned with ends as such. It is equally important that its preoccupations should be sharply distinguished from those of the technical arts of production. This raises certain issues of considerable complexity, which it is desirable to examine at some length (Robbins 1945, 32).

The proponents of the materialist definition had difficulties in understanding the relationship between economics and the technical arts of production.

Chapter VI: Robbins: Ends, Means, And Scarcity

It is clear that the technical arts of production are concerned with material welfare. Yet, the distinction between art and science does not seem to exhaust the difference. So much scientific knowledge is germane to the technical arts of production that is foreign to Economic Science. Yet where is one to draw the line? Sir William Beveridge has put this difficulty very clearly in his lecture on Economics as a Liberal Education. 'It is too wide a definition to speak of Economics as the science of the material side of human welfare. A house contributes to human welfare and should be material. If, however, one is considering the building of a house, the question of whether the roof should be made of paper or of some other material is a question not of Economics but the technique of house building.' Nor do we meet this difficulty by inserting the word 'general' before 'causes of material welfare.' Economics is not the aggregate of the technologies. Nor is it an attempt to select from each the elements common to several (Robbins 1945, 32).

But, from the point of view of the definition we have adopted, the connection is perfectly definite. The technical arts of production are simply to be grouped among the given factors influencing the relative scarcity of different economic goods. The technique of cotton manufacture, as such, is no part of the subject matter of Economics, but the existence of a given technique of various potentialities, together with the other factors influencing supply, conditions the possible response to any valuation of cotton goods and consequently influences the adaptations which it is the business of Economics to study (Robbins 1945, 33).

This inference might be challenged because "the theory of production is one of the central preoccupations of economic analysis." Therefore, this line of reasoning might be interpreted as excluding a vital component of the subject matter of economics.

However, this objection "involves a complete misapprehension—a misapprehension which it is important finally to dispel."

> The attitude we have adopted toward the technical arts of production does not eliminate the desirability of an economic theory of production. For the influences determining the structure of production are not purely technical in nature. No doubt, technique is very important. But technique is not everything. It is one of the merits of modern analysis that it enables us to put technique in its proper place. This deserves further elucidation. It is not an exaggeration to say that, at the present day, one of the main dangers to civilization arises from the inability of minds trained in the natural sciences to perceive the difference between the economic and the technical (Robbins 1945, 34).

Robbins illustrates the point by referring to Crusoe's dilemma with a small stock of wood. We can see the nature of the economic problem he encounters if we assume that the supply of wood cannot be increased for the time being. He will have no difficulty in deciding how to use this limited stock if he has only one purpose, such as making a fire or fencing the cabin. For, he will burn the wood for as long as it lasts or make the fence as wide as he can. In both cases, the problem is technical concerning fire-making and fencing, which he knows well. However, if this limited stock is to be used for both purposes, then he will be confronted with a problem—deciding how much wood to use for the fire and how much for the fence. In this resource use situation, the problem is no longer a purely technical problem; it an economic problem.

> Or, to put the matter in more behaviouristic terms, the influences on his disposal of wood are no longer purely technical. Conduct is the resultant of conflicting

psychological pulls acting within an environment of given material and technical possibilities. The problem of technique and the problem of economy are fundamentally different problems. To use Professor Mayer's very elegant way of putting the distinction, the problem of technique arises when there is one end and a multiplicity of means, the problem of economy when both the ends and the means are multiple (Robbins 1945, 35).

It has been established that "ends are various and that most of the scarce means at our disposal are capable of alternative application" in the world in which we live.

This applies not only to scarce products. It applies still more to the ultimate factors of production. The various kinds of natural resources and labour can be used for an almost infinite variety of purposes. The disposition to abstain from consumption in the present releases uses of primary factors for more than one kind of roundabout process. And, for this reason, a mere knowledge of existing technique does not enable us to determine the actual "set" of the productive apparatus. We need to know also the ultimate valuations of the producers and consumers connected with it. It is out of the interplay of the given systems of ends on the one side and the material and technical potentialities on the other, that the aspects of behaviour that the economist studies are determined (Robbins 1945, 36).

Although "all this sounds very abstract," it merely states the "facts which are well known to all of us." If asked why a particular commodity is produced in a specific area in such an amount, we usually answer in terms of prices and costs that are "the reflection of relative valuations, not of merely technical conditions." Similarly, if a commodity, which can be easily produced, is not being produced, we explain the reason in terms of its expected price and production costs. Thus, the difference between economics and technology is sufficiently clear. However, all this brings us "back to the proposition from which we started."

> Economists are not interested in technique as such. They are interested in it solely as one of the influences determining relative scarcity. Conditions of technique "show" themselves in the productivity functions just as conditions of taste "show" themselves in the scales of relative valuations. But there, the connection ceases. Economics is a study of the disposal of scarce commodities. The technical arts of production study the "intrinsic" properties of objects or human beings (Robbins 1945, 38).

6.2.4.1 Critical Commentary

The first difficulty with this section is that Robbins continues to accuse the conventional wisdom about a fancied materialist conception of the nature and scope of economics, which has been corrected long ago. Second, in Section I, Chapter III, Neville illustrates the connection between the positive political economy and physical sciences, including agriculture and manufacturing. Nevertheless, Robbins does not say a word about Neville, which raises curiosities about his objective of dealing with the issue in the *Essay*. More specifically, the manner of his presentation seems to suggest that he is determined to discredit the conventional wisdom to publicize his conception.

According to Robbins, there is no conflict between economics and technology in the scarcity conception because it only groups the factors influencing the relative scarcity of different economic goods. For example, the technique of cotton manufacturing is not part of the subject matter of economics. However, techniques of various potentialities and other supply factors influence the possible response to any valuation of cotton goods, which is the business of economics. This position does not undermine the role of production theory in economics. The attitude "adopted toward the technical arts of production does not eliminate the desirability of an economic theory of production." The factors "determining the structure of production are not purely technical in nature." Techniques are indispensable in production but "not everything."

Robbins's logic presented in the section appears less than convincing because he fails to see the different meanings of two related words—science and technology. Science is all about cause-and-effect relations, while technology refers to the sum of techniques, skills, methods, and processes used to produce goods or services. In other words, technology is the art of production, which represents the application of scientific knowledge to resolve problems of practical life.

Given this difference, science may be understood as developing theories, while technology refers to applying those theories to satisfy human needs and demands. An economist working at a university may not know how a car is manufactured, but an economist working for a car manufacturing firm must know the details about how cars are manufactured. These details are indispensable for settling both production and pricing problems. They are supposed to determine optimum input combinations to produce the optimal output level at minimum costs. In marketing, they must determine a pricing scheme to maximize profit. The automobile corporation is not a price-taker like a producer in our micro model. However, economists are concerned about how cars are manufactured in the plant. This is the job of automobile engineers.

The preceding line of reasoning suggests that Robbins's arguments are fallacious on several counts. Firstly, he confuses science with technology. Secondly, he fails to see the roles economists play in their different professional responsibilities. As a university economist, he only considers economic theories he learned and ignores the roles economists play in their other employments. It is worth noting that individuals do not qualify to be engineers by merely obtaining engineering degrees; they are known as engineers through their professional activities. Robbins's proposed distinction between economics and technology appears unconvincing. His use of Crusoe's dilemma of the small wood stock is unsatisfactory to justify his claim.

Besides these faulty arguments, he commits other fallacies by tying the production issues with the first three conditions of the scarcity model—unlimited ends, limited means, and alternative employment capabilities—which also apply to all factors of production, such as labour, land, and natural resources and capital.

Difficulties in these arguments follow directly from overlooking the difference between input and output markets. In both markets, demand and supply factors determine the commodity price. The players of the output market—consumers and producers—are very different types of economic agents. Consider a very short-run market situation where supply is fixed. In this market, the price will be determined by the elasticity of the demand curve, which is derived from the proposition that consumers maximize the utility subject to the budget constraint. Consider a similar situation in the input market. Here consumers are the firm owners while workers are input suppliers. Given the fixed supply of labour, consumers (the firm owners) will determine the wage rate given profit prospects of their outputs, not their budget constraint. The strength of the consumers' budget depends on their incomes, while the credit market determines the producer's demand for labour. Therefore, it is tough to see how Robbins's definition of economics, which seems universally accepted in the modern economics profession, can describe the nature of economics to be practiced in a democratic society.

6.2.5 Economic Theory and Economic History (Section 5)

It follows from the argument of the preceding sections that the subject matter of Economics is essentially a relationship—a relationship between ends conceived as tendencies to conduct, on the one hand, and the technical and social environment on the other. Ends as such do not form part of this subject matter. Nor does the technical and social environment. It is the relationships between these things and not the things in themselves that are important for the economist (Robbins 1945, 38). This supposition introduces a new relationship between "economic history" and "economic theory," which removes all possible grounds of conflict between them.

> The nature of Economic Theory is clear. It is the study of the formal implications of this relationship of ends and means. The nature of Economic History should be no less evident. It is the study of the substantial instances in which this relationship shows itself through time. It is the explanation of the historical manifestations of "scarcity". Economic Theory describes the forms, Economic History the substance (Robbins 1945, 38-39).

> Therefore, it is illogical to classify events into groups and say that these are the subject matter of economic theory and those are the subject matter of economic history.

> The province of Economic History, equally with the province of Economic Theory, cannot be restricted to any part of the stream of events without doing violence to its inner intentions. But no more than any other kind of history does it attempt a comprehensive description of this stream of events; it concentrates upon the description of a certain aspect thereof—a changing network of economic relationships, the effect on values in the economic sense of changes in ends and changes in the technical and social opportunities of realizing them. If the Economic

Theorist, manipulating his shadowy abacus of forms and inevitable relationships, may comfort himself with the reflection that all action may come under its categories, the Economic Historian, freed from subservience to other branches of history, may rest assured that there is no segment of the multi-coloured weft of events which may not prove relevant to his investigations (Robbins 1945, 39).

Consider the Reformation in Europe as an illustrative example. Historians examine the nature and significance of this great movement from four different perspectives belonging to four different academic areas—religion, politics, culture, and economics. Religious historians analyze the significance of Reformation "on doctrine and ecclesiastical organization;" the interest of political historians "consists in the changes in political organization, the new relations of rulers and subjects and the emergence of the national states;" and the cultural historians study significant "changes both in the form and the subject matter of the arts in the spirit of modern scientific enquiry." However, the economic historians are chiefly interested in the "changes in the distribution of property, changes in the channels of trade, changes in the demand for fish, changes in the supply of indulgences, and changes in the incidence of taxes." They are not interested in "the changes of ends and the changes of means in themselves."

6.2.5.1 Critical Commentary

In Appendix C, titled *The Scope and Method of Economics*, Marshall examines the relationship between economic theory and economic history, where economic history is considered as part of general history that informs us about the nature of past social institutions and the consequences of their policies. For this purpose, economists do not require intensive analysis; an active and inquiring mind can easily do the job. Much of this work needs little more than common sense and wit, a sound sense of proportion, and extensive life experience, not detailed scientific inquiry. Thus, the difference and the relation between economic theory and economic history are clear.

However, without referring to Marshall's published arguments, Robbins strangely counters them. He holds that economic theory studies the formal relationship between ends and means, while economic history studies the notable instances in which this relationship shows itself through time. "It is the explanation of the historical manifestations of 'scarcity.' Economic Theory describes the forms, Economic History the substance." Therefore, it is illogical to classify economic events into two groups—economic theory and economic history.

Robbins's assertion demands more careful consideration than ever before because he contradicts himself and confuses his readers. First, consider his claim from Locke's empiricist perspective. Each word signifies a definite idea. Here, "economic" is an adjective that qualities two words—theory and history—in the same sense. Let us ignore the adjective and focus on the two abstract nouns—theory and history—and ask ourselves: Do these words signify the same or similar idea? It is impossible that they will convey the same or similar idea because these words are not synonyms.

Second, Robbins developed his economics definition by analyzing Crusoe's survival issues, where he was both producer and consumer. Therefore, his production and consumption decisions were guided by the same motive—his welfare, consisting of material and non-material components. However, when he takes on parrot-talking as a profession, he becomes a consumer, not a producer. As a consumer, his objective is to maximize utility (ends) subject to the budget constraint, i.e., income received from the parrot-talking business. The technical environment relevant to his profession concerns his skills in parrot-talking. If his skills are poor, he will have few customers. The "social environment" relevant to his profession concerns people's tastes in entertainment. If the people who live in his community like parrot-talking, he will undoubtedly have a prosperous business.

This argument suggests some ambiguity about the roles consumers and producers play in a market economy. Consumers maximize utility subject to budget constraint, which gives rise to the downward-sloping demand curve. On the other hand, producers maximize profits by minimizing costs, which generate an upward-sloping supply curve. If these conditions do not hold, we have no economic discipline. The statement "the subject matter of economics is essentially a relationship—a relationship between ends conceived as tendencies to conduct, on the one hand, and the technical and social environment on the other" seems very confusing.

Based on the proposition reported above, Robbins argues that the subject matter of economic history cannot be separated from that of economic theory. For, economic theory studies "the formal implications of this relationship of ends and means." On the other hand, economic history studies "the substantial instances in which this relationship shows itself through time. It is the explanation of the historical manifestations of 'scarcity.' Economic theory describes the forms, economic history the substance."

Robbins's rationale about the difference between the subject matter of economic theory and economic history seems unscientific because theory and history are two different academic subjects. From the empiricist perspective, a theory represents a cause-and-effect relation among matters of facts. Matters of facts relations vary depending on the type of physical objects under investigation. For this reason, theories are distinguished by using adjectives such as political theory, sociological theory, etc. As noted above, we have theories related to both demand and supply in economics, which create the basic microeconomics model. The demand theory predicts a negative relationship between the quantity of a commodity demanded and its price, while the supply theory predicts the opposite. To develop these theories, pioneering economists needed great insights into human nature and its manifestations in the social environment in which individuals in their roles, both as consumers and producers, revealed their behaviours.

On the other hand, history is a branch of knowledge that analyzes past events using rules of logic. Since past events differ in terms of number and importance, they need to be classified for the research. Thus, the history of Canada can be studied from different perspectives, including politics, economics, and culture. This will be done using the following adjectives: political, economical, and cultural. Those who wish to study Canada's economic history will do a better job if they first acquire some knowledge of economic theory. This knowledge is required to explain different economic events in different periods, which does not suggest that they must use the scarcity conceptions to do that. Therefore, the meanings and messages Robbins suggests in the following sentences, collected from pages 38-41, are not entirely clear. The subject matter of economic theory and economic history are intimately related but unambiguously separated by different objectives and methodology:

> *It is the explanation of the historical manifestations of "scarcity." Economic Theory describes the forms, Economic History the substance... So, too, in the field of "Descriptive Economics"— the Economic History of the present day— the main objective is always the elucidation of particular "Scarcity relationships"—although the attainment of this object often necessarily involves very specialized investigations.*

6.2.6 The Materialist Interpretation of History (Section 6)

Finally, we may notice the bearing of all this on the celebrated Materialist or 'Economic' Interpretation of History. For, from the point of view we have adopted, certain distinctions, not always clearly recognized, are discernible (Robbins 1945, 42).

Although conventional economics has been defined as materialist, "its content is not at all materialistic."

The change of definition which we have suggested, so far from necessitating a change of content, serves only to make the present content more comprehensible. The 'materialism' of Economics was a pseudo-materialism. In fact, it is not materialistic at all (Robbins 1945, 42-43).

The actual theory of "materialism" is the Marxist conception of history, which Robbins calls the Materialist Interpretation of History. In substance, it is

through and through materialistic. It holds that all the events of history, or at any rate all the major events in history, are attributable to "material" changes, not in the philosophical sense that these events are part of the material world, nor in the psychological sense that psychic dispositions are the mere epiphenomena of physiological changes— though, of course, Marx would have accepted these positions—but in the sense that the material technique of production conditions the form of all social institutions, and all changes in social institutions are the result of changes in the technique of production. History is the epiphenomenon of technical change. The history of tools is the history of mankind (Robbins 1945, 43).

Marx's theory, right or wrong, is undeniably materialistic. At the same time, it is also true that it has a slight relation to the science of economics.

It [Marx's theory] asserts quite definitely, not only that technical changes cause changes in scarcity relationships and social institutions generally—which would be a proposition in harmony with modern economic analysis—but also that all changes in social relations are due to technical changes—which is a sociological proposition quite outside the limited range of economic generalization. It definitely implies that all changes in ends, in relative valuations, are conditioned by changes in the technical potentialities of production. It implies that ultimate valuations are merely the by-product of technical conditions. If technical conditions alter, tastes, etc., alter. If they remain unchanged, then tastes, etc., are unaltered. There are no autonomous changes on the demand side. What changes occur are, in the end, attributable to changes in the technical machinery of supply. There is no independent "psychological" (or, for that matter, "physiological") side to scarcity. No matter what their fundamental make-up, be it inherited or acquired, men in similar technical environments will develop similar habits and institutions. This may be right or wrong, pseudo-Hegelian twaddle or profound insight into things which at the moment are certainly not susceptible of scientific analysis, but it is not to be deduced from any laws of theoretical Economics. It is a general statement about the causation of human motive, which, from the point of view of Economic Science, is completely gratuitous. The label 'Materialist' fits the doctrine. The label 'Economic' is misplaced. Economics may well provide an important instrument for the elucidation of history. But there is nothing in economic analysis that entitles us to assert that all history is to be explained in 'economic' terms if 'economic' is to be used as equivalent to the technically material. The Materialist Interpretation of History has come to be called the Economic Interpretation of History because it was thought that the subject matter of Economics was 'the causes of material welfare.' Once it is realized that this is not the case, the Materialist Interpretation must stand or fall by itself. Economic Science lends no support to its doctrines. Nor does it assume at any point the connections it asserts.

From the point of view of Economic Science, changes in relative valuations are data (Robbins 1945, 44-45).

6.2.6.1 Critical Commentary

Robbins concludes Chapter II by assessing Marx's materialist conception of history in light of his new definition of economics. Unfortunately, Robbins's nomenclature—the materialist interpretation of history—does not reflect Marx's theory. This point will soon be clear from the following discussion, conducted based on Marx's terminology—the materialist conception of history (MCH).

For several reasons, this concluding section commands significant interests from curious readers. First, Marx's complete view about structure and superstructure and the ultimate nature of social changes are built on the MCH, first presented in the *Manifesto of the Communist Party* (1848). The book's preamble begins with these revolutionary words:

> A spectre is haunting Europe—the spectre of communism. All the powers of old Europe have entered into a holy alliance to exorcise this spectre: Pope and Tsar, Metternich and Guizot, French Radicals and German police spies. Where is the party in opposition that has not been decried as communistic by its opponents in power? Where is the opposition that has not hurled back the branding reproach of communism against the more advanced opposition parties, as well as against its reactionary adversaries (Marx and Engels 1848).

Then Chapter I begins with these words:

> The history of all hitherto existing society is the history of class struggles. Freeman and slave, patrician and plebeian, lord and serf, guild-master and journeyman, in a word, oppressor and oppressed, stood in constant opposition to one another, carried on an uninterrupted, now hidden, now open fight, a fight that each time ended,

either in a revolutionary reconstitution of society at large or in the common ruin of the contending classes (Marx and Engels 1848).

These words underline Marx's motive for articulating the MCH. He believed that private property is the ultimate evil in a nation-state; economic justice cannot be established in this political society without eliminating this social institution. Finally, he believed that the technological progress in the capitalist mode of production would turn out to be the cause of its destruction because the technical development will make human labour so cheap that the proletariats will be forced to revolt against the bourgeois class.

Marx succinctly summarizes this monumental doctrine in his 1859 manuscript *A Contribution to the Critique of Political Economy*. In the Preface, he says:

> In the social production of their existence, men inevitably enter into definite relations independent of their will, namely relations of production appropriate to a given stage in the development of their material forces of production. The totality of these relations of production constitutes society's economic structure, the real foundation, on which arises a legal and political superstructure and to which correspond definite forms of social consciousness. The mode of production of material life conditions the general process of social, political, and intellectual life. It is not the consciousness of men that determines their existence, but their social existence determines their consciousness. At a particular stage of development, the material productive forces of society come into conflict with the existing relations of production or—this merely expresses the same thing in legal terms—with the property relations within the framework of which they have operated hitherto. From forms of development of the productive forces, these relations turn into their fetters. Then begins an era of social revolution. The changes in the

economic foundation lead sooner or later to transforming the whole immense superstructure (Marx 1859).

On closer examination, it becomes clear that Robbins does not correctly interpret Marx's maxims with his new title, "the materialist interpretation of history." In his words, MCH argues that all significant events in history are attributable to "material" changes:

> The material technique of production conditions the form of all social institutions, and all changes in social institutions are the result of changes in the technique of production. History is the epiphenomenon of technical change. The history of tools is the history of humanity (Robbins 1945, 43).

This interpretation of the MCH is both inaccurate and intentional. By materialist, Marx refers to the material production of the means of subsistence on which life depends. In civilized societies, the production of the means of subsistence is regulated by the two sets of forces, which Marx called "the means of production" and "the relations of production." The means of production includes all the four factors—land, labour, capital, and organization—required to produce a commodity. Among these four factors, the proletariats own only labour, while the bourgeois class owns the remaining. These two sets of forces together constitute the mode of production, which is the primary idea of Marx's MCH. The histories of human civilizations across the world testify that the changes in the mode of production have been driven primarily by improvements in the means of production, i.e., technology, which, in turn, cause changes in the relations of production. Eventually, these changes result in a new mode of production. This materialistic view is Marx's conversion of the Hegelian idealism—thesis, antithesis, and synthesis. In Marx, the MCH doctrine has only one motive: to eliminate private property institutions to establish economic justice, i.e., free the working people, the labour class in the classical and neoclassical economics, from exploitation.

Robbins's interpretation of the MCH suggests that he intentionally ignored to highlight this Marxian maxim. In other words, he ignored Marx's fundamental purpose of conceiving history in the way he did. Robbins's assertion, "History is the epiphenomenon of technical change. The history of tools is the history of mankind," is incorrect and intentional.

Second, Robbins asserts that Marx's MCH doctrine is not a "derivative from Economic Science as we know it." It is a sociological argument that claims that "technical changes" ultimately determine all social relations. However, his economic argument—technical changes cause changes in scarcity relationships and social institutions—is in harmony with the modern economic analysis. This is because Marx's sociological proposition overpasses the limited range of economic generalization.

These judgments appear both vague and controversial. Robbins analyzes Marx's historical materialism in the light of his "conception of ends," which signifies relative valuations. According to Marx, Robbins says, improvements in production technology change ends or relative valuations of the economic agents, meaning the "ultimate valuations are merely the by-product of technical conditions." If technical conditions alter, so do tastes. If they remain unchanged, then tastes, etc., are unaltered. There are no autonomous changes on the demand side. What changes occur are, in the end, attributable to changes in the technical machinery of supply. The scarcity of means has no independent "psychological" or "physiological" side.

> No matter their fundamental makeup, be it inherited or acquired, men in similar technical environments will develop similar habits and institutions (Robbins 1945, 44).

This "pseudo-Hegelian twaddle or profound insight into things" is "not susceptible to scientific analysis" nor can it be "deduced from any laws of theoretical Economics."

It is a general statement about the causation of human motive, which, from the point of view of Economic Science, is completely gratuitous. The label 'Materialist' fits the doctrine. The label 'Economic' is misplaced (Robbins 1945, 44).

Robbins's assessment of Marx's MCH raises a whole host of questions. First, ends or relative valuations, which have been proved to be both ambiguous and controversial, make good sense in consumer theory. Marx was nowhere involved in the demand side of the market economy. Therefore, criticizing someone for something that was never their intention violates the principles of critique in academic debate. Robbins did this because, as noted above, he failed to see the difference between the two blades of a shear. He derived this conception of the scarcity definition from Robison Crusoe's experience, ignoring the fact that there was no exchange institution on his isolated island. He was both a producer and a consumer.

The economy that both classical and neoclassical economists talk about is an exchange economy. An exchange market can only be explained if producers and consumers are considered different economic agents, having completely different motives. The consumer may not show interest in buying additional quantities of a commodity he is consuming if its price is not lowered. On the other hand, the producer will not increase the production level unless she sees higher price prospects. Scarcity is a significant factor in the demand analysis but not in the supply analysis. It is important to remember that when we talk about demand, we are talking about the labour market because the consumers obtain incomes by selling their skills.

On the other hand, when we talk about the supply side, we are referring to two markets—output and capital. The firm makes a production plan based on the output market prospects. Therefore, we will look at both the output price and the market size to determine her production plan. It has a good deal of flexibility in determining the plant's size because a bulk proportion of capital invested will come from the capital market. Thus, the nature of the resource scarcity issue encountered in the consumer theory must be distinguished from the producer theory.

Finally, this section demands profound curiosity because it raises doubts about Robbins's motive for writing the *Essay*. Here, he informs the readers that the conventional definition of economics, which he rejected, is not "materialistic" in the real sense. The "materialism" of economics in the orthodox definition is merely a pseudo-materialism; it is not materialistic.

This confession confuses the readers about his real motive behind writing the *Essay*. However, it seems fair to say that Robbins took the term "material welfare" both out of context and out of proportion. Restricting the jurisdiction of economic analysis to production, manufacturing, mining, and exploration does not prevent analyzing the service sector, which today is the most dominant component of the modern economy. This restriction is necessary to put a brake on the temptation of those economists interested in applying economic theories to study illegal and psychological activities such as crimes and happiness. Both Marshall and Neville recognized this truth and the scope of economic analysis in their respective treatises.

6.3 The Relativity of Economic "Quantities" (Chapter III)

The title of this chapter does not seem very clear because it does not refer to the topics discussed. However, this issue will hopefully resolve itself as we explore Robbins's ideas. This chapter is divided into six sections. However, only the first two sections—The Meaning of Scarcity and The Concept of an Economic Good—will be reviewed here because they elaborate on the implications of the scarcity conception that Robbins has developed in the preceding two chapters.

6.3.1 The Meaning of Scarcity

THAT aspect of behaviour which is the subject matter of Economics, is, as we have seen, conditioned by the scarcity of given means for the attainment of given ends. It is clear, therefore, that the quality of scarcity in goods is not an "absolute" quality. Scarcity does not mean mere infrequency of occurrence. It means a limitation in relation to demand. Good eggs are scarce because, having regard to the demand for them, there are not enough to go around. But bad eggs, of which, let us hope, there are far fewer in existence, are not scarce at all in our sense. They are redundant. This conception of scarcity has implications both for theory and for practice which it is the object of this chapter to elucidate (Robbins 1945, 45).

6.3.1.1 Critical Commentary

In this paragraph, Robbins describes both the denotation and the connotation of scarcity. In plain English, scarcity signifies an economic phenomenon created by the individual's limited means and unlimited wants. This is the denotation that seems meaningful to all economists. Its connotation, which drags Robbins into the controversy and criticism, is his assertion that this perception must guide the study of economics.

Let us examine his "quality of eggs" example. Good eggs are scarce relative to their demand, although millions of them are produced every day. However, bad eggs are not scarce, although a few bad eggs are produced or become outdated. "They are redundant."

This market interpretation appears highly unsound. First, the market demand for a commodity depends upon the utility it imparts to different consumers, which makes Robbins's scarcity conception extremely vulnerable as a barometer of defining economics. For example, consider beef and pork, which are religiously prohibited to Hindus and Muslims, respectively. Does this mean that they are like bad eggs, i.e., useless, to everyone? Similarly, the concept of scarcity is directly related to disposable income. To millions of people in the developing world, diamond or gold carries little value in their daily lives because they spend a significant portion of their income on food and clothing—the two indispensable commodities they need to survive and subsist. They are not concerned with the market price of diamonds or gold, but they certainly feel the consequences of a small increase in their staples' prices. Therefore, from the demand side, scarcity is a very unreliable barometer to define the nature and scope of economics.

Robbins presents the conception of scarcity as the unifying force in his free-market economics. This presumption faces even a more formidable conceptual hurdle from the supply side. Producers are profit-makers, meaning they plan all their production activities very calculatedly. Since bad eggs have no market demand, the farmers will not ship them to the grocery stores. Bad eggs are accidents that happen in the production process, meaning this kind of example does not work in describing the role of scarcity in the generation of demand and supply in a market economy.

6.3.2 The Concept of an Economic Good

It follows from what has just been said that the conception of an economic good is necessarily purely formal. There is no quality in things taken out of their relation to men, which can make them economic goods. There is no quality in services taken out of relation to the end served, which makes them economic. Whether a particular thing or a particular service is an economic good depends entirely on its relation to valuations.

Thus, wealth is not wealth because of its substantial qualities. It is wealth because it is scarce. We cannot define wealth in physical terms as we can define food in terms of vitamin content or calorific value. It is an essentially relative concept. For the community of ascetics discussed in the last chapter, there may be so many goods of certain kinds in relation to the demand for them that they are free goods—not wealth at all in the strict sense. In similar circumstances, the community of sybarites might be "poor." That is to say, for them, the self-same goods might be economic goods.

So, too, when we think of productive power in the economic sense, we do not mean something absolute—something capable of physical computation. We mean power to satisfy given demands. If the given demands change, then productive power in this sense changes also.

A very vivid example of what this means is to be found in Mr. Winston Churchill's account of the situation confronting the Ministry of Munitions at 11 a.m. on November 11th, 1918—the moment of the signing of the armistice. After years of effort, the nation had acquired a machine for turning out the materials of war in unprecedented quantities. Enormous programmes of production were in every stage of completion. Suddenly the whole position is changed. The "demand" collapses. The needs of war are at an end. What was to be done? Mr. Churchill relates how, in the interests of a smooth change-over, instructions were issued that material more than 60 percent, advanced was to be finished. Thus, for many weeks after the war was over we continued to disgorge upon the gaping world masses of artillery and military materials of every kind. "It was waste", he adds, "but perhaps it was a prudent waste." Whether this last contention is correct or not is irrelevant to the point under discussion. What is relevant is that what at 10:55 a.m. that morning was wealth and productive power, at 11:55 a.m. had become 'not-wealth,' an embarrassment, a source of social waste. The substance had not changed. The guns were the same. The potentialities of the machines were the same. From the point of view of the technician, everything was exactly the same. But from the point of view of the economist, everything was different. Guns, explosives, lathes, retorts, all had suffered a sea change. The ends had changed. The scarcity of means was different (Robbins 1945, 46-47).

6.3.2.1 Critical Commentary

To understand the meaning of this section, we need to read the first paragraph of the next section, *The Fallacy of Misplaced Concreteness,* carefully.

The proposition which we have just been discussing, concerning what may be described as the relativity of "economic quantities," has an important bearing on many problems of Applied Economics—so important, indeed, that it is worthwhile, here and now, interrupting the course of our main argument in order to examine them rather more fully. There can be no better illustration of the way in which the propositions of pure theory facilitate comprehension of the meaning of concrete issues (Robbins 1945, 48).

Here Robbins explains what he means by the title of this chapter. "Scarcity" is a relative term, which qualifies all commodities called "economic." Therefore, the "Relativity of Economic Quantities" simply means that the commodities studied in applied economics are relative, not absolute or concrete, in the same way, munitions become "bad eggs" or economic waste.

Robbins's proposition seems to suggest that economics has no real or concrete subject matter like other sciences. First, consider his conception of "economic good." This vocabulary is a requirement of classification of objects as it requires that all objects can be divided into different categories using an adjective. Thus, the adjective "economic" is used to distinguish goods from other goods so that they can be studied by the principles of economics. This is a convention of English grammar because no object can earn this status without being related to the conception of scarcity. Thus, wealth is an economic object because it is scarce. In other words, the qualification of a particular thing or a particular service to be treated as an economic good is entirely determined by its relation to valuations, which is the meaning of the title of this chapter.

Robbins's argument creates enormous difficulties in the sense that the role he assigns to scarcity makes the nature and the subject matter of economic inquiry very undefinable. First, consider Prime Minster Churchill's decision concerning the mass production of weaponry after the armistice was signed. A military program, developed after years of intensive efforts, became useless due to the change in demand. Churchill cancelled the program after consummating the production of the lot that was 60% complete. As a result, the materials, which were wealthy and productive, turned out to be an embarrassment, a source of social waste, after Churchill's decision. Nothing but the ends have changed due to the change in demand. The change in war phenomenon has initiated a new game in the nation's resource allocation issues, which the scarcity situation will again guide.

By this proposition, Robbins seems to contradict himself. His entire thesis about the definition and subject matter of economics is founded on Robinson Crusoe's behaviour, a natural and private person. His innate selfishness propels him to work for both material and non-material welfare, constrained by his physical ability and time. However, Churchill is not a private person; the profit motive does not guide his decision concerning munition production. The munitions he produces by using public money is a public good, not a private good. Therefore, two fundamental axioms of our economic model—private person and private good—are violated in Robbins's example.

So, Robbins's purpose in this chapter is not entirely clear. One of the primary objectives of his *Essay* is to show the connection between three ideas—ends, means, and scarcity—which creates choice-making as the necessary outcome in all economic inquires. Thus, when ends change, the whole matrix of economic activities changes as it has happened in the case of war. However, economic wastes, which Robbins describes as "redundant," can occur without the change in ends. This is particularly true in the case of the production of the necessities of life—food and medicine. Both these commodities are produced regularly because our survival depends on them. However, these items are regularly disposed of as wastes when their recommended dates expire. The producers do not seem to be aware of any scarcity law, which they can use to reduce the size of this waste.

Second, a critical survey of the evolutionary history of science will reveal that all sciences, natural or social, are founded on some fundamental innate/natural characteristics of the objects under investigation. Physics studies the characteristics of material objects concerned with the generation and distribution of energy, while chemistry studies the composition and chemical properties of the substance. In social sciences, these characteristics are revealed through human actions and behaviour. Thus, political science studies human actions and behaviour concerned with politics and governance, while sociology studies individuals' relationships in different social organizations—family, community, nation, religion, etc. Economics studies human actions and behaviour that are directly connected with the production, exchange, and consumption of wealth—both material and monetary. Economists assume that these actions and behaviours are guided by selfishness, believed to be a universal attribute present in all individuals. Scarcity is a social concept, not a natural characteristic of human nature. Therefore, the foundation of economics would be weak if we accept scarcity as the fundamental feature that controls our actions connected with those activities. This is because individuals' actions concerning the production, exchange, and consumption of wealth vary dramatically due to natural and social factors.

6.4 Conclusion

The reader is at liberty to draw their own conclusions about the review presented above. However, our discussion about Robbins will end with a thought-provoking question. We have critically examined the doctrines of three authors, whom we could consult for understanding the definition and subject matter of economics. (The auxiliary verb, could, has been used to underline that Neville is untouchable in this discussion.) The modern economists have accepted Robbins's idea of the definition and scope of economics: Economics is a science of choice because the scarcity of resources is relative to demands and desires. Why? What in Robbins's conception has captivated our minds in his favour?

This question can only be answered by seeking Hume's wisdom: *Reason is, and ought only to be the slave of the passions, and can never pretend to any other office than to serve and obey them.* We kill animals for food daily but react angrily when the same action is performed on a person. This is because our consciousness tells us that this action is morally unacceptable. If this feeling is removed, we will see no difference between killing an animal and a human being.

The difference between Marshall, JNK, and Robbins lies in their perception of the role of public welfare in studying economics. Within the classical framework of political economy, Marshall and Neville had tried to inject a sense of economic justice in the selfish activities humans conduct to create and own wealth. Robbins began his disinterested efforts by condemning the idea of public welfare in the study of economics. When we choose Robbins over Marshall and JNK, we do not simply approve his logic; we, in fact, endorse his moral judgment that social welfare has no business in the economics profession.

CHAPTER VII

JOHN MAYNARD KEYNES: GENERAL THEORY AND THE SCOPE OF ECONOMICS

7.1 Introduction

There is perhaps no better way to assess Maynard's purpose of writing *The General Theory*, as it relates to our discussion than reproducing his words spoken at Marshall's obituary:

> The study of economics does not seem to require any specialized gifts of an unusually high order. Is it not, intellectually regarded, a very easy subject compared with the higher branches of philosophy and pure science? Yet good, or even competent, economists are the rarest of birds. An easy subject, at which very few excel! The paradox finds its explanation, perhaps, in that the master-economist must possess a rare combination of gifts. He must reach a high standard in several different directions and must combine talents not often found together. He must be a mathematician, historian, statesman, philosopher—to some degree. He must understand symbols and speak in words. He must contemplate the particular in terms of the general and touch abstract and concrete in the same flight of thought. He must study the present in the light of the past for the purposes of the future. No part of man's nature or his institutions must lie entirely outside his regard. He must be purposeful and disinterested in a simultaneous mood, as aloof and incorruptible as an artist, yet sometimes as near the earth as a politician (DeLong 2017).

With these words, JMK described himself as an economist. His personal and professional profiles confirm this truth. This chapter intends to highlight his contributions to the scope and methodology of economics by pinpointing the fact that public policy is the testing ground for the social scientists and economists in particular. It is here the economists apply their theories to resolve both micro and macro problems. JMK's approach toward economic inquiry testifies that he was specifically interested in the economic issues with which the governments and societies of the day were grappling.

During the two world wars, the most challenging economic environments that the western countries experienced were German repatriations and worldwide depression. In the *Economic Consequence of the Peace*, JMK explained the possible fallouts of the harsh financial penalties imposed on Germany. Before the western world could resolve this issue and recover from the devastations caused by WWI, it became overwhelmed by the deadly depression that began in 1929 and lasted for a decade.

This Great Depression constituted the context of JMK's approach to macroeconomic management under the classical paradigm. The following paragraphs attempt to summarize this approach, undertaken to convince his colleagues that they need to re-examine their beliefs:

> For if orthodox economics is at fault, the error is to be found not in the superstructure, which has been erected with great care for logical consistency, but in a lack of clearness and generality in the premises. Thus, I cannot achieve my object of persuading economists to re-examine critically certain of their basic assumptions except by a highly abstract argument and also by much controversy. I wish there could have been less of the latter. But I have thought it important not only to explain my own point of view but also to show in what respects it departs from the prevailing theory. Those who are strongly wedded to what I shall call "the classical theory" will fluctuate,

I expect, between a belief that I am quite wrong and a belief that I am saying nothing new. It is for others to determine if either of these or the third alternative is right. My controversial passages are aimed at providing some material for an answer, and I must ask forgiveness if, in the pursuit of sharp distinctions, my controversy is itself too keen. I, myself, held with conviction for many years the theories which I now attack, and I am not, I think, ignorant of their strong points (Keynes 1936, 4).

7.2 The General Theory (Chapter 1)

In a one-paragraph introduction, JMK describes the nature and the purpose of his book:

I HAVE called this book the *General Theory of Employment, Interest, and Money,* placing emphasis on the prefix *general.* The object of such a title is to contrast the character of my arguments and conclusions with those of the *classical* theory of the subject, upon which I was brought up and which dominates the economic thought, both practical and theoretical, of the governing and academic classes of this generation, as it has for a hundred years past. I shall argue that the postulates of the classical theory are applicable to a special case only and not to the general case, the situation which it assumes being a limiting point of the possible positions of equilibrium. Moreover, the characteristics of the special case assumed by the classical theory happen not to be those of the economic society in which we actually live, with the result that its teaching is misleading and disastrous if we attempt to apply it to the facts of experience (Keynes 1936, 9).

The title of the book is most illuminating. Employment is the pivotal concept in JMK's thought system—the key concept in classical theory developed by the master economists, including J.B. Say, David Ricardo, J.S. Mill, and Marshall. The two other related concepts are interest and money. Second, JMK declares that "the postulates of the classical theory" are not general; they constitute "a special case only," meaning the economy-wide equilibrium suggested by the classical theory is a limiting case.

7.3 The Postulates of Classical Economics (Chapter 2)

This chapter examines two postulates on which the classical employment theory is founded. First, "the wage is equal to the marginal product of labour," which suggests that

> ... the wage of an employed person is equal to the value which would be lost if employment were to be reduced by one unit (after deducting any other costs which this reduction of output would avoid); subject, however, to the qualification that the equality may be disturbed, in accordance with certain principles, if competition and markets are imperfect (Keynes 1936, 11).

Second, "the utility of the wage when a given volume of labour is employed is equal to the marginal disutility of that amount of employment."

> That is to say, the real wage of an employed person is that which is just sufficient (in the estimation of the employed persons themselves) to induce the volume of labour actually employed to be forthcoming; subject to the qualification that the equality for each individual unit of labour may be disturbed by a combination between employable units analogous to the imperfections of competition which qualify the first postulate. Disutility must be here understood to cover every kind of reason which might lead a man, or a body of men, to withhold their labour rather than accept a wage which had to them a utility below a certain minimum (Keynes 1936, 11).

In short, the first postulate describes the demand schedule for labour (employment), while the second gives us its supply schedule. The labour market determines the equilibrium level of employment at the point where the utility of the marginal product balances the disutility of the marginal employment.

From this understanding, JMK deduces four possible measures to increase employment in an economy: (a) reducing "frictional" unemployment through improving organization or foresight, (b) decreasing the marginal disutility of labour, i.e., the real wage, to diminish "voluntary" unemployment, (c) increasing the marginal physical productivity of labour, and (d) increasing the price of non-wage-goods, relative to wage-goods and shifting the expenditure of non-wage-earners from wage-goods to non-wage-goods. JMK was primarily concerned with the first two employment environments—frictional and voluntary unemployment.

7.3.1 Weaknesses of the Classical Postulates

The first postulate is not "true" because the available labour force may not have the opportunity to work up to the level it wants at the going wage rate due to the lack of effective demand. The classical school seems to counter this criticism with the second postulate:

> While the demand for labour at the existing money-wage may be satisfied before everyone willing to work at this wage is employed, this situation is due to an open or tacit agreement amongst workers not to work for less, and that if labour as a whole would agree to a reduction of money-wages more employment would be forthcoming. If this is the case, such unemployment, though apparently involuntary, is not strictly so and ought to be included under the above category of 'voluntary' unemployment due to the effects of collective bargaining, etc. (Keynes 1936, 13).

This classical counterpoint calls for two critical observations. The first relates to the workers' actual attitude toward money-wages:

Let us assume, for the moment, that labour is not prepared to work for a lower money-wage and that a reduction in the existing level of money-wages would lead, through strikes or otherwise, to a withdrawal from the labour market of labour which is now employed.

This scenario does not suggest that "the existing level of real wages accurately measures the marginal disutility of labour." For, a reduction in the existing money-wage might cause a withdrawal of labour, but does not imply "a fall in the value of the existing money-wage in terms of wage-goods" that were supposed to "rise in the price of the latter."

In other words, it may be the case that within a certain range, the demand of labour is for a minimum money-wage and not for a minimum real wage. The classical school have tacitly assumed that this would involve no significant change in their theory. But this is not so. For if the supply of labour is not a function of real wages as its sole variable, their argument breaks down entirely and leaves the question of what the actual employment will be quite indeterminate. They do not seem to have realized that, unless the supply of labour is a function of real wages alone, their supply curve for labour will shift bodily with every movement of prices. Thus, their method is tied up with their very special assumptions and cannot be adapted to deal with the more general case (Keynes 1936, 13).

It seems a typical case that the labour stipulates (within limits) for a minimum money-wage, not a real minimum wage. The workers indeed resist a reduction in their money-wages but do not withdraw their labour whenever "there is a rise in the price of wage-goods." Theoretically, it will be illogical to assume that workers resist the reduction in money wages but not the reduction in their real wages. Nevertheless, this precisely is what happens in the real labour market. The classical model cannot explain this practical situation because it concludes that all unemployment is either frictional or voluntary. The solution to this practical paradox requires us to show that all atypical unemployment is "involuntary." Section iii below explains how it could be.

If, indeed, it were true that the existing real wage is a minimum below, which more labour than is now employed will not be forthcoming in any circumstances, involuntary unemployment, apart from frictional unemployment, would be non-existent. But to suppose that this is invariably the case would be absurd. For more labour than is at present employed is usually available at the existing money-wage, even though the price of wage-goods is rising and, consequently, the real wage falling. If this is true, the wage-goods equivalent of the existing money-wage is not an accurate indication of the marginal disutility of labour, and the second postulate does not hold good (Keynes 1936, 15).

However, the classical theory of employment faces "a more fundamental objection." According to the second postulate, "the real wages of labour depend on the wage bargains which labour makes with the entrepreneurs." Therefore, the real-wage is not independent of the corresponding money-wage. This theoretical relation between the two wage rates causes problems in the classical employment theory.

Thus, the classical theory assumes that it is always open to labour to reduce its real wage by accepting a reduction in its money-wage. The postulate that there is a tendency for the real wage to come to equality with the marginal disutility of labour clearly presumes that labour itself is in a position to decide the real wage for which it works, though not the quantity of employment forthcoming at this wage (Keynes 1936, 15).

In other words, the labour market is perfectly competitive, meaning the wage is determined in the market through the free interplay between demand and supply curves, in which both entrepreneurs and workers are the price-taker. Therefore, the real wage and the marginal disutility of labour are to be equal in the long run.

> The classical conclusions are intended, it must be remembered, to apply to the whole body of labour and do not mean merely that a single individual can get employment by accepting a cut in money-wages that his fellows refuse. They are supposed to be equally applicable to a closed system as to an open system and are not dependent on the characteristics of an open system or on the effects of a reduction of money-wages in a single country on its foreign trade, which lie, of course, entirely outside the field of this discussion ... They are based on the belief that in a closed system a reduction in the general level of money-wages will be accompanied, at any rate in the short period and subject only to minor qualifications, by some, though not always a proportionate, reduction in real wages (Keynes 1936, 16).

The classical assumption that "the general level of real wages depends on the money-wage bargains between the employers and the workers" is not obviously true.

> For it is far from being consistent with the general tenor of the classical theory, which has taught us to believe that prices are governed by marginal prime cost in terms of money and that money-wages largely govern marginal prime cost. Thus, if money-wages change, one would have expected the classical school to argue that prices would change in almost the same proportion, leaving the real wage and the level of unemployment practically the same as before, any small gain or loss to labour being at the expense or profit of other elements of marginal cost which have been left unaltered (Keynes 1936, 6).

Nevertheless, the classical economists seemed to have left this line of thought, partly because of the belief that "labour is in a position to determine its own real wage" and partly preoccupied with "the idea that prices depend on the quantity of money." Thus, they maintain that the real wage will always "correspond to full employment, i.e., the maximum quantity of employment that is compatible with a given real wage."

> To sum up: there are two objections to the second postulate of the classical theory. The first relates to the actual behaviour of labour. A fall in real wages due to a rise in prices, with money-wages unaltered, does not, as a rule, cause the supply of available labour on offer at the current wage to fall below the amount actually employed prior to the rise of prices. To suppose that it does is to suppose that all those who are now unemployed though willing to work at the current wage will withdraw the offer of their labour in the event of even a small rise in the cost of living. Yet, this strange supposition apparently underlies Professor Pigou's Theory of Unemployment, and it is what all members of the orthodox school are tacitly assuming (Keynes 1936, 17).

7.3.2 Involuntary Unemployment

If the classical conception of "voluntary" unemployment is rejected, we need to define the third category of unemployment, which the classical theory overruled. This third category is "involuntary unemployment."

> Clearly, we do not mean by 'involuntary' unemployment the mere existence of an unexhausted capacity to work. An eight-hour day does not constitute unemployment because it is not beyond human capacity to work ten hours. Nor should we regard as 'involuntary' unemployment the withdrawal of their labour by a body of workers because they do not choose to work for less than a certain real reward. Furthermore, it will be convenient to exclude 'frictional' unemployment from our definition of 'involuntary' unemployment. My definition is, therefore,

as follows: Men are involuntarily unemployed if, in the event of a small rise in the price of wage-goods relatively to the money-wage, both the aggregate supply of labour willing to work for the current money-wage and the aggregate demand for it at that wage would be greater than the existing volume of employment. An alternative definition, which amounts, however, to the same thing, will be given in the next chapter (Keynes 1936, 19).

This definition suggests the classical equality between the real wage and the marginal disutility of employment presupposed in the second postulate refers to the absence of "involuntary" unemployment. It is called "full" employment, which fits well with other characteristics of the classical theory, regarded as a theory of distribution in conditions of full employment. Involuntary unemployment cannot occur as long as the classical postulates hold; involuntary unemployment cannot occur in the above sense.

Thus, writers in the classical tradition, overlooking the special assumption underlying their theory, have been driven inevitably to the conclusion, perfectly logical on their assumption, that apparent unemployment (apart from the admitted exceptions) must be due at the bottom to a refusal by the unemployed factors to accept a reward that corresponds to their marginal productivity. A classical economist may sympathize with labour in refusing to accept a cut in its money-wage, and he will admit that it may not be wise to make it to meet conditions that are temporary, but scientific integrity forces him to declare that this refusal is, nevertheless, at the bottom of the trouble (Keynes 1936, 19).

Obviously, however, if the classical theory is only applicable to the case of full employment, it is fallacious to apply it to the problems of involuntary unemployment—if there be such a thing (and who will deny it?). The classical theorists resemble Euclidean geometers in a non-Euclidean world who, discovering that in experience straight lines apparently parallel often meet, rebuke the lines for not keeping straight as the only remedy for the unfortunate collisions that are occurring. Yet, in truth, there is no remedy except to throw over the axiom of parallels and to work out a non-Euclidean geometry. Something similar is required today in economics. We need to throw over the second postulate of the classical doctrine and to work out the behaviour of a system in which involuntary unemployment in the strict sense is possible (Keynes 1936, 19).

7.3.3 Supply Creates Its Own Demand

The classical economists, following Say and Ricardo, have been preaching the dogma that "supply creates its own demand," meaning "the whole of the costs of production must necessarily be spent in the aggregate, directly or indirectly, on purchasing the product." As Mill says in his famous *Principles of Political Economy*:

> What constitutes the means of payment for commodities is simply commodities. Each person's means of paying for the productions of other people consist of those which he himself possesses. All sellers are inevitably, and by the meaning of the word, buyers. If we could suddenly double the productive powers of the country, we should double the supply of commodities in every market, but we should, by the same stroke, double the purchasing power. Everybody would bring a double demand as well as supply; everybody would be able to buy twice as much because everyone would have twice as much to offer in exchange (Quoted in Keynes 1936, 21-22).

A corollary of this doctrine concerns the relation between saving and investment. Any act of abstaining from the current consumption results in the creation of capital input, which is invested in other production enterprises. As Marshall says in his *Pure Theory of Domestic Values*:

> The whole of a man's income is expended in the purchase of services and of commodities. It is indeed commonly said that a man spends some portion of his income and saves another. But it is a familiar economic axiom that a man purchases labour and commodities with that portion of his income which he saves just as much as he does with that he is said to spend. He is said to spend when he seeks to obtain present enjoyment from the services and commodities which he purchases. He is said to save when he causes the labour and the commodities that he purchases to be devoted to the production of wealth from which he expects to derive the means of enjoyment in the future (Quoted in Keynes 1936, 22).

This doctrine underlies classical economics, although it is no longer stated in this crude form today.

Contemporary economists, who might hesitate to agree with Mill, do not hesitate to accept conclusions that require Mill's doctrine as their premise. The conviction, which runs, for example, through almost all Professor Pigou's work, that money makes no real difference except frictionally and that the theory of production and employment can be worked out (like Mill's) as being based on 'real' exchanges with money introduced perfunctorily in a later chapter, is the modern version of the classical tradition. Contemporary thought is still deeply steeped in the notion that if people do not spend their money in one way, they will spend it in another.[11] Post-war economists seldom, indeed, succeed in maintaining this standpoint consistently, for their thought today is too much permeated with the contrary tendency and with facts of experience too obviously inconsistent with their former view.[12] But they have not drawn sufficiently far-reaching consequences; and have not revised their fundamental theory (Keynes 1936, 23).

This doctrine rests on the "false analogy" between the non-exchange Robinson Crusoe economy and the modern exchange economy, where money plays the most critical role. Even if this doctrine is accepted for the sake of argument, the proposition it leads to is difficult to agree with:

> income derived in the aggregate by all the elements in the community concerned in a productive activity necessarily has a value exactly equal to the value of the output (Keynes 1936, 23-24).

The above doctrine also argues that the individual act concerning saving must necessarily enrich the whole community because the "act of individual saving inevitably leads to a parallel act of investment." In other words, "the sum of the net increments of the wealth of individuals must be exactly equal to the aggregate net increment of the wealth of the community."

> Those who think in this way are deceived, nevertheless, by an optical illusion, which makes two essentially different activities appear to be the same. They are fallaciously supposing that there is a nexus that unites decisions to abstain from present consumption with decisions to provide for future consumption, whereas the motives which determine the latter are not linked in any simple way with the motives which determine the former.

It is, then, the assumption of equality between the demand price of output as a whole and its supply price, which is to be regarded as the classical theory's 'axiom of parallels'. Granted this, all the rest follows—the social advantages of private and national thrift, the traditional attitude toward the rate of interest, the classical theory of unemployment, the quantity theory of money, the unqualified advantages of laissez-faire in respect of foreign trade, and much else we shall have to question (Keynes 1936, 23-24).

7.4 The Principle of Effective Demand (Chapter 3)

JMK concluded Chapter 2 by stating three assumptions on which the classical theory is founded: (i) the real wage is equal to the marginal disutility of the existing employment; (ii) there is no such thing as involuntary unemployment in the classical system; and (iii) supply creates its own demand, meaning the aggregate demand price is equal to the aggregate supply price for all levels of output and employment.

> These three assumptions, however, all amount to the same thing in the sense that they all stand and fall together, any one of them logically involving the other two (Keynes 1936, 24).

JMK criticizes the classical theory in Chapter 3 by arguing that the environment of involuntary unemployment is a real possibility in an economy founded on the institution of private property. This possibility is created by the dearth of "effective demand," which is a new term JMK introduced in the science of economics. This novel conception became so popular among politicians and policymakers that the economics profession brought about a revolutionary change in the way it thinks about private and public economic activities. The first section of this chapter appears to be the most interesting and important segment of the book.

In any given state of techniques, resources, and costs, an entrepreneur incurs two kinds of production expenses. The first is called *factor cost*, which includes the payments made to three types of production factors—land, labour, and capital. The second is called the *user cost*, which involves payments made to other entrepreneurs who supply the necessary equipment and the owned services. Thus, the entrepreneur's profit or *income* is the difference between the value of the output sold and the sum of the factor and user costs. The factor cost is not different from the factor income when looked at from the perspective of the owners of the factors of production. Therefore, the total income generated by an entrepreneur by employing a given amount of labour is the sum of the factor cost and the entrepreneur's profit.

The entrepreneur's profit thus defined is, as it should be, the quantity which he endeavours to maximize when he is deciding what amount of employment to offer. It is sometimes convenient, when we are looking at it from the entrepreneur's standpoint, to call the aggregate income (i.e., factor cost plus profit) resulting from a given amount of employment the proceeds of that employment. On the other hand, the aggregate supply price of the output of a given amount of employment is the expectation of proceeds which will just make it worth the while of the entrepreneurs to give that employment (Keynes 1936, 25-26).

This scenario suggests that the total amount of employment at any level—firm, industry, and nation "depends on the amount of the proceeds which the entrepreneurs expect to receive from the corresponding output. For entrepreneurs will endeavour to fix the amount of employment at the level that they expect to maximize the excess of the proceeds over the factor cost."

Let Z be the aggregate supply price of the output from employing N men, the relationship between Z and N being written $Z = \varphi(N)$, which can be called the Aggregate Supply Function. Similarly, let D be the proceeds which entrepreneurs expect to receive from the employment of N men, the relationship between D and N being written $D = f(N)$, which can be called the Aggregate Demand Function (Keynes 1936, 26-27).

Given this formulation, the entrepreneurs will be tempted to increase their labour demand if the expected proceeds from $D = f(N)$ are greater than $Z = \varphi(N)$, i.e., if D is higher due to increased factor costs. Therefore, the volume of employment in the economy will be determined by the intersection of the aggregate demand and supply functions because the entrepreneurs' expected profits are maximized at that point. The volume of labour demand at this point of intersection will be called the "effective demand."

Since this is the substance of the General Theory of Employment, which it will be our object to expound, the succeeding chapters will be largely occupied with examining the various factors upon which these two functions depend.

The classical doctrine, on the other hand, which used to be expressed categorically in the statement that "Supply creates its own Demand" and continues to underlie all orthodox economic theory, involves a special assumption as to the relationship between these two functions. For "Supply creates its own Demand" must mean that f(N) and φ(N) are equal for all values of N, i.e. for all levels of output and employment; and that when there is an increase in Z(= f(N)) corresponding to an increase in N, D(=f(N)) necessarily increases by the same amount as Z. The classical theory assumes, in other words, that the aggregate demand price (or proceeds) always accommodates itself to the aggregate supply price so that whatever the value of N may be, the proceeds D assume a value equal to the aggregate supply price Z which corresponds to N. That is to say, effective demand, instead of having a unique equilibrium value, is an infinite range of values all equally admissible; and the amount of employment is indeterminate except in so far as the marginal disutility of labour sets an upper limit.

If this were true, competition between entrepreneurs would always lead to an expansion of employment up to the point at which the supply of output as a whole ceases to be elastic, i.e., where a further increase in the value of the effective demand will no longer be accompanied by an increase in output. Evidently, this amounts to the same thing as full employment. In the previous chapter, we have given a definition of full employment in terms of the behaviour of labour. An alternative though equivalent criterion is that at which we have now arrived, namely a situation in which aggregate employment is inelastic in response to an increase in the effective demand for its output. Thus, Say's law, that the aggregate demand price of output as a whole is equal to its aggregate supply price for all volumes of output, is equivalent to the proposition that there is no obstacle to full employment. If, however, this is not the true law relating to the aggregate demand and supply functions, there is a vitally important chapter of economic theory that remains to be written and without which all discussions concerning the volume of aggregate employment are futile (Keynes 1936, 27-28).

7.5 Critical Commentary

The preceding discussion was a modest attempt to summarize the key features of JMK's revolutionary approach to fight the post-WWI dogged depression, which argues that the existence of "involuntary unemployment" is a real possibility in an economy founded on the institution of private property. The classical school fails to recognize this truth because their prognostication—the aggregate demand price equals the aggregate supply price for all output and employment levels—is unsustainable. In other words, "supply does not create its own demand," as the classical theory suggests.

JMK argues that the only explanation of this dogged depression is the principle of effective demand, which says that involuntary unemployment may be created in an economy due to the dearth of aggregate demand in the output market. Since the aggregate demand for the final goods and services is a function of labour employed, a fall in aggregate demand necessarily means a fall in labour demand, which implies "involuntary unemployment." The classical theory cannot explain this employment dilemma because of its assumption that "supply creates its own demand."

In this scenario, JMK's policy recommendations supplied a glimmer of hope to the government leaders and policymakers across the Atlantic to end this economic evil and revitalize their economies. He suggested massive public works for utilizing the burgeoning unemployed labour force, which was cautiously carried out both at the domestic and international levels. The labour obtained disposable incomes from public work programs, which stimulated the aggregate demand for final goods and services. In turn, the private sector responded by increasing the aggregate demand. The increased private demand for labour simultaneously decreased unemployment and increased wage compensations. Both individuals and society became economically better off.

JMK's name is now engraved in the western world's economic history; he is known as the mastermind behind the Golden Age of Capitalism. This is an era of economic prosperity that began after World War II in 1945 and continued to the early 1970s when the Bretton Woods monetary system collapsed (United Nations 2017). This period is marked by the appreciable achievements of sustained economic growth, a high level of labour productivity and a low unemployment level. This is when world institutions like the International Monetary Fund, the World Bank, the United Nations Conference on Trade and Development (UNCTAD), the United Nations Industrial Development Organization (UNIDO), the GATT, the FAO, the WHO, and many others were established.

As the Golden Age took off beginning in the 1950s, Keynesianism developed as the policy regime of western democracies, which encouraged the economics profession to divide economics into micro and macroeconomics. The classical theoretical framework of microeconomics was improved by developing the demand-side of the market. The new market model—developed to explain how production, consumption, and prices are simultaneously determined in the commodity market—earned the name neoclassical economics.

The insights that JMK supplied in his *General Theory* are now fully integrated into macroeconomics, which provides the basic economic framework for macroeconomic management, i.e., stabilizing the economy by reducing the risks of unwarranted involuntary unemployment. Few economists argue against JMK's suggestions for undertaking massive public works to revitalize the western world's war-ravaged economies. However, legitimate objections have been raised against using his theory as a sort of permanent macroeconomic management model whenever the business cycle's downside destabilizes the economy. For example, Paul Samuelson wrote *A Centrist Proclamation* in the 19th edition of his famous book *Economics*, founded on the idea of "mixed economy."

This idea seems to have created controversy in macroeconomics, critically examined in the next chapter. Here JMK's doctrine enunciated in the *General Theory* is critically examined from two perspectives, positive and normative, as Neville described in his book. The positive analysis will criticize JMK's doctrine from the theoretical viewpoint to see how much it differs from the classical theory. The normative assessment will involve determining its public policy implication under the democratic system of governance. This analysis is most critical in this era of the COVID-19 economy because it will show the defects of using Keynesian policy measures to overcome the COVID-19-led depression.

7.5.1 Theoretical Novelty in the Keynesian Model

In the *General Theory*, JMK recognizes that his book will be highly controversial because it challenges the entire orthodox establishment. However, his appeal to the readers' sympathy is not entirely unfair when he says that the classical theory supporters might reject his view either as "quite wrong" or that it "says nothing new." This statement seems tantamount to implying that anyone who disagrees with his conclusions is "wedded to the classical school"—clearly an *ad hominem* fallacy.

However, after more than a century, the current generation of economists is neoclassical, meaning they are no longer die-hard classical school supporters. Some of them are indeed monetarists, but they cannot be accused of being wedded to the classical school of thought. Moreover, as Paul Krugman (2006) says, JMK's ideas are not surprising to the modern practitioners of economic policy because his policy suggestions are followed whenever the economy of a "non-socialist" country suffers from the ebbs of the business cycle.

To develop this critical analysis, the first point to be noted is that the model JMK uses is not different from the classical one. In other words, he uses the same old classical economic model to present his views about salvaging the economy from the curse of despicable depression. This model is the familiar Robinson Crusoe economy where exchanges are introduced in the name of rescuing him from his home of an isolated island.

Mr. Crusoe retains all his natural qualities, i.e., being totally selfish concerning his economic activities, but lives in a civilized society using the market to meet his consumption needs and fulfil his economic ambitions. In other words, this natural person is not under any legal or moral obligation in generating and spending incomes. More specifically, the classical school presupposes an economy that is owned and operated entirely by private entrepreneurs. In this economy, the government exists for administering law and order situations, which it does by collecting various taxes.

In this economy, involuntary unemployment is unthinkable because the aggregate demand and aggregate supply prices are the same. In other words, the slope of the aggregate demand and aggregate supply functions is the same. This classical proposition is preposterous because the aggregate demand and supply functions constitute the aggregated individual market demand and supply functions. JMK's principle of effective demand suggests that involuntary unemployment is entirely possible in this model because the economy can settle at an equilibrium level where aggregate demand for labour is lower than its aggregate supply. The private sector, which is propelled by a profit-making motive, cannot resolve the resulting unemployment problem. To solve this problem, the government must start a massive public works program to boost aggregate demand for labour.

JMK's analysis encounters an insurmountable logical flaw. He criticizes the classical school for failing to recognize the difference between the aggregate demand and the aggregate supply functions but makes a similar mistake in that the government has no active role in economic activities performed in the country. As mentioned above, it exists mainly as law and order maintaining authority and keeping individuals safe from both foreign and domestic violence. Thus, the government's job is to collect taxes to finance its activities; it neither helps the individual create wealth nor monitors how the wealth is distributed among the individuals who join to create it. Pareto's efficiency criteria, treated as the tenets of welfare economics, constitute the best example of the distribution principles of modern mainstream economics.

If the government is asked to financially help the labour class employed in the private sector during the depression and the recovery phases of the business cycle, it must also monitor how the sector's wealth is distributed between the labour and the entrepreneur. Otherwise, the private property principle, set forth by John Locke, will be violated, and society will see the worst kind of economic injustice in wealth consumption. More specifically, the national wealth will be concentrated in a small proportion of the population, while the government will immerse into ever-increasing public debt.

7.5.2 The Social Contract Theory: Hobbes and Locke

The above statement is illustrated next. However, before coming to this discussion, the history of modern democratic governance will be recounted briefly with the hope that it will make the distinction between classical and Keynesian schools more straightforward.

The states worldwide used to be governed under one political institution—hereditary monarchy—founded on the spiritual theory that everything on earth belongs to God, the Creator. Monarchs are His representatives on earth, taking on the solemn responsibility of maintaining law and order. Therefore, disobedience to the monarch is tantamount to disobeying God's command.

This spiritual theory came under serious challenge during the European Enlightenment Era. The monarchs' hypocritical and tyrannical activities in different countries made both the general public and political elites antagonistic to the prevailing political establishments. From the intellectual perspective, the new challenge turned out to be justifying monarchy based on civil consent. Hobbes (1588–1679), a passionate royal loyalist, constructed the hypothetical social contract theory to justify absolute monarchy. He argued that life in the State of Nature is "solitary, poor, nasty, brutish, and short." To come out of this sorrowful situation, men enter a "social contract" with a powerful individual or authority to end this chaotic community affair. They surrender their natural freedoms in exchange for the safety of life. Without a "sovereign," life in society would be difficult. Since the monarchy was the governing institution, Hobbes argued that the institution of the monarchy is founded on the "social contract," not the spiritual common sense as everyone believes. This controversial political theory was published in his classic *Leviathan: The Matter, Forme, and Power of a Commonwealth Ecclesiatical and Civil* in 1651, which is believed to be the outcome of the British Civil War 1642–1651.

Leviathan's central message is crystal-clear—the institution of hereditary monarchy is established by public consent, meaning the institution is a perpetual governance system. Locke agreed with Hobbes that modern civil societies must be ruled with their people's consent but disagreed with the second part of his conclusion.

Locke, who was about 44 years Hobbes's junior, grew up during the British Civil war (1642–1651) and played a very significant intellectual role in the political events leading to the Glorious Revolution of 1688. He is also known as the "father of liberalism" both in intellectual and political thinking. All this indicates that the two progenitors' moral makeup of the social contract theory was polarly different. This fact needs to be carefully considered in assessing the merits of their political theories.

Locke changed Hobbes' social contract theory in two ways. First, instead of treating the State of Nature as an anarchic social organization, he assumed that all men are free to "order their actions, and dispose of their possessions and persons as they think fit, within the bounds of the law of Nature." This is because the State of Nature has a Law of Nature to govern it with "reason."

Second, despite this unfettered freedom, the State of Nature suffered from one irremediable difficulty—there was no human authority to punish the law transgressors. To overcome this inconvenience, men voluntarily made a social contract among themselves to establish a civil society (nation-state in modern political vocabulary) in which every member was equal in terms of their rights. This condition suggests that people living in the State of Nature surrendered their persons and possessions to the civil society created by the contract. In other words, civil society was a sovereign association founded on the principle of equality of membership. Since civil society or body politic is a general body, it cannot execute its sovereign power. For this reason, people's sovereign power is vested in the institution of government. However, being the owner of this supreme institution, the body politic elects deputies to formulate laws and policies and administer its daily activities.

This sovereignty has two inviolable properties—inalienability and indivisibility (Rousseau 1762). Because of these properties, the elected leaders cannot consolidate their hold on the power beyond their tenure; they must seek voters' consent for another term.

To sum up, the social paradigm on which Hobbes and Locke's political theories of governance are founded is the conception of "social contract." Since they have stipulated different provisions in the contract, their analyses led to two different governance systems: Hobbes established an absolute monarchy as the form of government in a nation-state, while Locke created a republic for the same purpose. To see the difference between the classical and the Keynesian schools, we need to identify the nature of provisions inserted in the two.

7.5.3 The Economic Virtue of the Keynesian Model

Based on the previous discussion, the first issue to be resolved for understanding the difference between classical and Keynesian schools is to determine the paradigm on which modern economics is founded. Every economist believes that there is no such need because our paradigm is well spelled out over the two and a half centuries.

This view is an honest mistake at best, and at worst, it is a malignant ignorance. For, our reasoning centres around the institution of private property, which is a political issue, not an economic one. Owning and accumulating private property and consuming private wealth are matters of civil rights granted and guaranteed by the state. Once these rights are enacted into law, economists analyze human behaviour to explain and predict possible changes in market variables as the endogenous and exogenous variables alter. Thus, the Cuban or the North Korean economists analyze their countries' macro and microeconomic issues and suggest policy measures to their governments. However, these analyses and policy recommendations are very different from those conducted in an advanced democratic country because individuals' rights concerning owning and accumulating private property are very different.

Based on this argument, the science of economics does seem to have an entirely independent paradigm like other natural and social sciences, including physics, chemistry, sociology, and psychology. For its paradigm must be consistent with that of the political system which it will serve. Accordingly, economics studied in advanced democratic countries is supposed to develop its laws and theories based on the principles of democracy, whether these principles are practiced or not. Thus, an appropriate debate in this context is to answer two general questions: (i) does the science of economics, developed over the past two and a half centuries, have a paradigm? (ii) what does this answer, if negative, imply when preaching and practicing this science in a democratic political society?

These questions are too complicated to analyze satisfactorily at this short pace. Therefore, no attempt will be made to answer these questions here. Instead, some summary views are submitted, which might suffice for our purpose.

First, except for a few countries, besides Cuba and North Korea, all others have adopted the democratic framework to govern them. Accordingly, the paradigm of economics studied in these countries is supposed to be suggested by John Locke. Men create private property from natural objects, given freely in common, by mixing their labour to make them useful for human use. For this reason, owning and accumulating property is an inviolable individual right that the civil government must protect and promote.

Given this premise, the economic paradigm of democracy is that the institution of private property is its fundamental pillar for the production, distribution, and consumption of wealth. Accordingly, the economist's first job is to formulate laws and theories to make the system fair, i.e., consistent with the fundamental principle of democracy—equality in sharing benefits of all wealth-creating activities. In other words, all commodities produced jointly by several individuals must be distributed according to their contributions in terms of labour skills. Since the nature of these skills varies from one individual to another, the distribution of proceeds cannot be equal. However, this distribution cannot be so unequal that it instantly appears "unjust" or "unfair." What we see today is not economic inequality; its appropriate designation is "economic injustice."

Locke's private property doctrine seems to be the primary inspiration behind articulating the classical labour theory of value, which describes laws of distribution and exchange under the institution of private property. However, this theory does not reflect Locke's economic paradigm because classical economists departed from his line of thought in two fundamental ways. First, as Weldon (1988, 15) says:

> Classical theorists borrowed their stage setting from the durable institutions of their everyday experience. Industrial capitalism in primitive or developed form as part of their system but always lived in company with a large traditional economy and many arrangements for transfer payments.

The truth of this statement can be confirmed by reading all eminent classical authors, including Adam Smith, Thomas Malthus, David Ricardo, and J.S. Mill. For example, consider J.S. Mill's *Principles of Political Economy*, first published in 1848. The *Principles* is divided into five books consisting of 214 chapters, of which the first three respectively deal with production, distribution, and exchange. Among these three topics, the most important one is the first book, concerned with commodity production. The two other issues become relevant for economic analysis only after a commodity is produced and transported for exchange in the market.

Production means the creation of wealth, which, in turn, is owned and accumulated as private property. Therefore, Locke's economic paradigm directly concerns activities related to commodity production. A horrendous kind of goods and services is produced and consumed in a civilized society. However, they are of little concern to the economics profession because they do not enter the market for exchange. In other words, these goods and services are not commodities in the sense economists understand them. They are private property by Locke's definition, which means no one can claim their ownership. Accordingly, when a commodity is produced by applying labour and skills of several individuals, a question naturally arises as to how the surplus value earned from the exchange of the commodity is to be distributed among those who participated in its production. The only solution to this question is to apply Locke's doctrine about the creation of private property.

The classical economists did not approach the distribution issue from this theoretical perspective. Instead, as Weldon said, they took the prevailing distribution of private wealth as the benchmark point and theorized how to distribute the total production among the suppliers of three production factors—land, labour, and capital. As Mill says,

> Since [labour, capital, and land] may be separately appropriated, the industrial community may be considered divided into landowners, capitalists, and productive labourers. Each of these classes, as such, obtains a share of the produce: no other person or class obtains anything except by concession from them (Weldon 1988, 15).

These shares are called rent, interest, and wage, which are determined in their respective factor markets. The interest rate is determined by the demand and supply of loans, while the productivity of the marginal land determines rent. Finally, the wage rate is determined by the subsistence requirement of the labour, the amount of money required for their survival and reproduction.

In this system, the capitalists, and in JMK's word, entrepreneurs, organize the whole production process. They buy necessary fixed and variable inputs by borrowing money from the financial institutions at the market rate of interest, paying wage to general labourers and salaries to other employees providing other skills required in the enterprise. Because all production factors have been paid their market-determined remunerations, the finished commodity rightfully belongs to the capitalist who organized its production. Therefore, the capitalist is entitled to retain the entire sum of profit or incur a loss, which might be the case when the commodity is sold out.

The classical theory may be compared with Hobbes and Locke's social contract theory. Hobbes articulated his version of the social contract theory to save his preferred political institution—the institution of the monarchy—in the rapidly changing religious and political climate. On the other hand, Locke believed that hereditary monarchy could never deliver peace and prosperity in the modern world. Therefore, he rejected the prevailing political paradigm and proposed a new one that made people the state's sovereign authority and the elected government leadership as its administrator. He also proclaimed that private property should be the fundamental pillar of the economy of this political system because the property is created through human labour, which belongs to only the person himself.

The classical economists violated this fundamental tenet of the institution of private property by endorsing the existing wealth distribution in the economy. Even if this wealth distribution is accepted by Locke's standard, their distribution theory does not satisfy his criterion for generating new wealth in the economy.

Since JMK used the same classical model to justify the government's active role in breaking the depression ice, he is not immune from the defects described above. To echo Hume's sentiment, he added no new idea to the classical model to justify the government's massive public work. If we take Russell's view articulated in his *History of Western Philosophy*, we should say that JMK was lucky because the western governments in his time were eagerly looking for the Keynesian policy recommendation. This is a very different assessment of the *General Theory* than the one that prevails in the relevant literature.

Secondly, Keynesian economics' implication seems more critical from the normative viewpoint compared to its positive insinuation. This point becomes evident when his business cycle theory is scrutinized carefully. In the words of Samuelson and Nordhaus (2009, 429):

> Business cycles are economy-wide fluctuations in total national output, income, and employment, usually lasting for 2 to 10 years, marked by widespread expansion or contraction in most sectors of the economy.

More specifically, business cycles are divided into two main phases: recession and expansion, with peak and trough marking the turning points. The recession—a repeated declining duration in total output, income, and employment—represents the business's downturn, which usually lasts from 6 to 12 months.

This feature is typical of all advanced industrial economies founded on the institution of private property. As discussed above, the classical economists believed that the downside phase of the long-run trend relationship between full employment, aggregate demand, and the general price level is transitory because the market will eventually readjust to eliminate this unemployment. The Great Depression came as a sort of evidence that classical economists are not correct. In the *General Theory*, JMK argued that the government must get involved in this national economic condition to stimulate aggregate demand through public works. His theory led to the creation of macroeconomics, the second window of economics. This is a science of public policy, which was adopted as one of the measures to fight recession in the modern economics of the non-communist world.

The Keynesian policy prescription has an ominous implication for managing the national economy under democracy, which was ignored for about eight decades. In the classical model, the government has no active economic role because all three production factors—land, labour, and capital—are privately owned. Its primary responsibility is to maintain law and order in the country for which it collects taxes from the public members. In this situation, it can undertake public works only by running a deficit budget, which suggests that the government will accumulate public debt at an increasing rate. The tax revenues collected after the economy begins to function normally may not be good enough to begin repaying the old debt, or the incumbent government may decide to spend this tax revenue for other purposes (increasing the government's military might, for example) instead of repaying the debt.

Consider the gross government debt and GDP ratios in the OECD countries. In 2018, Japan's national debt amounted to about 237% of the gross domestic product, which is projected to 263% in 2021 (Statista 2020). For all OECD countries, the gross government debt to GDP ratio was 110% in 2017.

These figures highlight the ugly manifestations of Keynesian economics. In the classical model, which JMK used and standardized today under the name of mainstream economics, the government does not own any production factor, meaning it has no claim on the vast wealth generated by the country's labour force. Given this, the first question that naturally arises concerns the justification of public debt in this kind of economy. Under what condition do we ask the government to revitalize the economy when the private sector alone is responsible for creating its booms and busts? Classical economics appears to be a standard case of the "free-rider problem" that economists often discuss.

Second, today, the nature and extent of economic inequality is a global concern. For example, in 2017, the combined wealth of three Americans—Jeff Bezos, Warren Buffett, and Bill

Gates—was higher than the bottom half of its population (Kirsch 2017). This kind of distributional injustice can crop up only in the classical model of economics being practiced globally. Marx had ingeniously explained how this classical model exploits the working class to generate surplus value. Marx had to labour for many years to describe and demonstrate how the classical political economy creates opportunities for the capitalists to exploit the labour class. Today, this process is crystal clear to every curious observer but does not seem to be unfair, let alone unacceptable to them.

Some examples may be given to underline the irrationality of the distribution policy under the current economic model. First, take the case of book publishing. No one can doubt the role and contribution of the author(s) in writing the manuscript. What percentage of net revenue does an average author get from the sale of his/her book? How much do the CEO and other executive officers get from the publishing enterprise?

Second, every organization or institution is run by a supreme, not necessarily sovereign, leader, whose designation varies from one organization to another. Nevertheless, these supreme leaders may be described by a common title—Chief Executive Officer (CEO). One way to see the lack of logic in the prevailing model of mainstream economics is to compare the remuneration packages received by the CEOs of different organizations in the US. The President is the CEO of the wealthiest and the mightiest country in the world. Since 2001, the US President is paid an annual salary of 400,000.00 USD plus an extra expense allowance of $50,000 a year, a $100,000 non-taxable travel account, and $19,000 for entertainment (Elkins 2018).

Broadcom Inc. is a designer, developer, manufacturer, and global supplier of a wide range of semiconductor and infrastructure software products in the US. Founded in 1961, its gross and net revenues were respectively 22.6 and 2.74 billion USD in 2019. In that year, the corporation paid its CEO, Hock E. Tan, 103,211,163 USD. This means that the US President's total pay was only 0.55% of Broadcom Inc.'s CEO (As You Sow 2021). A curious and conscious mind is supposed to know the reason behind the nature of this kind of pay structure. However, they will get no answer from the economics profession. The current level of economic inequality is indeed a subject of great debate in the profession. Nevertheless, this debate does not go beyond the academic forum because there is no trace to its remedy under the current model of mainstream economics.

Finally, JMK wrote *The General Theory* to fight the Great Depression caused by various factors, including the 1929 stock market crash, banking panics and monetary contraction, the gold standard causing currency devaluation and decreased international lending and tariffs (Duignan 2021). Currently, the global community is grappling with a worldwide recession that has been caused by a disease called COVID-19. It belongs to a family of viruses, which cause illnesses ranging from the common cold to more severe diseases such as Middle East Respiratory Syndrome (MERS) and Severe Acute Respiratory Syndrome (SARS). COVID-19 has caused much concern among the public and policymakers because it has never been identified in humans before, and vaccines have not been developed for it. Consequently, COVID-19 caught the world off-guard.

Vaccines are now available for the disease. However, to see business as usual, we may have to wait until 2022. Natural scientists are responsible for this job, and they have done a spectacular job by inventing vaccines within a year, which typically takes about two years. To ensure that a similar situation does not happen again, the *first* question that needs to be answered is why the scientific community failed to accomplish this job in the case of COVID-19.

The answer is not difficult to find if we carefully look at our economic model and economic policy research. First, medical research is a responsibility of the private sector, which spends R & D on projects that show the greatest profit prospect. Naturally, the private sector will not allocate R & D for a vaccine whose demand prospect is virtually unknown. Second, the government collects revenue through various taxation, which is, therefore, limited by the size and performance of the economy. On the other hand, it must choose between different national priorities, meaning the government will apply the same principles of the consumer theory to choose its priorities. In the consumer theory, the purchasing priorities are pre-set by natural laws—we must meet our natural needs and then, if money is available, make choices based on our tastes. In the case of the government budget allocation, the tastes of the people in power mainly determine the nature of this allocation. For example, the health sector has never had priority in the government budget allocation. Emerging as a superpower after WWII, the successive US governments always put greater emphasis on their military than any other sector. The reason behind the medical community's failure to prepare the world to fight this medical emergency is the government's negligence or the lack of commitment to protecting and promoting public health. This inference is valid only if made by a citizen of a democratic country. From the perspective of mainstream economics, it has little academic merit because the job of giving scientists the right incentives and equipment is the private sector's responsibility, not the government's.

Second, to avoid repetition, each democratic government needs a public health policy for its citizens that is consistent with its political principles. In other words, Locke's social contract theory is supposed to be taken as the paradigm of governance, which will, in turn, help appropriate the health policy. There is no scope for developing such a public health policy under the framework of modern mainstream economics, which has created two types of anomalies in the study of health economics, developed over the past half-century or so. First, the conceptual foundation of health economics is unempirical in that the characteristics of human health are significantly different from the ordinary commodities that are the subject matters of mainstream economics. For example, the modern theory of the consumer equilibrium (tangency between the budget line and an indifference curve) primarily reflects Robbins's scarcity theory. We have already noticed that his theory is subject to serious criticism. Thus, developing the health policy of a democratic country is not logically unsound but also politically unacceptable. If we want to leave out politics from our discussion, then we should forget the government because it is a political organization by nature.

Second, the entire economic community is eager to know how soon the government could resolve this health crisis. Thanks to the miracles of information and communications technology (ICT), academics and the general public can now hear and watch the giants of current generations of economics giving their well-articulated views through webinars and electronic media. The general theme in these discussions is common. They detail the economic damage caused by the pandemic and predict what might happen if this virus is not subdued soon. Most economists agree with the government policy to do whatever is necessary to contain the spread of the virus, but there are some who recognize the downside of the lockdowns and deficits created due to the COVID-19 emergency relief programs (Cutler 2020).

The position of the economic profession in the COVID-19 era seems highly contradictory because the government has no active role in their model. Therefore, their business cycle model cannot explain the COVID-19-induced recession. However, COVID-19 has exposed the contradiction inherent in the burgeoning science of health economics that was not so clear before.

Take the case of Canada. It practices a universal healthcare policy under which all citizens and permanent residents enjoy free access to medical care services. To keep the program sustainable, the Canadian government has also enacted the Canada Health Act, which effectively discourages the private sector from participating in the health care industry.

All this suggests that the Canadian government has separated its medical care industry from the mainstream economic model that regulates the Canadian economy. However, Canadian universities teach courses on health economics, which treat the medical care markets at par with other commodity markets, meaning Canadian health economics directly disregard the country's health policy. This practice raises questions about the value and virtue of health economics being taught in Canada and other countries that practice a universal healthcare policy.

CHAPTER VIII
PAUL SAMUELSON:
SCARCITY, EFFICIENCY, AND MIXED ECONOMY

8.1 Introduction

Paul Anthony Samuelson is the final author in our research on the chronological developments in the definition and scope of economics. From Chapter II, we know that his moral makeup was different from Marshall, JNK, and JMK, although his intellectual ability was comparable with theirs. However, his professional outlooks are much closer to Robbins, the author of the scarcity conception in economics. This connection implicates him with the same irrationalities that Robbins's pioneering notion does. Samuelson's contribution consists of mathematizing the language of economics. To be more specific, at the risk of oversimplification, he has translated Robbins's verbal discussion of resource scarcity in mathematical language.

Has he been able to dispel the controversies and contradictions that constitute the subject matter of this book? The following discussion critically examines this question. However, it needs to be noted that Samuelson does not appear clear about his moral/subjective view concerning the nature of economics to be studied in a democratic society. In his 1970 Nobel Lecture, Samuelson calls himself "a *modern* economist… in the right wing of the Democratic New Deal economists in terms of economic philosophy" (Samuelson 1970). In the 19th edition of *Economics*, he declared himself as a "centrist" and advocated establishing a "mixed economy" in western democracies, including the US.

For two reasons, Samuelson's *Economics* seems more important from positive and normative perspectives than any textbook written on the discipline. First, he began working on the book shortly after WWII, when the economics profession was in a sort of vacuum. Over six decades, he saw developments in both theory and practice. Political economy, which started its journey as a branch of moral sciences, progressed into a social science at the hands of economists like Alfred Marshall by the time WWI ended. Political chaos and wars disrupted developments in the science, like all other fields of intellectual industry. The end of WWII initiated a new era in the global village with three most notable political and intellectual developments—the end of colonial rule, the start of the cold between two belligerent western and eastern blocs, and the unprecedented developments in science and technology. Samuelson's book is of utmost interest to us because it records all these developments in the study and practice during this turbulent and tantalizing period. Second, what happened before the beginning of this century is interesting from an academic perspective. However, what is happening today is of practical concern to the profession. It is of particular concern for the social scientists who dare to wish to see a revolutionary change in the modern democratic world for peace and justice in the global village.

Samuelson describes the framework of his ideal economic system—the Mixed Economy—in Part 1 of *Economics* titled *Basic Concepts*. This part is divided into three chapters, which are summarized below for critical assessment.

8.2 The Central Concepts of Economics (Chapter 1)

8.2.1 Definition of Economics

The central concepts of economics relate to twin themes—scarcity and efficiency—meaning they constitute the pivotal terminologies in his definition:

Economics is the study of how *societies* [emphasis added] use scarce resources to produce valuable goods and services and distribute them among different individuals (Samuelson and Nordhaus 2010, 4).

8.2.1.1 Scarcity

Although economics is currently a humongous discipline dealing with diverse topics, the two ideas stated above are germane in all studies that qualify to be called "economic."

Ours is a world of scarcity, full of economic goods. A situation of scarcity is one in which goods are limited relative to *desires* [emphasis added]. An objective observer would have to agree that, even after two centuries of rapid economic growth, production in the United States is not high enough to meet everyone's *desires*. If you add up all the wants, you quickly find that there are simply not enough goods and services to satisfy even a small fraction of everyone's *consumption desires* [emphasis added]. Our national output would have to be many times larger before the average American could live at the level of the average doctor or major-league baseball player. Moreover, outside the United States, particularly in Africa, hundreds of millions of people suffer from hunger and material deprivation (Samuelson and Nordhaus 2010, 4).

8.2.1.2 Efficiency

Because of this situation, an economy must make the best use of its limited resources, indicated by the word efficiency. "Efficiency denotes the most effective use of a society's resources in satisfying people's wants and needs."

Economic efficiency requires that an *economy* [emphasis added] produce the highest combination of quantity and quality of goods and services, given its technology and scarce resources. *An economy is producing efficiently when no individual's economic welfare can be improved unless someone else is made worse* [emphasis added].

The essence of economics is to acknowledge the reality of scarcity and then figure out how to organize society to produce the most efficient use of resources. That is where economics makes its unique contribution [emphasis added] (Samuelson and Nordhaus 2010, 4-5).

8.2.1.3 Microeconomics and Macroeconomics

The scope of economics is divided today into two primary subfields—microeconomics and macroeconomics. Microeconomics studies "the behaviour of individual entities such as markets, firms, and households."

In *The Wealth of Nations* (1776), Smith considered how individual prices are set, studied the determination of prices of land, labour, and capital, and inquired into the strengths and weaknesses of the market mechanism. Most important, he identified the remarkable efficiency properties of markets and explained how the self-interest of individuals working through the competitive market could produce a societal, economic benefit. Microeconomics today has moved beyond the early concerns to include the study of monopoly, the role of international trade, finance, and many other vital subjects (Samuelson and Nordhaus 2010, 5).

Macroeconomics is concerned with the overall performance of the economy.

Macroeconomics did not even exist in its modern form until 1936, when John Maynard Keynes published his revolutionary *General Theory of Employment, Interest and Money*. At the time, England and the United States were still stuck in the Great Depression of the 1930s, with over one-quarter of the American labour force unemployed. In his new theory, Keynes developed an analysis of what causes business cycles, with alternating spells of high unemployment and high inflation. Today, macroeconomics examines a wide variety of areas, such as how total investment and consumption are determined, how central banks manage money and interest rates, what causes international financial crises, and why some nations rapidly grow while others stagnate. Although macroeconomics has progressed far since his first insights, the issues addressed by Keynes still define the study of macroeconomics (Samuelson and Nordhaus 2010, 5).

8.2.2 Market, Command, and Mixed Economies

Given that resources are limited relative to human *desires*, all societies must resolve three vital problems—what commodities to produce, how to produce them, and for whom to produce them. These are the three fundamental questions of economic organization—what, how, and for whom.

What are the different ways that a society can answer the questions of what, how, and for whom? *Different societies are organized through alternative economic systems and economics studies the various mechanisms that a society can use to allocate its scarce resources* [emphasis added] (Samuelson and Nordhaus 2010, 8).

It is customary in economics to identify two polar ways of organizing an economy.

At one extreme, the government makes most economic decisions, with those on top of the hierarchy giving economic commands to those further down the ladder. At the other extreme, decisions are made in markets, where individuals or enterprises voluntarily agree to exchange goods and services, usually through payments of money (Samuelson and Nordhaus 2010, 8).

The first category is called command economy, while the second one is called market economy. However, no "contemporary society" completely fits either of these polar models, suggesting the existence of a third category that characterizes all societies. This category is called "mixed economy," which inherits some elements of both market and command economy.

Economic life is organized either through a hierarchical command or decentralized voluntary markets. Today most decisions in the United States and other high-income economies are made in the marketplace. But the government plays an important role in overseeing the functioning of the market; governments pass laws that regulate economic life, produce educational and police services, and control pollution. Most societies today operate mixed economies [emphasis added] (Samuelson and Nordhaus 2010, 8).

8.3 The Modern Mixed Economy (Chapter 2)

8.3.1 The Market Mechanism

In most high-income countries, maximum economic activities occur in private markets without any coordinated effort or direction of any single authority, private or public. Here, myriads of business firms and consumers engage in voluntary trade with the sole intent to improve their economic goals, whose actions "are invisibly coordinated by a system of prices and markets." Nevertheless, there is little chaos or irregularities in these markets except occasional booms and busts.

"A market is a mechanism through which buyers and sellers interact to determine prices and exchange goods, services, and assets (Samuelson and Nordhaus 2010, 26)." It accomplishes this job by determining the commodity's price under consideration, which is simply the amount of money per unit paid by the buyer to the seller. Therefore, this price is a signal to both the producer and the consumer to adjust their supply and demand schedules.

This principle is equally applicable to the factor markets for determining prices—rent, wage, interest, and profit.

> Prices coordinate the decisions of producers and consumers in a market. Higher prices tend to reduce consumer purchases and encourage production. Lower prices encourage consumption and discourage production. Prices are the balance wheel of the market mechanism (Samuelson and Nordhaus 2010, 27).

The market's fundamental function is to determine the commodity price to resolve three problems of economic organization. Samuelson summarizes this process as follows:

> The market mechanism works as follows to determine the *what* and the *how*: The dollar votes of people affect prices of goods; these prices serve as guides for the amounts of the different goods to be produced. When people demand more of a good, its price will increase, and businesses can profit by expanding the production of that good. Under perfect competition, a business must find the cheapest method of production, efficiently using labour, land, and other factors; otherwise, it will incur losses and be eliminated from the market.
>
> At the same time that the what and how problems are being resolved by prices, so is the problem of *for whom*. The distribution of income is determined by the ownership of factors of production (land, labour, and capital) and by factor prices. People possessing fertile land or the ability to hit home runs will earn many dollar votes to buy consumer goods. Those without property or with skills, colour, or sex that the market undervalues will receive low incomes (Samuelson and Nordhaus, 2017, pp.41-42).

8.3.2 The Dual Monarchy

Although there is no official ruler of a market economy, it is, in the end, coordinated by "the dual monarchs of tastes and technology."

> *One fundamental determinant is the tastes of the population. These innate and acquired tastes—as expressed in the dollar votes of consumer demands— direct the uses of society's resources. They pick the point on the production-possibility frontier (PPF). The other major factor is the resources and technology available to a society. The economy cannot go outside its PPF. You can fly to Hong Kong, but there are no flights yet to Mars. Therefore, the economy's resources limit the candidates for the dollar votes of consumers. Consumer demand has to dovetail with the business supply of goods and services to determine what is ultimately produced* [emphasis added] (Samuelson and Nordhaus, 2017, p.28).

8.3.3 The Invisible Hand

This section ends by applauding Smith's theory of the invisible hand and highlighting its limitations in the modern market economies. Smith was the first economist who recognized and demonstrated how "a market economy organizes the complicated forces of supply and demand." He defined the economy as the science of the legislators and wrote for the legislators of his time. However, after about two and a half centuries, the utility of this general market model has significantly declined.

> We know that there are "market failures" that markets do not always lead to the most efficient outcome. One set of market failures concerns monopolies and other forms of imperfect competition. A second failure of the "invisible hand" comes when there are spillovers or externalities outside the marketplace— positive externalities such

as scientific discoveries and negative spillovers such as pollution.

A final reservation comes when the income distribution is politically or ethically unacceptable. When any of these elements occur, Adam Smith's invisible hand doctrine breaks down, and the government may want to step in to mend the flawed invisible hand (Samuelson and Nordhaus, 2017, p.30).

8.3.4 Trade, Money, and Capital

Modern economies must be distinguished from those of the 1700s because they utilize three factors most intensively—trade, money, and capital. This changed scenario of economic organization has, in turn, created three critical features of the modern market economy—exchange, specialization, and the division of labour.

As economies develop, they become more specialized. Division of labour allows a task to be broken into a number of smaller chores that can each be mastered and performed more quickly by a single worker. Specialization arises from the increasing tendency to use roundabout methods of production that require many specialized skills. As individuals and countries become increasingly specialized, they tend to concentrate on particular commodities and trade their surplus output for goods produced by others. Voluntary trade, based on specialization, benefits all.

Trade in specialized goods and services today relies on money to lubricate its wheels. Money is the universally accepted medium of exchange—including primarily currency and checking deposits. It is used to pay for everything from apple tarts to zebra skins. By accepting money, people and nations can specialize in producing a few goods and can then trade them for others; without money, we would waste much time negotiating and bartering.

Capital goods—produced inputs such as machinery, structures, and inventories of goods in process—permit roundabout methods of production that add much to a nation's output. These roundabout methods take time and resources to get started and therefore require a temporary sacrifice of present consumption in order to increase future consumption. The rules that define how capital and other assets can be bought, sold, and used are the system of property rights. In no economic system are private-property rights unlimited (Samuelson and Nordhaus 2010, 42).

8.3.5 The Visible Hand of Government

Adam Smith's doctrine ends right here because it cannot explain the problems of economic organization in the modern market economies. During Smith's time, the invisible hand had just begun to show what it could do to an economy founded on the institution of private property. Today, we know what this market mechanism can do to us. Modern science and technology have achieved miraculous improvements in the means and methods of material production. By employing Smith's doctrine of natural selfishness, the capitalist class has amassed amazing quantities of wealth with the help of its supporting forces in academia, the public, and politics. However, the overwhelming majority of people, who participate in this production process, have little access to this Himalayan stock of wealth. SN identify three significant factors for this kind of economic growth—*market failures*, *externalities*, and *wealth distribution*. To prevent this scenario from worsening, the government must correct the imperfections inherent in the output and input markets.

Although the market mechanism is an admirable way of producing and allocating goods, sometimes market failures lead to deficiencies in the economic outcomes. The government may step in to correct these failures. Its role in a modern economy is to ensure efficiency, to correct an unfair distribution of income, and to promote economic growth and stability.

Markets fail to provide an efficient allocation of resources in the presence of imperfect competition or externalities. Imperfect competition, such as monopoly, produces high prices and low levels of output. To combat these conditions, governments regulate businesses or put legal antitrust constraints on business behaviour. Externalities arise when activities impose costs or bestow benefits that are not paid for in the marketplace. The government may decide to step in and regulate these spillovers (as it does with air pollution) or provide for public goods (as in the case of public health) (Samuelson and Nordhaus 2010, 42).

Markets do not necessarily produce a fair distribution of income; they may spin off unacceptably high inequality of income and consumption. In response, governments can alter the pattern of incomes (the for whom) generated by market wages, rents, interest, and dividends. Modern governments use taxation to raise revenues for transfers or income-support programs that place a financial safety net under the needy.

Since the development of macroeconomics in the 1930s, the government has undertaken a third role: using fiscal powers (of taxing and spending) and monetary policy (affecting credit and interest rates) to promote long-run economic growth and productivity and to tame the business cycle's excesses of inflation and unemployment.

8.4 Basic Elements of Supply and Demand (Chapter 3)

This is the final chapter of Part 1 of SN's *Economics*. The first chapter titled, *The Central Concepts of Economics*, sets the stage for the intellectual inquiry that goes by the name "economics," which used to be called "political economy" before Marshall made the two terms synonymous. Here, SN tell us that the study of economics centres around the twin themes—scarcity and efficiency—which supply the necessary economic environment for formulating laws and theories to resolve three fundamental problems of economic organization that all societies must deal with. They also state that three theoretical models of economic organization have been developed to resolve this—market, command, and mixed economies. However, few countries practice the first two types of economic organization, meaning the third type is the one practiced in the modern global village.

Chapter 2 then describes the salient features of the mixed economy under three sections—market mechanism, the role of money, trade, and capital, and the government's participation under the title—the visible hand of the government. In the first section, SN describe how the market system operates in a mixed economy by the "twin" themes of economic life, while the second section explains how money works as a "lubricator" in employing capital and facilitating trade. However, instead of allocating the scarce resources efficiently and distributing equitably, the unbridled "invisible hand" causes serious side-effects, including market failures, pollution, and economic inequality. This scenario demands the government's regulative role to correct the market imperfections and the issues of inequity in the factor market, the labour market to be more specific.

We also saw that the modern mixed economy relies primarily on a system of markets and prices to solve the three central problems. *Recall that the fundamental building blocks of an economy are the dual monarchy of tastes and technology* [emphasis added]. 'Consumer sovereignty' operating through dollar votes determines what gets produced and where the goods go, but technologies influence costs, prices, and what goods are available. Our task in this chapter is to describe in detail how this process works in a market economy (Samuelson and Nordhaus 2010, 45).

Accordingly, SN introduces the notions of supply and demand in this chapter and show how they operate in competitive markets for individual commodities. The chapter begins with the two sides of the market mechanism—demand and supply curves—and explains how their intersection determines the market price. "It is the movement of prices—the price mechanism—which brings supply and demand into balance or equilibrium."

8.4.1 Market Mechanism

Chapter 3 is divided into three sections, which have been summarized at the end of the chapter. These summaries are quoted below for the reasons explained before.

8.4.1.1 The Demand Schedule

A demand schedule shows the relationship between the quantity demanded and the price of a commodity, other things held constant. Such a demand schedule, depicted graphically by a demand curve, holds constant other things like family incomes, tastes, and the prices of other goods. Almost all commodities obey the law of downward-sloping demand, which holds that quantity demanded falls as a good's price rises. This law is represented by a downward-sloping demand curve.

Many influences lie behind the demand schedule for the market as a whole: average family incomes, population, the prices of related goods, tastes, and special influences. When these influences change, the demand curve will shift (Samuelson and Nordhaus 2010, 60).

8.4.1.2 Supply Schedule

The supply schedule (or supply curve) gives the relationship between the quantity of a good that producers desire to sell—other things constant—and that good's price. Quantity supplied generally responds positively to price, so the supply curve is upward-sloping.

Elements other than the good's price affect its supply. The most important influence is the commodity's production cost, determined by the state of technology and by input prices. Other elements in supply include the prices of related goods, government policies, and special influences (Samuelson and Nordhaus 2010, 60).

8.4.1.3 Equilibrium of Supply and Demand

The equilibrium of supply and demand in a competitive market occurs when the forces of supply and demand are in balance. The equilibrium price is the price at which the quantity demanded equals the quantity supplied. Graphically, we find the equilibrium at the intersection of the supply and demand curves. At a price above the equilibrium, producers want to supply more than consumers want to buy, which results in a surplus of goods and exerts downward pressure on price. Similarly, too low a price generates a shortage, and buyers will therefore tend to bid price upward to the equilibrium.

Chapter VIII: Paul Samuelson: Scarcity, Efficiency, And Mixed Economy

Shifts in the supply and demand curves change the equilibrium price and quantity. An increase in demand, which shifts the demand curve to the right, will increase both equilibrium price and quantity. An increase in supply, which shifts the supply curve to the right, will decrease price and increase quantity demanded.

To use supply-and-demand analysis correctly, we must (a) distinguish a change in demand or supply (which produces a shift of a curve) from a change in the quantity demanded or supplied (which represents a movement along a curve); (b) hold other things constant, which requires distinguishing the impact of a change in a commodity's price from the impact of changes in other influences; and (c) always look for the supply-and-demand equilibrium, which comes at the point where forces acting on price and quantity are in balance.

Competitively determined prices ration the limited supply of goods among those who demand them (Samuelson and Nordhaus 2010, 60-61).

The three chapters of Part 1 summarized above constitute the background of economics that is learned, taught, and researched worldwide. In other words, SN present the conventional wisdom of economics in Part 1 of their textbook. This is also the part of the economics texts immersed in deep controversy, as Robbins complains in his *Essay*. There is little scope of controversy in the rest of the discussions as they are founded on rigid and rigorous assumptions, meaning we can disagree with their assumptions but not with the analysis.

Part 2 is titled *Microeconomics: Supply, Demand, and Product Prices,* which describes the consumer and producer theories to explain how the market demand and supply curves are derived. Both these theories begin with a single economic agent, which used to be called *the economic man.* In consumer theory, this economic man is a consumer who maximizes utility subject to budget constraint. The indifference curve technique and the price consumption curves show how the consumer's demand curve for a particular commodity is derived under the perfectly competitive market condition, which bears an inverse relationship between the quantity of commodity demand and its price. The slope of this curve will be different for different economic men, but the demand-price relationship's direction will not change. By horizontally aggregating the individual demand curves of all the market participants, we get the well-behaved market demand curve.

In the producer theory, the firm or the entrepreneur is a profit-maximizer. Therefore, she will sincerely try to find the least cost combination of the input-output relationship with the help of the isoquant and isocost line. The individual supply curve is the upward-sloping portion of the marginal cost curve from above the U-shaped minimum average variable cost curve. Thus, the market supply curve is again obtained horizontally, aggregating the individual supply curve.

The critical points to be noted here are that under perfect competition, the concerned commodity is homogenous, and both the consumer and the producer are price takers.

8.5 Critical Commentary

The main reason for reviewing the previous four authors is historical because these chronological developments need to be reviewed to resolve the debate on the nature and scope of economics in this era of globalization and political polarization. However, Samuelson's ideas and arguments are of practical importance to us because he was the author who helped reformulate the science of economics we study today. Accordingly, a selected number of basic concepts discussed in Part 1 are critically examined below with the hope that this critical review will help us better understand the meaning and message of his economics.

8.5.1 Society, State, and Government

Let us first look closely at SN's definition: *Economics is the study of how societies use scarce resources to produce valuable goods and services and distribute them among different individuals.* This is a representative definition of economics in that its theme is common in almost all modern introductory economics texts. The difference among different authors basically involves the use of different vocabularies.

The critical concept in this definition is "society" because everything else pivots around it. Society is the gravitational force that employs its scarce resources efficiently and distributes the outputs produced equitably. Naturally, understanding the meaning of society is critical for understanding the nature and scope of economics. Unfortunately, few authors take the trouble to spell out the meaning they imply by this term. In other words, authors articulate their arguments and opinions based on the idea of society they have in their minds, and we, the readers, interpret them in the way we understand it. This intellectual scenario has created an unending course of confusion and controversy.

Accordingly, this word has raised some serious questions about its meaning and function. The ambiguity in its meaning becomes evident when we juxtapose three social institutions implying a similar signification but performing different functions—society, the state, and the government. They all refer to the same idea. Society, a common noun, signifies formal and informal human organizations, whose commonality lies in the fact that each of them has definite rules and customs, written and/or unwritten, that all its members are supposed to respect. In a broader sense, both the state and the government are society but in the political category. Therefore, their functions become distinguishable from others only when they are considered in the political context. The state is a geographically demarcated, internationally recognized land and sea territory that is ruled by a well-organized government. In a democracy, its sovereign authority belongs to the people living there. The people is a general body of individuals commanding equal rights and obligations. This feature makes it unfit to exercise their sovereign power. From a theoretical perspective, this is the reason for establishing the institution of government in a nation-state (Locke's civil society), empowering the state's sovereign authority and periodically choosing some fellow voters through the general election to run its administration.

Thus, an economy is created automatically when a state is established and is operated by the political principles by which the government governs itself. In other words, the nature of a nation-state's economy cannot be separated from its fundamental principles of governance. Consider the United States of America. It is a sovereign state, not a society in its ordinary usage. The sovereign power of the Union is vested in the Government of the United States of America, whose CEO is the President. The President, who governs with Congress's help, does not dictate the course of the US economy. Millions of small and large business firms make the overwhelming portion of the nation's production decisions, which is true today in most countries in the global village. This fact evidently and immediately contradicts the idea of "society" SN have attached in the definition.

Second, after WWII, two primary political philosophies dominated the government establishments throughout the world—Locke's theory of "civil society" and Marx's theory of socialism. The principal difference between them concerns the role that the private property institution plays in the economy. Locke's system is founded on this institution, meaning the creation and accumulation of private property is the fundamental pillar of the economy. On the other hand, Marx's socialist superstructure is established by abolishing the institution of private property, meaning the government performs the solemn responsibility of commanding the economy to generate employment and meet the essential needs of its people—food, accommodation, health, and education. Which system is the most beneficial for the ordinary people is not the concern of the economics discipline. It is a political decision reserved for the voters, meaning we can participate in this political debate as a voter, not as a professional. As an economist, our job is to explain how an economy is supposed to operate, i.e., create and distribute wealth under this political system and recommend most efficient and equitable measures to resolve different economic policy issues with which the nation is grappling.

From this point of view, SN's conception of "society" seems closer to Marx's political philosophy than that of John Locke, on which all governments of the Western hemisphere are founded. In current Cuba and North Korea, the government indeed makes all the critical decisions concerning the allocation of the country's "scarce resources to produce valuable goods and services and distribute them among different individuals." On the other hand, the economic policy that China is pursuing since 1979 is consistent with SN's conception of mixed economy but entirely inconsistent with Locke's theory explained above. At the Third Plenum of the National Party Congress in 1978, the leadership of the ruling Communist Party of China decided to open the vast Chinese economy to foreign trade and investment and permitted its citizens to undertake private economic ventures (MacFarquhar 1987). From the political perspective, the Chinese system is a complete hotch-potch because it has abandoned its socialist goal of creating a classless society. On the other hand, it certainly does not follow democracy's twin principles—political equality and liberty. In 2019, the total membership of the Chinese Community Party was 91.91 million, which is roughly 7% of the population of the country. In the People's Republic of China, 91.91 million individuals govern the country's 1.394 billion citizens.

This line of reasoning apparently leads to an ugly and unfortunate inference: the modern economics portrayed in SN's book does not represent economies of the Western hemisphere.

8.5.2 Scarcity and Efficiency

SN define economics in terms of twin themes—scarcity and efficiency. Therefore, the clarity of these conceptions is critical to understanding their conception of economics and its scope.

8.5.2.1 Scarcity

To see the difficulty in SN's scarcity conception, we first need to notice the difference between the ideas implied by two words—desire and demand. One way to do so is to treat "desire" as a jargon of psychology and moral philosophy and demand as what economists use to analyze the market economy. This approach is necessary because the two words have entered everyday vocabulary and are typically used synonymously in ordinary usage.

In commonplace language, desire signifies a strong feeling of wanting something or wishing for something to happen. However, from a psychological perspective, it is an emotion similar to craving, wanting, or longing for something—person, object, or outcome (Wikipedia 2021). This intense feeling has two vital features that distinguish it from similar other feelings like hunger and thirst and the economic jargon, demand. First, desire is always excited by the thought or prospect of excitement or entertainment. Second, it has little connection with a person's financial ability, what we call budget constraint. The English word, desire, is derived from the Latin word, *desiderare*, which means "to long or wish for." This term comes from *de sidere*, meaning "from the stars," which suggests that the original sense is "to await what the stars will bring" (Burton 2014).

Chapter VIII: Paul Samuelson: Scarcity, Efficiency, And Mixed Economy

Desires constantly arise in the human mind and are replaced continuously by others.

Without this continuous stream of desiring, there would no longer be any reason to do anything: life would grind to a halt, as it does for people who lose the ability to desire. An acute (short-term) crisis of desire corresponds to boredom and a chronic crisis to depression. It is desire that moves us and gives our life direction and meaning—perhaps not meaning in the cosmic sense, but meaning in the more restricted narrative sense. If you are at all reading this book, this is because, for whatever reason or reasons, you have formed a desire to read it, and this desire motivates you to read it (Burton 2014).

On the other hand, demand is the ultimate output of the consumer theory, which is obtained through an indifference curve analysis that includes consumer equilibrium and the derivation of the price consumption curve. As explained in the preceding paragraph, the fundamental feature that distinguishes it from desire is that it is backed by the consumer's purchasing power. Without this quality, the term has little use in economics.

Therefore, the following two sentences in SN's statement are confusing: *An objective observer would have to agree that, even after two centuries of rapid economic growth, production in the United States is not high enough to meet everyone's desires. If you add up all the wants, you quickly find that there are simply not enough goods and services to satisfy even a small fraction of everyone's consumption desires.*

This difference between the two terms makes SN's conception of scarcity genuinely confusing. To see this clearly, SN's words are reproduced below:

> A situation of scarcity is one in which goods are limited relative to *desires*. An objective observer would have to agree that, even after two centuries of rapid economic growth, production in the United States is not high enough to meet everyone's *desires*. If you add up all the

wants, you quickly find that there are simply not enough goods and services to satisfy even a small fraction of everyone's *consumption desires* [emphasis added]. Our national output would have to be many times larger before the average American could live at the level of the average doctor or major-league baseball player. Moreover, outside the United States, particularly in Africa, hundreds of millions of people suffer from hunger and material deprivation.

SN's idea of scarcity described here seems entirely inconsistent with the consumer theory they detail later.

8.5.2.2 Efficiency

From the perspective of economics, scarcity is a condition of demand, not desire, because it depends upon the individual's willingness to buy a commodity backed by purchasing power. It does not depend upon the quantity of the commodity available, explained by the famous water-diamond paradox.

In turn, the scarcity condition creates another theme of the market economy, efficiency, which refers to the supply side. However, SN's definition of efficiency seems confusing: *Economic efficiency requires that an economy produce the highest combination of quantity and quality of goods and services given its technology and scarce resources. An economy is producing efficiently when no individual's economic welfare can be improved unless someone else is made worse.*

The first point to be noted here is that both scarcity and efficiency are micro concepts. A commodity becomes scarce to the consumer when she needs to choose its quantity due to budget constraints. A millionaire does not have to bother about how much money she needs to allocate for a weekly food budget, but an ordinary worker must. In other words, scarcity is an individual phenomenon created primarily by the level of income. The consumer theory teaches us that a consumer's efficient allocation of her budget is indicated by the tangency between the budget line and an indifference curve.

On the other hand, commodity production involves financial outlays to pay for the factor services used in the production process. Each of these factors is capable of alternative employment, meaning they have opportunity costs. Thus, the business must consider these costs when combining them to produce a given commodity. There are two such combination principles—least-cost combination and profit maximization. In the producer theory, the least-cost combination is indicated by the tangency between the isocost line and an isoquant, in which the profit-maximizing level of output is indicated by the marginal cost and revenue curves.

Both these concepts are taught in microeconomics, which is concerned with a single market. However, market economy or national economy is the subject matter of macroeconomics. Thus, a question naturally arises how the micro concepts can help resolve the macro issues of aggregate production and consumption efficiency. In the old days, our macroeconomics tutors told us in the beginning classes that microeconomics has resolved two fundamental themes of modern economics—scarcity and efficiency. Based on this assumption, macroeconomics deals with three "big" issues of public policy—full employment, stability, and economic growth.

Second, it is interesting to note that SN have used the Paretian welfare condition of public policy efficiency in an introductory textbook meant for the college freshmen: *An economy is producing efficiently when no individual's economic welfare can be improved unless someone else is made worse.* One may not fail to be curious about its purpose because welfare economics—whose obituary has been announced by several eminent economists—is ordinarily taught at the graduate level or in the final semesters of the undergraduate curriculum. Then, we should not ignore the fact that the Pareto welfare criterion is both confusing and controversial.

8.5.2.3 Economy: Market, Command, and Mixed

Among the basic concepts SN treated in *Economics*, these three are most critical because they describe the economic policy pursued in a political system. In other words, they are directly related to the political paradigm in which the science of economics is supposed to be studied. To understand their true nature and significance, we should revisit Hume's conclusion detailed above: *Human understanding has no other office than to serve human passions, controlled by our morals.*

Economics is defined as a science of choice because the resources are scarce. However, we hardly think that this maxim appropriately explains the nature of choice we make in our intellectual industry. Intellectual ability is a special kind of skilled labour input used to produce a sophisticated commodity called human knowledge. In its initial stage, this human labour-power is the rarest of all the gifts from Nature. However, the full flourishing of this labour-power critically depends upon both socio-economic opportunities and personal ambition.

Therefore, each intellectual worker chooses their profession after fair calculation of opportunity costs of different options available to them. By choosing to teach economics, we set our feet in the world of intellectual industry, which is fundamentally a science of combining, comparing, and relating ideas. No act or enterprise can be freer than this because we are the boss; none can dictate what to think.

We read, think, and write. Before beginning to write, we consult countless ideas, some supplied to us by our fellow scientists and philosophers, and some suggested to us by our faculty of understanding. Samuelson had avowed himself as a centrist and placed his trust in a mixed economy. Hume's philosophy can help us explain why he chose to be a centrist and advocated the middle path in practicing economic policy. Our job here is to critically examine the clarity of the mixed economy system, which has become a source of unending disagreement in the discipline, most of the time polite but often very violent.

In the second half of the 19th century, Karl Marx revolutionized the political and intellectual atmosphere in Europe by introducing the (in)famous capitalism vs. socialism debate, which eventually culminated in the establishment of socialism as the political system in the former USSR in 1917. Under the able leadership of Vladimir Ilyich Lenin, the Bolshevik Party overthrew the Tsarist rule in Russia and converted it into a socialist republic by virtually abolishing the institution of private property. In Europe, capitalism, which undermined the prevailing feudal economic order, was already under intense political pressure because of its unfair distribution principles and repressive work ethics. The Russian Revolution added more fuel to this exploding political situation in Europe.

This is the context in which the idea of mixed economy arose in the UK political discourse as early as the 1930s (Reisman 1994). As SN describe, the policy prescription came as a compromise between the command economy of socialism and the laissez-faire market economy of capitalism. These conceptualizations eventually resulted in a tripartite classification of economic systems—command economy, market economy, and mixed economy—accepted in the profession without critical review.

If we accept this conventional wisdom, then there is very little we can add to this controversial debate. In other words, we need to raise questions about the rationality of this tripartite classification to see why the debate goes on unabated.

There is indeed an unavoidable ground for suspecting this classification, which is being overlooked since the beginning of the debate. This ground is the treatment of the institution of private property in the two political systems. In the *Discourse on Inequality*, Rousseau (1755) concludes that the "civil society" was established when men began to claim ownership of land and other objects useful to them, i.e., they created the institution of private property. Locke (1689) gave moral justification to this institution that men used their labour and skill in creating a property. Since human labour and skills are personal, the objects where men used them must be private. Thus, a democratic country's government is contractually and constitutionally obligated to protect and promote private property as a fundamental right of the people living in the state. In other words, the institution of private property is the fundamental pillar of the economic system of a democratic political society.

On the contrary, the socialist government leaders believe that private property is the source of all evil in human society, and the socialist superstructure is needed to abolish this institution. However, the function of the economic system is the same whether the government admires or admonishes the institution of private property. It is concerned with the production, exchange, distribution, and consumption of wealth. The difficulty with the idea of a mixed economy lies in the fact that two different kinds of economic agents are involved in the wealth creation and distribution process. In the Lockean system of government, the bulk of national wealth is created in the private sector. Therefore, the motivation of owing wealth mainly guides the wealth creation process in the Lockean system. In the Marxian political system, the government owns the economy's principal sectors and operates them according to national objectives. Since the national and private objectives are supposed to be different, a logical question naturally arises concerning the idea of creating a mixed economy by combing some features of both political systems.

On the other hand, there is no reason to continue this debate if there is no difference between private and public wealth creation motives. To attest to the truth of this statement, we can look at Adam Smith's famous maxim, partly quoted by SN:

> Every individual necessarily labours to render the annual revenue of the society as great as he can. He generally, indeed, neither intends to promote the public interest nor knows how much he is promoting it. By preferring

the support of domestic to that of foreign industry, he intends only his own security; and by directing that industry in such a manner as its produce may be of the greatest value, he intends only his own gain, and he is in this, as in many other cases, led by an invisible hand to promote an end which was no part of his intention. Nor is it always the worse for the society that it was no part of it. By pursuing his own interest, he frequently promotes that of the society more effectually than when he really intends to promote it. I have never known much good done by those who affected to trade for the public good (Joyce 2001).

This is the first problem with the conception of the mixed economy. In both economies, ordinary consumers' nature is the same, but the nature of the primary wealth owners and production decision-makers is very different. In socialism or the command economy, politicians and bureaucrats make all the major resource allocation decisions. It will be a miracle if these people, by chance, become gifted with entrepreneurial and managerial abilities needed to perform big decision-making jobs. On the other hand, the clear majority of individuals possessing these qualities will lose their natural talents and social ambitions as they must work simply as hired workers. The passions for owning and accumulating property are natural. Therefore, when individuals lose this right, they become disinterested in their creativity.

There is also a second problem in the conception of the mixed economy. An economy is automatically created when a sovereign state is established. This state is governed by a political system, which is democracy in our case, meaning the principles of democracy determine the nature and principles of government that determines the economic policy to be practiced in its economy. In a democracy, creating and accumulating property is an individual right. When we use the word, right, we must remember that it means an individual's prerogative or claim established and protected by law. Thus, an individual can create and accumulate property in democracy under its law. This law is Locke's theory that property is relative to labour contribution in its creation. Regrettably, modern economics never think of expanding Locke's idea of the property. However, the western world has progressively refined his political theory of government that President Lincoln famously said—by the people, of the people, and for the people.

Democracy treats the creation and accumulation of private property as an individual right, which facilitates this institution's growth in the market economy. This general framework is elastic enough to accommodate all kinds of modifications needed to achieve the state's objective, which the American Declaration of Independence beautifully proclaims: security of life, liberty, and the pursuit of happiness of the individual. For example, all democratic governments pursue "the ability to pay principle" to finance their revenue and development expenditures and transfer income from the rich to the poor. In executing this general principle, successive administrations might differ drastically, which could create gruesome inequality issues. However, this issue will be resolved over time because a country cannot remain politically stable by creating unfair economic inequality. It is wrong to characterize any political initiative to raise progressive tax rates as socialistic because it has nothing to do with the socialistic system of government.

This suggests that democracy is a very robust political system that needs to borrow features from socialism. The problem we are having with modern democracy is that our governments are failing to guide the institution of private property in the way Locke theorized it.

We cannot also introduce the principles of market economy in the economy of a socialist country because the political principles are diagonally different: Democracy protects and promotes the institution of private property, which is destined to divide the state into different social classes. On the other, socialism is determined to abolish the institution of private property to reach its ultimate goal of the boundary-less global village. If it allows its citizens to own and accumulate private property, it will have no political philosophy—socialism or capitalism. Modern China is a classic example of this hotch-potch.

8.5.2.4 Adam Smith's Invisible Hand

In his famous book *The Structure of Scientific Revolutions*, Thomas Kuhn (1962) says that science progresses through shifting paradigms, which he defines as "universally recognized scientific achievements that, for a time, provide model problems and solutions for a community of practitioners." Economics is a social science. This statement challenges us with the question: What is its paradigm? Is it Adam Smith's invisible hand? If so, what did the great philosopher mean by the metaphor? Is it still relevant after two and a half centuries? How do modern economists interpret his maxim today?

The following paragraphs intend to examine these questions. Adam Smith is the undisputed father of modern economics, which was then called political economy. He defined political economy—production, exchange, distribution, and consumption of wealth—as a branch of study for the legislators because they are responsible for determining a sovereign country's economic policy. Smith, a liberal moral philosopher, admired John Locke and was a close friend of David Hume. Naturally, he articulated his theory of the economic system based on Locke's philosophy of "civil society" and explained how property is created in it.

The fundamental premise of his political economy is generally understood as the invisible hand theory. This theory ties up Locke's theory of private property with human nature to suggest the philosophy of economic policy to be pursued by the government ruling at his time. Smith's system of thought may be described in the following way: Human beings are by nature selfish; they always endeavour to employ their physical and mental resources to the most profitable enterprises as described above. Therefore, a government, which rules by collecting tax revenues from private property owners, would do better both to itself and society if it refrains from interfering in economic activities of the private people.

When John Locke published his political philosophy in the 18th century, the Industrial Revolution had not yet been incepted. The first Industrial Revolution occurred in Europe when Adam Smith wrote his book about a century later. This Revolution gave him the fundamental idea and inspiration to develop the edifice of his political economy theory—the division of labour. This historical information is critically important for understanding the difference between Smith's political economy and the mainstream economics we study today.

Once again, we need to consult Hume's empiricist philosophy, supplemented by Jeremy Bentham's observation on human nature: Nature has placed mankind under the governance of two sovereign masters, "pain and pleasure." These masters, naturally, control our morals by which we conduct our civil life. Social conditions, defined in their broadest sense, cause psychological pain and pleasure, meaning our morality is directly related to the time and society in which we live. Adam Smith wrote for the legislators and intellectuals of his time. Accordingly, the modern interpretation of Smith's paradigm demands critical scrutiny.

Smith's philosophical clarification—that the economic policy, founded on the institution of private property, is more consistent with its political ideology and faster economic growth—was interpreted as the laissez-faire state policy advocated by the French Physiocrats. This French phrase, which means "leave us alone," recommended a policy of minimum governmental interference in individuals and society (The Editors of Encyclopedia Britannica 2019). The classical economists, including J.B. Say, David Ricardo, and J.S. Mill, converted Smith's idea of economics into a pure laissez-faire theory: Supply creates its own demand. The neoclassical economists, including J.M.

Keynes and Paul Samuelson, consolidated the classical theory by incorporating Adam Smith's premise in the micro and macro models.

SN lucidly describe the nature of the modern version of Smith's invisible hand in Chapter 2 with the help of Figure 2-1 titled, "The Market System Relies on Supply and Demand to Solve the Trio of Economic Problems." To understand the meaning of this market mechanism and how the invisible hand operates in a market economy, the figure is reproduced here for critical review.

Figure 1. The Market System Relies on Supply and Demand to Solve the Trio of Economic Problems

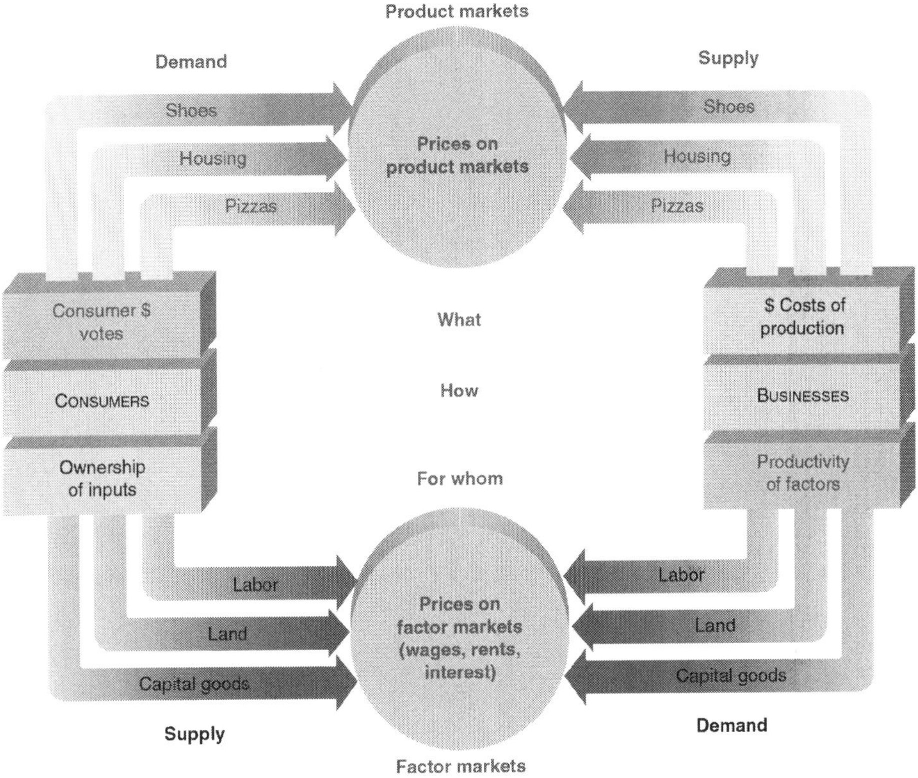

Source: Samuelson and Nordhaus (2010, 29, Figure 2-1)

SN's market economy consists of two kinds of economic agents—consumers and businesses— involved in two kinds of economic activities: consumption and production. Consumers own all production factors—land, labour, and capital goods—which they sell to the businesses in exchange for returns called rents, wages, and interests. On the other hand, the businesses organize these production factors to produce goods and services demanded—*not desired*—by the consumers. In other words, consumers use their factor incomes to buy goods and services produced by the businesses. This is the economic mechanism of how goods and services are produced and consumed in a market economy. In SN's words:

> We see here the circular flow of a market economy. Dollar votes of consumers (households, governments, and foreigners) interact with business supply in the product markets at the top, helping to determine what is produced. Business demand for inputs meets the supply of labour and other inputs in the factor markets below, determining wage, rent, and interest payments; incomes thus influence for whom goods are delivered. Business competition to buy factor inputs and sell goods most cheaply determines how goods are produced (Samuelson and Nordhaus 2010, 29).

A closer look at the figure seems to reveal several ambiguities in SN's model that deserve to be critically scrutinized. First, SN's figure is a micro-macro mix-up. In microeconomics, the unit of analysis is a market where a commodity is exchanged between the producers (sellers) and consumers (buyers). Here, individual demand and supply curves are aggregated to obtain the market demand and supply curves, which simultaneously determine the commodity's market price. The same process happens in each factor market that determines the factor price. When this aggregation process is extended to the economic level, we get aggregate demand and supply curves and the general price level. These are the concepts of macroeconomics, not microeconomics.

This observation may be illustrated with the following open-economy income flow model used in macroeconomics. This is a five-sector open-economy model of a country. Two exogenous sectors—the government and the rest of the world—are located respectively at the top and bottom of the circle representing a market economy. Three endogenous sectors—households, financial institutions, and firms—lie at the diameter passing through its centre. The model shows how the GDP of a country is produced and consumed, but it can say little about the efficiency of the allocation of scarce national resources. This is because the allocation and the efficiency problems, which SN argues following Robbins, can be studied only in the context of a commodity market—both factor and product.

Figure 2: The Circular Flow of Income in an Open Economy

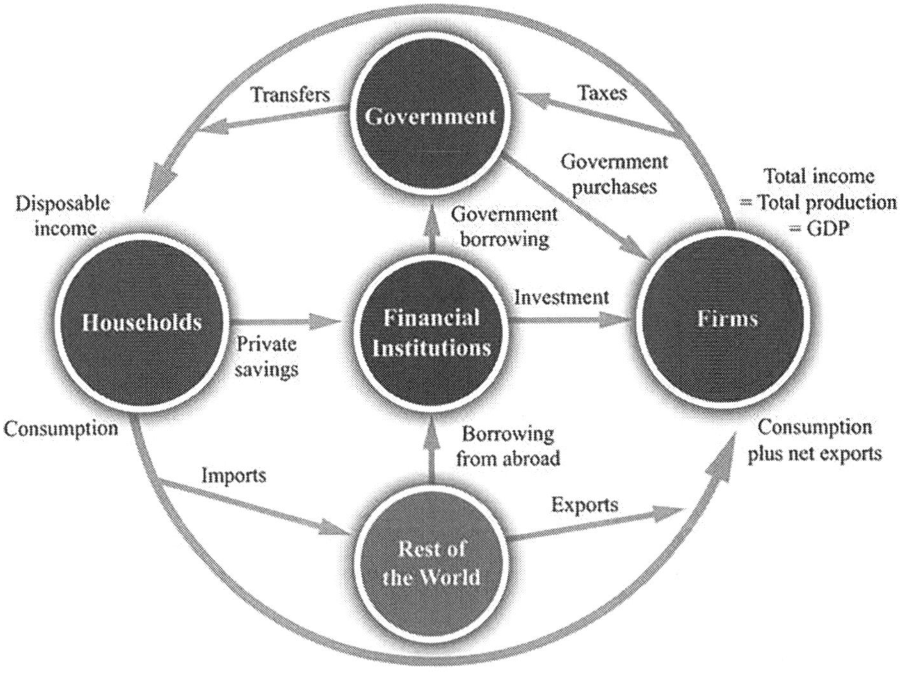

Source: Creative Commons (2021). Available from https://2012books.lardbucket.org/books/theory-and-applications-of-macroeconomics/s20-16-the-circular-flow-of-income.html (accessed on January 22, 2021).

Second, the economy is divided into two types of markets—product and factor—consistent with two types of economics agents: business and consumers. As noted above, consumers own all three production factors—land, labour, and capital goods—while businesses own all products. If the product and factor markets are perfectly competitive, the supply and demand will determine equilibrium prices in both markets, which will result in equilibrium in this economy. SN argue:

> Adam Smith discovered a remarkable property of a competitive market economy. Under perfect competition and with no market failures, markets will squeeze as many useful goods and services out of the available resources as is possible. But where monopolies or pollution or similar market failures become pervasive, the remarkable efficiency properties of the invisible hand may be destroyed (Samuelson and Nordhaus 2010, 30).

This is the modern version of Adam Smith's invisible hand theory. Did Smith intend to mean what the modern economists tell us to believe? We can form an informed opinion about this question, which would become another academic debate topic. However, from both theoretical and policy perspectives, the critical question concerns its relevance for the economy in which all actively participate. This is a grave and urgent question of market analysis for the economy of a democratic country.

Again, consider the US economy. The first point is that it exists because there is a sovereign state by this name. Thus, the US economy operates in the way the US government allows it to function. This is the macroeconomic aspect of our market economy. However, the US economy is a conglomeration of millions of markets, broadly divided into three kinds—public, private, and non-profit or charity. Consider the US defence industry. Although private firms are the primary producers of the defence materials, the government is its primary consumer. Thus, the motivational factor of the consumer theory does not apply here. Second, the industry is highly regulated, meaning the assumption of perfect competition is invalid in this case.

Adam Smith carefully maintained the distinctions among different markets in his theory of the invisible hand. He made this abundantly clear with the first two sentences of the book:

> The annual labour of every nation is the fund that originally supplies it with all the necessaries and conveniences of life that it annually consumes, which consist always either in the immediate produce of that labour or in what is purchased with that produce from other nations. Accordingly, therefore, as this produce, or what is purchased with it, bears a greater or smaller proportion to the number of those who are to consume it, the nation will be better or worse supplied with all the necessaries and conveniences for which it has occasion (Smith 1776).

Two points may be noted from the preceding discussion. First, the British and French monarchies were the major colonial powers, which used the mercantilist trade policy to accumulate species. Adam Smith argued against this beggar-thy-neighbour policy in favour of the French physiocrats' liberal trade policy. He argued that the mercantilist policy might boomerang to the home country. Second, the government should refrain from interfering in the private economic activities that mainly concern the production of necessities and conveniences of general people, which was the primary concern of both government and the business people. Modern economists grossly misinterpret Adam Smith by treating him as the prophet of laissez-faire domestic and foreign trade policy.

The second point concerns the modern economists' linearity hallucination. Adam Smith's ideas are used in modern debates without considering the fact that the world has dramatically changed during the last two and a half centuries. Smith articulated his economic philosophy when monarchs ruled their subjects, and the Industrial Revolution began to transform the feudal economy. Today, citizens govern themselves with their elected representatives, and the economies of the western hemisphere are fully industrialized. In this situation, Smith's invisible hand theory conflicts, at least partially, with modern democracies' economic policy.

Consider Canada. The country pursues a universal healthcare policy under which private participation in the healthcare industry is strictly limited. This feature cannot be accommodated in SN's invisible hand model, which can be demonstrated by replacing three products in SN's figure— pizzas, housing, and shoes—with food, healthcare, and utilities. People have little choice in food and healthcare as they are necessary for survival. They earn enough to buy necessary food items and can choose from available utilities.

Nevertheless, expensive medical care is not covered by regular payslips. Being incidental, it is covered by the accompanying benefits package as health insurance coverage. In Canada, each provincial and territorial government administers a universal health insurance program for all its residents. From the Canadian perspective, SN's model used in the health sector does not fit in this country, although the Canadian universities teach this model in health economics courses.

On the other hand, this model partially describes the health policy in the US. Most US residents employed in different public and private organizations receive health insurance for themselves and their family members as their benefits package. Accordingly, those who are not employed live without health insurance if they cannot afford it themselves. In modern times, this policy could have been a severe source of civil discontent as numerous junior and senior citizens, who require most medical care, would have been the victims of this undemocratic health policy. This potential civil unrest has been avoided by enacting two public healthcare programs—Medicaid and Medicare. Although the clear majority of the American public and policymakers are satisfied with this unique health policy, its political and economic justifications are still unknown. Politically, this policy is inconsistent with the principles of democracy as it clearly discriminates the US citizens based on their income and age. Economically, it is one of the most inefficient healthcare systems among the OECD countries, which has been demonstrated repeatedly.

However, the bottom line is that SN's interpretation of Smith's invisible hand theory, running the mixed economy's market mechanism, is subject to scathing criticisms.

8.5.2.5 The Visible Hand of the Government

SN begin Chapter 2, titled *The Mixed Economy,* by illustrating the operating mechanism of the market economy governed by the principles of the invisible hand and ends with describing the visible hand of the government, indicating it is a mixed economy. Their approach is similar to that of JMK, who first argued that the government has a critical role in streamlining the market economy that is propelled by entrepreneurs' profit-greed and the government's non-interfering economic policy. He articulated his arguments in the context of the great depression. SN generalized their vision by suggesting that the invisible hand cannot operate independently for three factors—"market failures," "externalities," and "inequitable income distribution"—which disturb the market condition. Therefore, the government must actively participate in managing the market economy by diminishing the ill effects of these undesirable economic events with its fiscal and monetary instruments. SN describe this public role as the visible hand of the government. When the government performs this role, the market economy turns into a mixed economy.

This is the general theory that has gradually developed after WWII, meaning it represents the general belief and philosophy of modern economists. Therefore, it will be unfair to credit this idea to SN alone. However, this general professional stand raises one unwarranted question: *Does this model represent the economies of modern democratic countries around the world?* The question is simply gargantuan, meaning it needs in-depth independent research to do it justice. However, some summary observations may be made in our context.

First, as noted above, this modern mixed-economy version of the classical theory originated from Ricardo's treatise on economics. To see the difference between Ricardian and modern economics, we need to underline two facts—one practical and another intellectual. The practical fact is concerned with the prevailing socio-economic and political milieus when Ricardo and his followers theorized this analysis. At that time, monarchs governed with their military powers and feudal lords; general people were subjects, not citizens. Therefore, Ricardo's classification of the production factors—land, labour, and capital—was consistent with the political and social systems of the time. As an input in the production process, human labour was not so different from other inputs, including animal labour. Thus, Ricardo had some logic in treating human labour as an input in the production process and paying it subsistence wages.

Today, we live in a democracy where we are all equal citizens in terms of rights. Therefore, everything accomplished by the participation of several individuals must be based on a voluntary contract. At the bottom, the institution of family is a voluntary contract between a man and a woman. At the top, the state is a political association founded on the social contract. Naturally, all production or wealth generated by different services supplied by several individuals is supposed to be accomplished by voluntary contracts among these individuals. By this analogy, labour cannot be treated as a factor of production in the same way land or capital is. We encounter this difficulty because we have not adjusted our model with the revolutionary changes in our social and political lives. We are no longer subjects; we are now citizens, and we govern ourselves by our own representatives. Therefore, every act or action that requires the participation of more than one individual is supposed to be based on a voluntary contract.

To clarify the point, SN is again quoted from Part 3 that deals with the factor markets—labour, land, and capital:

America is a land of extremes of income and wealth. If you are one of the 400 richest Americans, you are likely to be a 60-year-old white male with a degree from a top university and a net worth of about $4 billion. This tiny sliver of American society owns about 3 percent of the total wealth of the country.

At the other extreme are forgotten people who never make the cover of *Forbes* or *People* magazines. Listen to the story of Robert Clark, homeless and unemployed. A roofer and Vietnam veteran, he came to Miami from Detroit looking for work. He slept on the city streets on a piece of cardboard covered by a stolen sheet. Every day he and other homeless men crept out of the culverts into the daylight to work for temporary employment firms. These firms charged clients $8 to $10 an hour, paid the men the minimum wage, and then took most of the money back for transportation and tools. Clark's pay stub showed earnings of $31.28 for 31 hours of work.

How can we understand these extremes of income and wealth? Why are some people paid $10 million a year, while others net only $1 an hour? Why is real estate in Tokyo or Manhattan worth thousands of dollars a square foot, while land in the desert may sell for but a few dollars an acre? And what is the source of the billions of dollars of profits earned by giant enterprises like Microsoft and General Electric? (Samuelson and Nordhaus 2010, 229).

SN's mixed-economy model cannot explain this pay-structure scenario, although it appears to them morally offensive and economically unjustifiable. Robert Clark suffered this plight because there was no voluntary contract between the temporary-employment firm and him. From the perspective of mixed economy, this wage rate is not unfair because the labour of Robert Clark is treated as a commodity like any other commodity exchanged in the market economy.

However, this problem does not arise if we start our analysis based on the premise that reflects the way we conduct our daily lives: We live in a democratic society where everyone is equal in terms of rights. Thus, when we enter an agreement to operate a business, the voluntary contract demands that each of us is paid compensation commensurate to the value of their services. The service of a manual worker is less costly than the CEO of the company, meaning they must not be paid a similar salary package. However, this difference cannot be as high as SN shows in their book. Therefore, it seems to be a reasonable inference that the model of modern economics is inconsistent with the political society in which we live.

CHAPTER IX
ECONOMICS FOR DEMOCRCAY IN THE 21ST CENTURY: A PARADIGM SEARCH

"We can't solve problems by using the same kind of thinking we used when we created them." –Albert Einstein

9.1 Introduction

This penultimate chapter of the review book intends to achieve two objectives. First, it intends to see where our distinguished authors differ regarding the definition and scope of economics and why this century-long debate continues unresolved. For this purpose, we will juxtapose the definitions of four authors (JMK is excluded because he did not directly address the issue).

Second, we have now entered the third decade of the 21st century, which presents a remarkable social atmosphere for global humanity to live in peace and prosperity. A Greek proverb says that "man is the means and measure of everything." Our long journey from ancient Greece to the modern world has amply clarified the meaning and the message of this proverb. Natural science and technology have developed to such an unprecedented extent that they can deliver all kinds of benefits to humanity if we use it appropriately. Finally, our knowledge of history is supposed to convince us that democracy is the only political system that has the potential to ensure our rights to "security of life, liberty, and the pursuit of happiness." Unfortunately, our understanding and beliefs are being continuously tested because we interpret democracy as a system of governance to fit our interest or perception. More specifically, we fail to distinguish between three social concepts—capitalism, socialism, and democracy.

Given all kinds of economic chaos disturbing peace and stability in the lands of affluence, the critical issue before us is to think about the kind of economics that are supposed to be taught and learned in an advanced democratic state. The prevailing coronavirus pandemic was supposed to inspire us in this regard. Unfortunately, this does not seem to be the case.

The coronavirus pandemic is a health issue, which was not considered in theorizing the modern mixed economy model. In this model, both the employees and employers are assumed to be in perfect health, looking eagerly to employ their physical and mental skills in the most profitable enterprises. COVID-19 demonstrates that people may not be able to achieve their economic ambitions even if they are not sick. JMK told us that economic depression is the outcome of inadequate aggregate demand, which demands government intervention to avoid massive human miseries and economic stagnation. In the case of COVID-19, the fall in aggregate supply is contracting national output by affecting aggregate demand.

This supply-side contraction has created two challenging macroeconomic policy issues. First, the massive unemployment created by COVID-19 is affecting the government—the visible hand in SN's mixed economy—in two ways. First, it reduces the government's tax revenue due to the declining GDP. Second, the government needs more money to pay unemployment benefits and help low-income citizens. This revenue and expenditure scenario is creating a monumental fiscal policy crisis. The government is forced to increase its budget deficit, meaning increasing its debt. The so-called sovereign debt crisis is already a cause of serious concern in many western countries. For example, Japan's national debt amounted to about 237% of the gross domestic product in 2018, which is the highest in the world. In the US, the debt to the GPD ratio was 106% in that year, which is expected to reach 136% in 2020 (Amadeo 2020).

This is undoubtedly a dangerous national fiscal situation, which has dire political implications. The national economy is growing continuously, producing two diagonally different wealth implications. To help improve the health of the private sector, the government is getting increasingly indebted. This growth situation would have caused no alarm if the wealth generated by this policy was equitably distributed. The ugly fact of our civilized life is that the private sector's wealth is being concentrated in a tiny proportion of private citizens. This fiscal scenario is consistent with the economic model developed over the past two and half centuries. This is perhaps why the economics profession is not worried about "sovereign" indebtedness, although a section of the profession seems to be very vocal about income distribution in the private sector.

As noted before, the COVID-19 pandemic was supposed to strike professional ethics. This is not happening. On the one hand, the general body of economists is advising the government to do whatever necessary to eliminate the virus so that the economy could bounce back to its previous state. This general body ignores the history of pandemics, which shows that another kind of pandemic could crop up any time in the future. In this context, the health economists are playing the most regrettable and reprehensible role. Being the specialists in the crisis, they were supposed to take the lead in the pandemic research. However, "solemn silence" seems to be the phrase that describes their reaction in this situation.

PART I: THE CONVENTIONAL WISDOM

9.2 Definition and Scope of Economics

For over a century, the economics profession has been debating the definition and scope of its discipline. It has turned out to be a frustrating experience as some economists are prepared to abandon the debate for good. The conclusion of Backhouse and Medema (2009), cited in Chapter I, is reproduced below for reference:

> Modern economists do not subscribe to a *homogeneous* [emphasis added] definition of their subject. At a time when economists are tackling subjects as diverse as growth, auctions, crime, and religion with a methodological toolkit that includes real analysis, econometrics, laboratory experiments, and historical case studies, and when they are debating the explanatory roles of rationality and behavioural norms, *any concise definition* [emphasis added] of economics is likely to be inadequate. *This lack of agreement on a definition does not necessarily pose a problem for the subject* [emphasis added]. Economists are generally guided by pragmatic considerations of what works or by methodological views emanating from various sources, not by formal definitions: to repeat the comment attributed to Jacob Viner—economics is what economists do—... adhering to a specific definition may constrain the problems that economists believe it is legitimate to tackle and the methods by which they choose to tackle them.

This conclusion is unfortunate for three reasons. First, economics is taught around the world. The above statement seems to suggest that we need not tell our students what they are studying. Second, it must be unfortunate for any science discipline to have no well-agreed definition—a statement explaining the meaning or the essential features implied by its title. Third, Backhouse and Medema's statement appears very odd from the perspective of the modern dictionary. For, if there is a word, we can find its definition in appropriate dictionaries, which may vary across different lexicons due to differences in perspective.

Accordingly, this review work has taken the challenge to investigate where our distinguished authors differ and if there is any reason to believe that this disagreement is the product of our incorrect paradigm. If the answer is affirmative, we should redefine economics in light of both its practical utility and theoretical consistency.

With this objective, the book surveyed the opinions and arguments of five significant authors—Marshall, JNK, Robbins, JMK, and Samuelson—on the definition and scope of economics from three novel perspectives. First, economics is infamous for its legendary disagreements. Therefore, different views of these five authors about the definition and scope of economics are treated as a part of its broader debate: why economists disagree. Second, unlike the previous studies, this book examines the nature of these disagreements in light of John Locke and David Hume's empiricist philosophy. Finally, the book takes a diagonally different approach to examine the definition and scope of economics. The conventional wisdom derives the theories and laws of economics by studying Robinson Crusoe's behaviour—a natural person who pursues self-interests without any regard to the country's laws, let alone the interests of his fellow human beings and the welfare of the society in which he lives.

On the contrary, this book treats all economic agents as citizens of a democratic state, meaning they have both rights and responsibilities. Their rights include creating and accumulating private property, while their responsibilities include complying with the state's law and respecting fellow citizens' rights. Mr. Crusoe does not need to respect these requirements. His behaviour is "economically rational" whether he runs an agricultural firm or leads a vicious smuggling gang.

Table 1: Definition and Scope of Economics: Marshall, JNK, Robbins, and Samuelson

Author	Definition
Marshall	Political Economy or Economics is a study of mankind in the ordinary business of life; it examines that part of individual and social action which is most closely connected with the attainment and use of the material requisites of well-being. **Fundamental Concepts**: ordinary business, material well-being.
JNK	Political Economy or Economics is a body of doctrine relating to the economic phenomena or economic activities directly related to the creation, appropriation, and accumulation of wealth (slightly modified). **Fundamental Concepts**: creation, appropriation, and accumulation of wealth.
Robbins	Economics is the science that studies human behaviour as a relationship between ends and scarce means that have alternative uses. **Fundamental Concepts**: unlimited ends, scarce means, and alternative uses.
Samuelson	Economics is the study of how societies use scarce resources to produce valuable goods and services and distribute them among different individuals. **Fundamental Concepts**: society, scarce resources, production of valuable goods, and services and distribution.

9.2.1 Northern Approach

The definitions given by our four acclaimed authors are reproduced in Table 1. Before discussing the similarities and differences among these definitions, it may be worth saying a few words about how they are interpreted today. In this regard, we see two different approaches—which may be called northern and southern approaches—fully knowing that this division is arbitrary. First, consider the northern approach to teaching the definition of economics. About three decades ago, Harrison, Smith, and Davies (1992, 1) wrote in their *Introductory Economics*:

> There are many definitions of economics, each trying to encapsulate the fundamentals of the subject. No completely satisfactory definition has yet been derived, but most definitions that have been suggested emphasize the point that economics is about the allocation of scarce resources which have alternative uses.

SN's *Economics* reviewed in this book contains similar warnings and opinions. The book begins with a definition—*Economics is the study of how societies use scarce resources to produce valuable goods and services and distribute them among different individuals.* However, the authors note that economics has expanded to include a vast array of topics over the past half-century, for which the textbook authors often define economics in a narrower sense underlining their topical interests. Nevertheless, on a critical examination, all these definitions boil down to the one stated above.

9.2.2 Southern Approach

In the South, introductory economics, taught at the college and university levels, are ordinarily written by local authors, who treat its definition quite differently. Perhaps, it will not be wholly incorrect to characterize the southern approach as historical and the northern approach as contemporary.

Adam Smith created modern economics as a separate social science branch in 1776. Since then, successive generations of economists have been extending its scope of study by increasing topics on both practical and theoretical aspects. For example, agricultural economics—defined as the application of economics principles to the special field of agriculture—was established as the first branch of economics. The reasons were its characteristics and policy importance. Then, economics was divided into two fundamental branches under the title micro and macroeconomics. Today the *Journal of Economic Literature* (JEL) classifies different economics fields into twenty major categories, which are again broken down into sub-categories. Some of these categories have developed mainly because of theoretical importance. For example, the economics of happiness and economics of crime are more of theoretical curiosity than the topics' practical policy relevance.

These historical developments in economics seem to be related to various interpretations concerning the discipline's definition and scope. For example, the economics of crime, which treats a criminal's behaviour as "rational," cannot be developed if we do not assume that economics does not bother with "social welfare." However, these theoretical issues are of little importance in the South, specifically from studying and teaching economics. Thus, based on their northern colleagues' received knowledge, the southern economists have classified the definition of their discipline into three categories—wealth, welfare, and scarcity (Dewett and Nahalur 2006).

9.2.3 Wealth Definition

This definition is directly related to Adam Smith. Because of his book's title, it is generally believed that economics is a science of wealth. We can find this notion among the early classical economists, including J.E. Cairnes, J.B. Say, and F.A. Walker. More specifically, the scope of the study of economics is limited to human activities concerned with the creation of physical wealth. In his words:

> Political economy, considered as a branch of the science of a statesman or legislator, proposes two distinct objects; first, to provide a plentiful revenue or subsistence for the people, or, more properly, to enable them to provide such a revenue or subsistence for themselves; and, secondly, to supply the state or commonwealth with a revenue sufficient for the public services. It proposes to enrich both the people and the sovereign (Smith 1776)

As observed in Chapter VI, Robbins lucidly described the difficulty that arises when the study of economics is defined in that way. Some economists, notably Ludwig von Mises (1881–1973) and Philip Wicksteed (1844–1927), raised objections to Adam Smith's conception of wealth.

9.2.4 Welfare Definition

Alfred Marshall is the most influential economist who introduced the term "material well-being" in this definitional debate. As a socially concerned economist, he argued that the study of economics is supposed to improve the welfare of ordinary people, which he justified with some impeccable reasons. Unfortunately, few studies notice his purpose of highlighting "material well-being" as the primary objective of economics. Perhaps, it will be useful to highlight this weakness by citing the relevant passage of Marshall's work:

> Those who have been called the Residuum of our large towns have little opportunity for friendship; they know nothing of the decencies and the quiet, and very little even of the unity of family life, and religion often fails to reach them. *No doubt their physical, mental, and moral*

ill-health is partly due to other causes than poverty: but this is the chief cause [emphasis added].

And, in addition to the Residuum, there are vast numbers of people both in town and country who are brought up with insufficient food, clothing, and house-room; whose education is broken off early in order that they may go to work for wages; who thenceforth are engaged during long hours in exhausting toil with imperfectly nourished bodies, and have therefore no chance of developing their higher mental faculties ... But, for all that, their poverty is a great and almost unmixed evil to them. Even when they are well, their weariness often amounts to pain, while their pleasures are few; and when sickness comes, the suffering caused by poverty increases tenfold. And, though a contented spirit may go far toward reconciling them to these evils, there are others to which it ought not to reconcile them. Overworked and under-taught, weary and careworn, without quiet and without leisure, they have no chance of making the best of their mental faculties.

Slavery was regarded by Aristotle as an ordinance of nature, and so probably was it by the slaves themselves in olden times. The dignity of man was proclaimed by the Christian religion: it has been asserted with increasing vehemence during the last hundred years: but, only through the spread of education during quite recent times are we beginning to feel the full import of the phrase. *Now, at last, we are setting ourselves seriously to inquire whether it is necessary that there should be any so-called "lower classes" at all: that is, whether there need be large numbers of people doomed from their birth to hard work in order to provide for others the requisites of a refined and cultured life; while they themselves are prevented by their poverty and toil from having any share or part in that life* [emphasis added].

The hope that poverty and ignorance may gradually be extinguished derives indeed much support from the steady progress of the working classes during the nineteenth century. The steam-engine has relieved them of much exhausting and degrading toil; wages have risen; education has been improved and become more general; the railway and the printing-press have enabled members of the same trade in different parts of the country to communicate easily with one another, and to undertake and carry out broad and far-seeing lines of policy; while the growing demand for intelligent work has caused the artisan classes to increase so rapidly that they now outnumber those whose labour is entirely unskilled. A great part of the artisans have ceased to belong to the "lower classes" in the sense in which the term was originally used, and some of them already lead a more refined and noble life than did the majority of the upper classes even a century ago.

This progress has done more than anything else to give practical interest to the question of whether it is really impossible that all should start in the world with a fair chance of leading a cultured life, free from the pains of poverty and the stagnating influences of excessive mechanical toil; and this question is being pressed to the front by the growing earnestness of the age [emphasis added] (Marshall 1890).

9.2.5 Scarcity Definition

The final category of definition that the southern economists discuss in detail is our familiar scarcity definition. Since this definition has been examined in the relevant chapters, the discussion is not repeated here.

9.3 Summary

The preceding paragraphs reveal two lines of development regarding the definition of economics, which have been identified as the northern and southern approaches. The northern approach has placed its entire trust on Robbins's scarcity concept. The reason seems obvious. After WWII, leading economists, including Samuelson, devoted their mathematical talents to rigorize the language of economics. It may not be entirely inappropriate to describe their efforts as making economics a branch of applied mathematics. The post-WWII leading economists leaned toward Robbins, not because of his passionate arguments, but because the scarcity conception is most aggregable to their mathematical passions. On the other hand, although trained in the northern, a clear majority of southern economists prefer a historical approach where they divide the definitions of the prominent authors into three different versions described above.

The point to be noted here is that both the northern and southern approaches are controversial. The difficulties in the northern approach have been detailed above. The fault with the southern approach is that the characterization of economics in three different manners is a misconception of the meaning and scope of the discipline. Wealth is the undisputed subject matter of economics. However, there is a difference of opinions about how to study the production of consumption of wealth. Classical economists believed that social welfare ought to be the criterion or the principle to determine the kinds of goods and services that are to be included in the study of economics. On the other hand, Robbins believed that subjective judgment is inconsistent with the methodology of science. Therefore, he argued that scarcity is the unifying criterion in the study of economics.

9.4 The Fundamental Cause of Definitional Debate

The critical survey in this book began with two promises: (i) to treat the definitional debate as one case of legendary disagreements in the economics profession and (ii) to examine the causes of these disagreements in light of Locke and Hume's empiricist philosophy. These promises are fulfilled in this subsection, which will begin by identifying the points on which our authors agree and disagree.

Following Locke's empiricist philosophy, this book divided the entire process of creating human knowledge into two steps—private and public. Private knowledge is generated by the faculty of human understanding, which makes it impossible for a person to disagree with their ideas. On the other hand, public knowledge is created through language. For two reasons, this fact creates a constant source of disagreements among the experts. First, we have no way of knowing the ideas an author intended to express with his words. Second, we may disagree about the meaning of other individuals' written or spoken words for a variety of reasons, including our moral differences.

With this understanding of the nature of the academic debate, the following paragraphs identify the areas of agreements and disagreements among our authors over the definition of economics.

9.4.1 Agreements

First, the definition of economics must somehow involve the production, exchange, distribution, and consumption of wealth. This is true even though there are differences of opinion about its meaning. Second, the institution of private property must be the fundamental pillar of the economy so that individuals can create and accumulate private wealth. Third, all authors agree that the system of property ownership is most consistent with human nature. Fourth, the role of government in the creation of wealth is limited because individuals own most of the nation's natural and manufactured resources.

These are the areas of agreement that form the background of discussion on the definition and scope of economics, i.e., they are not discussed with sufficient importance in the text, if discussed at all. Adam Smith did not elaborate on private property's role in his ground-breaking book, although the book is all about how this institution operates to enrich both the public and the "sovereign." His successors followed in his footsteps. Therefore, ordinary individuals' involvement in creating private wealth was a factor of production supplying human labour, not a partner in production to be eligible to share the net sale revenue. This approach of wealth production is very similar to Aristotle's theory of household management:

> Property is a part of the household, and the art of acquiring property is a part of the art of managing the household, for no man can live well, or indeed live at all, unless he be provided with necessaries. And as in the arts, which have a definite sphere, the workers must have their own proper instruments for the accomplishment of their work, so it is in the management of a household. Now instruments are of various sorts; some are living, others lifeless; in the rudder, the pilot of a ship has a lifeless, in the look-out man, a living instrument; for in the arts, the servant is a kind of instrument. Thus, too, a possession is an instrument for maintaining life. And so, in the arrangement of the family, a slave is a living possession, and property a number of such instruments; and the servant is himself an instrument which takes precedence of all other instruments (Aristotle 350 BCE).

In Aristotle's Athens, Greek citizens owned property, which mainly meant agricultural lands. Since they were mainly preoccupied with political, cultural, and military functions, slaves were used for farming. During the 18th century, when the idea of modern economics was conceived, Europe was in the process of transiting from feudalistic to the capitalist mode of production. This happened under the auspices of the Industrial Revolution, which is dated from 1760 to the end of 1840 (Wrigley 2018). The 1851 population census indicates that England and Wales's population was equally divided between rural and urban areas. In 1901, i.e., the beginning of the 20th century, the rural-urban population ratio came down to 22:78, which suggests a massive migration of rural people, particularly the young, to urban centres to work as wage labourers. Thus, two different systems of production relations existed during the 18th and 19th centuries when the political economy, a moral science, was being transformed into a social science.

Although the term "feudalism" is widely used, it does not have a universal definition because scholars have never agreed on a precise definition (Cartwrightby 2018). The following definition that Cartwrightby quoted from the *Oxford English Dictionary*, may help us understand the nature of this institution:

> The dominant social system in medieval Europe, in which the nobility held lands from the Crown in exchange for military service, and vassals were in turn tenants of the nobles, while the peasants (villeins or serfs) were obliged to live on their lord's land and give him homage, labour, and a share of the produce, notionally in exchange for military protection.

On the other hand, capitalism represents a mode of production where the whole population is divided into two classes—bourgeois and proletariat. The bourgeois owns all property, while the proletariat owns only their labour. Karl Marx (1859) describes the system in the following words:

> In the social production of their existence, men inevitably enter into definite relations independent of their will, namely relations of production appropriate to a given stage in the development of their material forces of production. The totality of these relations of production constitutes society's economic structure, the real foundation, on

which arises a legal and political superstructure and to which correspond definite forms of social consciousness. The mode of production of material life conditions the general process of social, political and intellectual life. It is not the consciousness of men that determines their existence, but their social existence that determines their consciousness. At a certain stage of development, the material productive forces of society come into conflict with the existing relations of production or—this merely expresses the same thing in legal terms—with the property relations within the framework of which they have operated hitherto. From forms of development of the productive forces, these relations turn into their fetters. Then begins an era of social revolution. The changes in the economic foundation lead sooner or later to the transformation of the whole immense superstructure.

Both feudalism and capitalism are founded on the institution of private property. The primary difference between the two modes of production is the dominance of the factors of production. Under feudalism, the land is the dominant factor of production, which the landlords own. Ordinary people work as vassals and serfs in landlords' lands for their physical protection and subsistence. Under capitalism, the dominant factor of production is capital, the stock of monetary wealth, which can buy all kinds of production factors. By Marx's deduction, the bourgeois class owns this domineering factor exclusively. On the other hand, the proletariats own only their labour-power, which is *sine qua non* for carrying out all ordinary production activities.

Two points are worth noting from the above discussion. Like Aristotle, the treatment of human labour as an ordinary commodity in the classical and neoclassical theories before WWII is founded on actual production relations prevailing in Europe. Therefore, the economic literature until the first half of the 20th century is not theoretically incorrect; here, human labour is treated as a commodity. Second, this factual supposition becomes unacceptable when we judge it from our moral perspective. Marshall, underlining his notion of "material well-being," pointed to this issue mentioned above.

This is where Hume's philosophy becomes so critical in understanding our disagreements. Marx could not accept this political and economic order because of his moral attitudes. However, he failed to convince his fellow Europeans to end the existing superstructures' atrocities because he vowed to destroy the institution of private property without giving enough good reasons. Firstly, he did not inquire why our ancestors established the institution of private property in the first place. If he did, he would have noticed that the kind of communism he dreamt of existed when the *homo sapiens* had been living in small groups in the wilderness. Second, he did not give enough thought to the economic consequences of establishing a socialist government on ordinary people for whom he recommended dismantling the institution of private property. Nor did he consider how the government leaders would use the sovereign power of the state.

9.4.2 Disagreements

What is so different in the definition of economics offered by our four celebrated economists so that we are now prepared to abandon the century-old definitional debate for good? This ought to be a curious question because all authors agree on the background that defines the nature and scope of our discipline. The first and foremost premise on which classical and neoclassical economics is founded is the institution of private property. It is impossible to develop the theory of the market economy without agreeing to this premise. We cannot draw an individual supply curve without the existence of private property, and without individual supply curves, there is no market supply curve. Both individual and market demand curves exist irrespective of the nature of the economy. We cannot attribute private producers' selfish nature to our public authority because the two words—public and private—would then imply the same idea. Finally, under a command economy, the public authority is responsible for making three fundamental production decisions—what to produce, how to produce, and for whom to produce. All these decisions will be arbitrary because a centralized authority cannot predict the exact goods and services different individuals would prefer no matter how judicious it is. Nevertheless, the socialist government must allocate its scarce resources among different sectors of the economy for the services it promised—health, education, production of necessities, and conveniences. This allocation will be influenced both by the regime characteristics and the moral make-up of the regime leaders. The history of socialist superstructure testifies that the so-called communist leaders were most interested in building up the country's military might than improving the conditions of livelihoods of their ordinary citizens. More specifically, the socialist superpowers were more interested in hegemonic politics than the socio-economic conditions of ordinary people.

The four definitions cited in Table 1 can be condensed into two categories—welfare and scarcity. First, Marshall and JNK's definitions fall in the first category. These Cambridge economists argue that the key criterion to define the nature and the subject matter of economics should be "material welfare." The reason behind their opinion has been explained in Chapter III. They are socially concerned intellectuals who studied economics for the general welfare of the society in which they lived.

On the contrary, Robbins began his definitional discourse by rejecting the conventional wisdom that has been well articulated in Marshall's definition. He does this by arguing that economics is a science that cannot be constrained by imposing value-judgment. Other than this, there is no fundamental difference between the welfare and scarcity conceptions of economics. Robbins described Marshall's definition as classificatory because it marks off the human behaviour specifically directed to procuring material welfare as the subject matter of economics. On the other hand, his scarcity definition is analytical in the sense that it "focuses attention on a particular aspect of behaviour, the form imposed by the influence of scarcity."

As already argued, Samuelson gave Robbin's conception a mathematical interpretation, which made the study of economics rigorous but very deductive. Thus, Samuelson's contribution in the definitional debate primarily consists of introducing mathematics and symbolic logic to the study of economics. All this leads to the conclusion that the primary difference between Marshall and Robins lies in their moral judgments. Marshall believed that the fundamental purpose of studying economics in a democratic society concerns eradicating poverty and economic slavery, which is supposed to define the nature of the discipline's substance. On the contrary, Robbins believed that imposing welfare requirements in determining the nature and subject matter of economics is unscientific, which will unnecessarily curtail the scope of economic analysis.

PART II: ECONOMICS FOR DEMOCRACY: A 21ST CENTURY APPROACH

Our objective in this part of the chapter is to search for the most eligible definition of economics to be practiced in the 21st-century democratic states. For this, we need not dig into any in-depth theoretical and semantic debate because we now know nearly everything about how the laws of economics operate under two competing political systems—socialism and democracy. In 1848, J.S. Mill offered a definition of the discipline, which was perhaps appropriate in the context of his political and intellectual milieus. After 84 years, Lionel Robbins made a similar venture, which has made the topic extremely controversial. The following exploratory effort is made under the feeble hope that it might help clear out these controversies and propose a definition of economics for the 21st century. More specifically, this book intends to analyze the issue from a different thought system, which might be called a paradigm change. Unlike conventional wisdom, the approach to be taken here is pragmatic, meaning the study of economics will be dictated by the state's political, cultural, and technological condition, not the innate characteristics of human beings.

9.5 Democracy in the 21st Century: The Political Paradigm

9.5.1 Individuals and Citizens

It is no longer necessary to explain the reason for our economic activities—whether we are stranded in Robinson Crusoe's isolated island or live in a busy modern megacity like New York or London. We know we do everything in our best interests. Thus, the individual is both subject and object of all kinds of activities in modern society, whose entire life cycle is divided into three phases—dependence, independence, and retirement. This life cycle story may be dramatized with the following quote from Rousseau:

> How rapid is our journey on this earth! The first quarter of life has been lived before one knows the use of it. The last quarter is lived when one ceased to enjoy it. At first, we do not know how to live; soon we can no longer live; and in the interval which separates these two useless extremities, three-quarters of the time remaining to us is consumed by sleep, work, pain, constraint and efforts of all kinds. Life is short, not so much because it lasts a short time as because we have almost none of that time for savouring it. The moment of death may well be distant from that of birth, but life is too short when this space is poorly filled (Rousseau 1979, 211).

Rousseau is quoted here to show the importance of analyzing the life cycle of an individual because our role as an economic agent differs remarkably. If this life cycle is not constantly kept in our active mental compass, any economic analysis predicting human behaviour in society is destined to err both conceptually and practically.

When a baby is born, she needs four necessities for healthy growth—food and clothing, accommodation, healthcare, and nursing. Of course, the parents are responsible for meeting all her nursing needs, which will gradually decline as she grows up. However, who will be responsible for satisfying the remaining needs as they depend upon the parents' economic and social status? We must also include schooling opportunities with these needs. The socialist movement developed during the last century has an answer to this question; governments, which replaced Czars and monarchs' rule, took over the responsibility for providing all the basic needs of life.

However, the science of political economy, which developed in 18th century Europe and flourished gradually worldwide, has convincingly demonstrated the capability of the market economy to accelerate economic affluence but hardly discusses the issue about the dependents' needs. Economists before WWII might have the excuse to argue that the topic was not relevant to the political and economic realities. However, modern economists cannot have this excuse because modern political culture and structure, economic affluence, and scientific developments favour addressing this question.

The seniors' scenario is quite different from that of the dependents. Being retired from the workforce, they become dependent on pension income and accumulated wealth. While their demands for material goods and services decline, the need for healthcare increases, often astronomically. From the economic sense, these needs are not demands as most seniors cannot afford them. Since these people no longer qualify as *homo economicus*, orthodox economics has little to say about their existence in society.

The theme idea that beams forth from this discussion is that modern economics—primarily focused on the idea of the economic man—is, at best, a partial analysis of the economic system of democracy. More specifically, it revolves around the middle portion of the individual's life cycle in which they begin and complete their independent financial lives—earn incomes, start families, and carry out all the yolks of social responsibilities, including running the government. This is what is supposed to happen, as this is how Nature has planned it for us. However, analyzing this part of the life cycle will not lead to a steady-state economy, let alone an orderly society, unless the first and last parts of the life cycle are kept continuously in mind. More specifically, this objective cannot be achieved unless we treat the individual as the *citizen* of a democratic country because they have rights and obligations, which change with the life cycle.

9.5.2 Democracy, Government, and the State

Citizenship is a political vocabulary, meaning the concept needs to be examined from the perspective of the state, government, and the system of governance. Perhaps it is redundant at this stage of our intellectual and political life to talk about the nature of the state and its relation with the government. However, a concise and precise discussion of democracy as a system of governance is critically important because it seems to be the source of all confusion and controversy. This intellectual impasse is the outcome of interpreting democracy as an electoral mechanism to change the political leadership of the government. This is not just a public perception about democracy; it is deeply rooted in the prevailing intellectual discourse, most importantly in political science.

This interpretation is the most mischievous perception in that it justifies inefficient and politically unjust performance under the title "democratic governance." The government excises the sovereign power of the people, meaning the elected political leaders are supposed to administer this supreme organization in the best interest of all citizens who are equal by the constitutional law. Therefore, governance does not become democratic if the political part of the government is elected following the constitution. The constitution of the country may be used to suit the wishes of the individuals in power. The present American dilemma, which has been characterized as the "*Divided* States of America," may be cited as an example of this interpretation.

Accordingly, if we genuinely believe in democracy and want it to function as an ideal political model, we must review its history to see where we are erring in understanding its true theory and principles. We would experience little trouble in finding such reviews because of its long history and importance; philosophical and social science literature is fraught with studies on democracy. Nevertheless, we may not find one piece that will meet our requirement because these reviews fail to interpret the political system in its contextual socio-economic milieu.

Consider ancient Athens—the birthplace of modern democracy—and examine Aristotle's analysis. He believed that happiness is the ultimate objective of human life, and individuals can find it only by living in a polis—a city-state. The city's sovereign power is vested in the political institution called government, which can be organized in six different ways depending on who rules and for whom. Table 2 describes Aristotle's classification of the forms of government.

Table 2: Aristotle's Classification of the Forms of Government

Purpose/Ruler	One Ruler	Few Rulers	Many Rulers
Common Interest	Monarchy	Aristocracy	Polity
Ruler's Interest	Tyranny	Oligarchy	Democracy

Based on the number of people exercising the state's sovereign power, Aristotle divided the administration of government into three categories, which, in turn, yielded six forms of government. The first row identifies the politically desirable form of government because the power is exercised in common interests. The second-row names the defective or "perverted" forms of government because people in power exercise their offices for self- and/or group-interests.

To Aristotle, the number of people running the government is of little consequence if the power is exercised for the common interest, the same idea that Locke and Rousseau highlighted in their books. However, in reality, we get the types of government named in the second row. Aristotle explicitly examines the nature of democracy because it was the prevailing system of governance in Athens. The following quote from *Politics* is intended to underline the most fundamental features of a democratic government that must remain unchanged if a genuinely democratic political system is to be practiced.

> The basis of a democratic state is liberty, which, according to the common opinion of men, can only be enjoyed in such a state; this they affirm to be the great end of every democracy. One principle of liberty is for all to rule and be ruled in turn, and indeed democratic justice is the application of numerical, not proportionate equality; whence it follows that the majority must be supreme and that whatever the majority approves must be the end and the just. It is said that every citizen must have equality,

and therefore in a democracy, the poor have more power than the rich because there are more of them, and the will of the majority is supreme. This, then, is one note of liberty which all democrats affirm to be the principle of their state. Another is that a man should live as he likes. This, they say, is the privilege of a freeman since, on the other hand, not to live as a man is the mark of a slave. This is the second characteristic of democracy, whence has arisen the claim of men to be ruled by none, if possible, or, if this is impossible, to rule and be ruled in turns; and so, it contributes to the freedom based upon equality.

Such being our foundation and such the principle from which we start, the characteristics of democracy are as follows the election of officers by all out of all; and that all should rule over each, and each in his turn over all; that the appointment to all offices, or to all but those which require experience and skill, should be made by lot; that no property qualification should be required for offices, or only a very low one; that a man should not hold the same office twice, or not often, or in the case of few except military offices: that the tenure of all offices, or of as many as possible, should be brief, that all men should sit in judgment, or that judges selected out of all should judge, in all matters, or in most and in the greatest and most important, such as the scrutiny of accounts, the constitution, and private contracts; that the assembly should be supreme over all causes, or at any rate over the most important, and the magistrates over none or only over a very few. Of all magistracies, a council is the most democratic when there is not the means of paying all the citizens, but when they are paid, even this is robbed of its power; for the people then draw all cases to themselves, as I said in the previous discussion. The next characteristic of democracy is payment for services;

assembly, law courts, magistrates, everybody receives pay when it is to be had; or when it is not to be had for all, then it is given to the law-courts and to the stated assemblies, to the council and to the magistrates, or at least to any of them who are compelled to have their meals together. And whereas oligarchy is characterized by birth, wealth, and education, the notes of democracy appear to be the opposite of these—low birth, poverty, mean employment. Another note is that no magistracy is perpetual, but if any such have survived some ancient change in the constitution, it should be stripped of its power, and the holders should be elected by lot and no longer by vote. *These are the points common to all democracies, but democracy and demos in their truest form are based upon the recognized principle of democratic justice, that all should count equally; for equality implies that the poor should have no more share in the government than the rich, and should not be the only rulers, but that all should rule equally according to their numbers. And in this way, men think that they will secure equality and freedom in their state* [emphasis added].

Now the foundation of a democratic state is liberty, and people have been accustomed to say this as if here only liberty was to be found, for they affirm that this is the end proposed by every democracy. But one part of liberty is to govern and be governed alternately; for, according to democratic justice, equality is measured by numbers, and not by worth: and this being just, it is necessary that the supreme power should be vested in the people at large; and that what the majority determine should be final: so that in a democracy the poor ought to have more power than the rich, as being the greater number; for this is one mark of liberty which all framers of a democracy lay down as a criterion of that state; another is, to live as everyone likes; for this, they say, is a right which liberty gives since he is a slave who must live as he likes not. This, then, is another criterion of a democracy. Hence arises the claim to be under no command whatsoever to anyone, upon any account, any otherwise than by rotation, and that just as far only as that person is, in his turn, under his also. This also is conducive to that equality that liberty demands.

These things being premised, and such being the government, it follows that such rules as the following should be observed in it, that all the magistrates should be chosen out of all the people, and all to command each, and each in his turn all: that all the magistrates should be chosen by lot, except to those offices only which required some particular knowledge and skill: that no census, or a very small one, should be required to qualify a man for any office: that none should be in the same employment twice, or very few, and very seldom, except in the army: that all their appointments should be limited to a very short time, or at least as many as possible: that the whole community should be qualified to judge in all causes whatsoever, let the object be ever so extensive, ever so interesting, or of ever so high a nature; as at Athens, where the people at large judge the magistrates when they come out of office, and decide concerning public affairs as well as private contracts: that the supreme power should be in the public assembly; and that no magistrate should be allowed any discretionary power but in a few instances, and of no consequence to public business. Of all magistrates, a senate is best suited to a democracy, where the whole community is not paid for giving their attendance; for in that case, it loses its power; for then the people will bring all causes before them, by appeal, as we have already mentioned in a former book. In the next place, there should, if possible, be a fund to pay all the citizens—who have any share in the management of public affairs, either as members of the assembly, judges, and magistrates; but if this cannot be done, at least the magistrates, the judges the senators, and members of the supreme assembly, and those officers who are obliged to eat at a common table ought to be paid. Moreover, as an oligarchy is said to be a government of men of family, fortune, and education; so, on the contrary, a democracy is a government in the hands of men of no birth, indigent circumstances, and mechanical employments. In this state, also no office should be for life; and, if any such should remain after the government has been long changed into a democracy, they should endeavour by degrees to diminish the power; and also, elect by lot instead of vote. *These things, then, appertain to all democracies; namely, to be established on that principle of justice which is homogeneous to those governments; that is, that all the members of the state, by number, should enjoy equality, which seems chiefly to constitute a democracy, or the government of the people: for it seems perfectly equal that the rich should have no more share in the government than the poor, nor be alone in power; but that all should be equal, according to number; for thus, they think, the equality and liberty of the state best preserved* [emphasis added] (Aristotle 350 BCE).

This extended quote from Aristotle is deemed necessary to remind us of the true nature of democracy as it was conceived in ancient Athens and the nature of democracy we have made it to be. The two fundamental features of democracy include liberty and equality, as one cannot exist without the other. The meanings of the two terms are critically important for understanding the democratic system of governance. Liberty means "free to choose" under the law. This law is the equality of rights of all citizens and the obligation of each citizen to all. A citizen in a democracy cannot claim any right without granting the same to all fellow citizens.

We do not seem to see the significance of this stipulation because economics is concerned with only the second category of citizens. These individuals take part in production, meaning they possess purchasing power that is required to be a consumer. Consider the dependents who are treated as citizens in modern democracy. They need proper medical care and schooling opportunities for developing their bodies and minds to enter the independent adult life cycle. Today, quality services in both areas are available if we can pay the right price. In other words, access to both healthcare and schooling facilities is conditional to purchasing power. Since these services are directly related to the security of life and the pursuit of happiness, the government violates its constitutional obligation by making the private sector responsible for their delivery.

9.5.3 Citizenship and the Evolution of Democratic Governance

Any governance system that claims to be democratic must have these two features because they cannot be separated. This is a logical truth, which does not mean that the nature of democracy of ancient Athens is similar to one that is being practiced currently. The definition of citizenship evolved gradually from including a few to all nationals of a country. Thus, in ancient Athens, only male Greeks of eighteen years of age and above were citizens; Greek women and children were not treated as citizens. On the other hand, a clear majority of the non-Greek population serving the Greek households were slaves. In the modern world, democracy began its journey with the independence of the US in 1776. At that time, voting rights were confined to the *land-owning white men aged 21 and older*. After 188 years of independence, universal suffrage was introduced in 1964 by passing the federal Civil Rights Act, which guarantees voting rights to all men and women aged 21 and older, regardless of colour, race, religion, or education.

This evolutionary change in the voting right is critically important to properly understand the nature of the definitional debate we are conducting in our profession. Unfortunately, modern economists hardly take this political factor seriously in evaluating the definitional issue historically. It is both incorrect and unfair to blame Aristotle for treating slaves as production instruments because it was a political and social culture in his time. However, it is indeed an unacceptable mistake to treat human labour as a commodity in the factor market in the 21st century.

The point in all this is that the nature of present citizenship must be considered as the primary principle to determine the nature of democratic governance being practiced in a country. In turn, this will dictate the type of economic system that can be developed in that country. Over the last century, the western world has succeeded in making citizenship free from its discriminatory system by pursuing a secular state policy. Universal suffrage, the most fundamental feature of democracy, is currently a fact in the western world. What is now required is to use this democratic value to shape the government policy so that its real benefit can be equitably distributed across all ranks and files in the country.

9.5.4 Locke's Theory of Social Contract and Civil Society

To achieve this objective, democratic governance needs a theory so that the country's constitution can be founded on a set of principles to establish people as the sovereign authority of the state and make the government serve its purpose. Aristotle did not do any such thing in his discussion on the systems of government, although his entire writing project was theoretical—the ultimate end of his philosophy was to define the principles of political society in which citizens could live *happily*. His writing about Greek democracy consists mainly of the shared beliefs and customs of the Athenian elites. Therefore, to examine and explain the nature of democratic governance in our time, we need a theory of democracy because our society and economy are dramatically different from those of ancient Athens. We need not develop this theory because John Locke had already articulated it in his *Second Treatise on Government*. However, we need a moral mind to understand his theory and direct our focus on making the democratic system of governance perform its assigned role.

9.5.4.1 Social Contract and Civil Society

Ancient Athens is rightly described as the cradle of western civilization because it was the birthplace of democracy. This passage can be interpreted in two different ways. The first one is moral and philosophical, which enshrines two fundamental social virtues of democracy—equality and liberty. Some significant philosophers firmly believed in this interpretation and explained the idea to both the public and political leaders so that they can use the idea to change the prevailing political system of government. For example, these words were used in the *American Declaration of Independence* because Thomas Jefferson and some other founders of the republic truly believed in the advanced stage of society under democracy.

The other interpretation that prevails today is scientific. From this perspective, democracy is a system of governance in which the political part of the government is periodically appointed through general elections based on universal suffrage. Following Rousseau, we can say that the progress in arts and sciences has converted a fundamentally political idea into a real scientific idea over the past two thousand years. It seems unnecessary to show evidence that ancient Athenian values and beliefs concerning their political system no longer exist in the modern world, although universal suffrage is the law today.

Philosophy and science are the two fundamental systems of thought, which describe the principles of two social systems on which modern human life rests. Philosophy defines the fundamental virtue of the political system, while science defines the same for an economic system. The common name of this virtue is justice. The principle of justice in a democracy is equality, which is a moral or political concept. No matter how scientific we claim to be, we can never derive the principle of equality among citizens by using the methods of science. It is a moral judgment that we must make if we want to develop a democratic political system.

On the other hand, economics deals with the production, distribution, exchange, and consumption of wealth. These are matters of science because they are concrete activities that follow specific natural and technical laws. For example, production means transforming some goods and services, called inputs, into other goods and services, called outputs. Depending upon the nature of the commodity involved, its production follows both natural and technical laws. Since the process involves costs, the concerned commodity must be produced efficiently, signifying the principle of cost-minimization or least-cost combination. Thus, efficiency is the virtue of production theory in economics.

Similarly, distribution involves partitioning profits resulting from the sale of output among the individuals involved in the production process. Here, equity or the principle of equitable distribution is the criterion of justice. Modern economics applies this principle of economic justice to the three production factors—land, labour, and capital—not to equal and free economic agents. This is a general understanding in economics, which makes it possible to treat human labour as input in the production process like land and capital. Individuals owning these production inputs sell them as a commodity in factor markets and receive market-determined prices called rent, wage, interest, and profit.

The two systems work hand in hand when the principles of philosophy and science are appropriately applied. In other words, they produce desirable social outcomes when these principles are respected in developing the democracy's governance system. Unfortunately, this is not the case. First, democracy is no longer a moral system of governance. The principle of governance includes the rules of public administration suggested by modern political science, which view that the state's sovereign authority belongs to the government, not to the people. The voting system has been created for appointing the political part of the government periodically, which has a greater chance of minimizing political disturbance in the country. Second, human labour is treated as an input in commodity production, like land, animal, and machine, because equality of citizenship is no longer an imposing requirement for democratic governance. In ancient Athens, working people were slaves; during feudalism, they were serfs; and nowadays, they are wage-labourers. During all these epochs, the just income of these people is the amount of money needed for their subsistence. Today, the governments in advanced democratic countries guarantee this subsistence income through the minimum wage legislation.

When we deeply reflect on the issue, we should see one single cause responsible for this unwarranted socio-economic situation, particularly in the economically and politically advanced western countries. This single causal factor is the *violation of the social contract.* It is indeed a startling statement, supposed to raise many eyebrows. However, this astonishment might disappear as we examine the idea of social contract more closely.

The English word *contract* is thought to have originated from two Latin roots— "con," meaning "with, together" and "trahere," meaning "to draw." Thus, its etymological meaning as a noun signifies drawing two or more people together (Khoury 2018). This is the sense in which the word was used around the 1400s. In the early 1600s, the word began to be used as a *legally binding agreement.*

A contract is formed when two or more people promise to do something for each other. These people are called "contracting parties," and they can be individuals, a group of people or a company. A contract is formed when there is a "meeting of the minds," meaning the parties have agreed on what each is supposed to do to respect the contract (Online Etymology Dictionary 2021).

This discussion would mean little if we fail to see the fundamental point—*voluntary*—that forms the foundation of a contract. From the perspective of democracy, a contract does not qualify to be "social" unless it is voluntary or volitional. To be volitional, the contracting parties must be treated as equal associates in the concerned contract. For example, in western culture, husband and wife are considered equal partners, meaning the marriage contract stipulates that partners of the opposite sex are equal and free. *In other words, equality and liberty—two inseparable virtues—are the cornerstones of any social contract.*

It is interesting to note that we accept this proposition without hesitation in the institution of marriage but not in the establishment of the state and government. The institution of marriage is the foundation of a civilized society. It is where babies are born, nursed and nurtured, and who eventually grow up as independent adults taking all kinds of responsibilities that support a free and fair society. Partners in marriage are not equal in the same way citizens are not equal in the social contract. Thus, it is difficult to explain the reasons for rejecting equality of citizenship if we accept the principle of equality in uniting two adults of the opposite sex in holy matrimony, as devoted religious people would say. The equality of citizenship only refers to social rights, not sharing the benefits of the activities performed with these rights. In marriage, equality of partnership includes the right of sharing the household wealth equally unless there is a prenuptial agreement.

9.5.4.2 The Birth of the Social Contract Theory

The word contract, mainly used in legal and ordinary usages, became a compelling concept in the political philosophy of the 17th and 18th centuries under the name *social contract.* The political context of this philosophical approach was inspired by religious and political protests against the monarchy in Europe. It was difficult to justify the monarch's *divine right theory* against their abuses and atrocities. In his controversial book *Leviathan* (1651), the English philosopher Thomas Hobbes first articulated the social contract theory as a hypothetical contract between the ordinary men (the ruled) and the monarch (their ruler) to end the state of war that characterizes the state of Nature. Hobbes was a staunch monarchist; accordingly, he mastered and marshalled all arguments favouring this political institution. We know from our previous discussion how morals affect the faculty of human understanding.

However, the version of social contract theory on which modern democracy stands was authored by John Locke in his *Second Treatise of Government* (1689). The following quote highlights his role in building the political society we live in today:

> No single individual is ever the sole founder of any major stance in political philosophy—or in any other field of human inquiry. For, knowingly or unknowingly, every theorist makes important use of ideas and contentions previously developed by other thinkers. Nevertheless, if one were forced to name the founder of the classical liberal perspective in political thought, one would have to point to the English philosopher John Locke (1632–1704) (Mack 2019, 3).

Regrettably, his theory, once thought to be politically appealing and intellectually sound, has lost its glory and glare in recent times. In the intellectual world, the social contract is merely a *Lockean contractual* thought as its merits are judged relative to other versions available, including John Rawls's theory of justice, which promotes his notion of *original position* developed in his famous book *A Theory of Justice* (1971). However, it should be noted that Locke's motive for developing the social contract theory was very different from Rawls's original position, founded on the assumption of *the veil of ignorance*. On the other hand, politicians consider the election system of democracy as a means to capture the leadership of the government. Once elected, nothing can stop them from using this power in their best intention and interest other than their inability to maneuver the public and their party. Accordingly, our purpose here is to revive the glory of this all-important political theory to address the political and economic chaos the modern democracies are experiencing.

Thus, it is imperative to see what is so significant in Locke's social contract theory that demands our exclusive attention. This query revolves around the state's sovereign power: Where does the sovereign power of the state rest? Is it in the government, whether ruled by a single person or a small number of individuals, elected or not elected?

This political issue ought to be the most profound question that we can discuss in our civilized life. If we believe that the state's sovereign power lies in the institution of government, then it makes little difference whether the government leadership is elected through universal suffrage or not. The elected official has no moral obligation to rule by the principle of General Will or the common good. On the other hand, there are more significant risks that the elected leadership will be inefficient and selfish because, as Rousseau says, the collectivity of voters is blind; it does not know what is "good" for it.

An answer to this puzzling question may be found by enumerating the critical features of Locke's social contract theory. First is the background. The European nations were ruled by the hereditary monarchy, which derived its power from the *divine right theory*. It says that kings derived their authority from God, meaning any earthly authority, such as the parliament, could not challenge their authority. The Age of Reason in Europe discredited this theory, in which John Locke played a very critical role.

An alternative to the divine right theory was to place the sovereign authority of the state on its citizens. Locke theorized how this transition could be justified.

Second, the state of Nature is the first type of political arrangement, made by God Himself, where our evolution to civilized human beings started. Therefore, the state of Nature must be the starting point of our political discourse, which concerns two questions. First, we need to envision our living conditions in this state of Nature, and second, we must idealize why we left this state. Locke describes the nature of living conditions with the following words:

> To understand political power right and derive it from its original, we must consider what state all men are naturally in, and that is, a state of perfect freedom to order their actions, and dispose of their possessions and persons, as they think fit, within the bounds of the law of nature without asking leave, or depending upon the will of any other man.
>
> A state also of equality, wherein all the power and jurisdiction is reciprocal, no one having more than another; there being nothing more evident, than that creatures of the same species and rank, promiscuously born to all the same advantages of Nature, and the use of the same faculties, should also be equal one amongst another without subordination or subjection, unless the lord and master of them all should, by any manifest declaration of his will, set one above another, and confer on him, by an evident and clear appointment, an undoubted right to dominion and sovereignty (Locke 1689, 4-5).

According to Locke, the chief defect of the state of Nature is the lack of a human authority to enforce the laws of Nature. These laws are moral, not positive, which makes everyone responsible for obeying their conscience. However, there is no guarantee that everyone would abide by these moral laws without a positive power to punish the law transgressors. This insecurity in the state of Nature persuaded men to leave the state and establish themselves under a civil organization. The only way to do so was by a social contract:

> Men being, as has been said, by nature, all free, equal, and independent, no one can be put out of this estate and subjected to the political power of another without his own consent. The only way whereby anyone divests himself of his natural liberty and puts on the bonds of civil society, is by agreeing with other men to join and unite into a community for their comfortable, safe, and peaceable living one amongst another, in a secure enjoyment of their properties, and greater security against any, that are not of it. This any number of men may do because it injures not the freedom of the rest; they are left as they were in the liberty of the state of Nature. When any number of men have so consented to make one community or government, they are thereby presently incorporated and make one body politic, wherein the majority have a right to act and conclude the rest (Locke 1689, 31).

Third, the parties to this contract are free and equal men as they were in the state of Nature. Moreover, the fundamental objective of this contract is the security of each contractee based on the principle of equality of membership. Locke asserts that this security issue involves three fundamental rights—life, liberty, and estate—which he together calls property. This point needs our honest attention because the term property ordinarily implies physical, financial, and mental assets.

Given these three features, Locke's theory of social contract may be explained by the following articles. First, membership in the proposed association is equal—one member, one vote. Second, this definition suggests that the contract is made among ordinary men, not between the ruler and the ruled. Third, this contract requires each contractee to surrender all their natural rights to the civil community—their person and possession.

Whosoever, therefore, out of a state of Nature unite into a community, must be understood to give up all the power, necessary to the ends for which they unite into society, to the majority of the community, unless they expressly agreed in any number greater than the majority. *And this is done by barely agreeing to unite into one political society, which is all the compact that is, or needs be, between the individuals that enter into or make up a commonwealth* [emphasis added]. And thus, that which begins and actually constitutes any political society is nothing but the consent of any number of freemen capable of a majority to unite and incorporate into such a society. And this is that, and that only, which did, or could give beginning to any lawful government in the world (Locke 1689, 32).

Fourth, Rousseau (1762) adds two more properties to these stipulations, which refer to the contract's sovereign authority. First and foremost, sovereignty is inalienable, meaning it cannot be separated from the people, its proper owner. The authority is vested in the institution of government because a general body cannot perform its executive role, meaning the government is not sovereign. Its leaders are no more than magistrates, who follow constitutional laws to carry out the organization's routine, regular, and long-term policies. By this condition, officials elected to legislative and executive branches of the government do not represent their electors; they are, in Rousseau's words, their deputies. Second, sovereignty is indivisible for the same reason it is inalienable. By this proposition, Rousseau suggests that people's sovereign power always refers to General Will or the common good.

9.5.4.3 The Relevance of Locke's Thought in the 21st Century

A good look at the relevant literature should reveal that both the past and modern scholars have debated the theory's intellectual virtue as a political idea; they did not consider the fact that Locke's actual motive was to address the political crisis that his country, England, had been grappling with. For this reason, the social contract theory appears an imaginary idea before the educated public as well as the politicians. To escape from this undesirable intellectual environment, we first need to justify our claim that the social contract idea is as critically important today as it had been when it was conceived in the 17th and 18th centuries.

This job requires us to concentrate on the fundamental features of democracy as we apply them in intellectual and political discussions. As Locke tells us, complex ideas generated in our minds are a primary source of human knowledge, which, when communicated among fellow people, are called words. Over time, a word may mean different ideas as they are used in different contexts. However, they must imply the same idea when the context is fixed.

Democracy is a political vocabulary, which is concerned with the system of governance. This is the context of our discussion and debate, which clearly shows the difference between the Athenian system and the system being practiced in modern times. Besides the monumental differences between ancient Athens and the modern world, it is critical to note that the idea implied by the word, democracy, is the same. Athens practiced direct democracy; we practice indirect democracy. In Athens, the ecclesia, or assembly, used to be held at the Pnyx, where citizens voted directly on all major policy issues. In our time, all policy decisions are taken by the legislators elected through general polls. There is no guarantee that the legislators would vote according to the oath they took in the swearing-in ceremony.

The relevancy of Locke's social contract theory refers to this condition of indirect democracy. The legislators and the executives must be held accountable to the voters in general, for which we need a theory. According to Locke, the government is accountable to the people because they own it, meaning the legislators and executives are their deputies. Thus, the elected government officials are constitutionally obligated to set aside their personal and party interests and vote according to the national interests.

The US can be used as a model example to highlight how much the principles of democracy have decayed in modern times. Since the federal elections on November 4th, 2020, the activities of the US Congress have raised questions about the meaning of democracy practiced in the country. Every political activity in the country, both by the public and the political leaders, is carried out in the name of its two parties—the Democratic Party and the Republican Party. Thus, the debate over impeaching the 45th President, Donald Trump, does not focus on his behaviour on January 6th as the President of the United States of America. Most, if not all, members of Congress—the House of Representatives and the Senate—agree in private that Mr. Trump had committed an impeachable crime under the United States constitution. However, when the issue comes to voting, most democrats see it as a golden opportunity to denigrate the Republican Party, while most Republicans are unwilling to disgrace their leader. The debate is about impeaching a Republican Party president, not the President of the United States of America.

9.5.5 The Paradigm of the 21st Century Democracy

The paradigm of the 21st century democracy is nothing other than the theory of social contract propounded by John Locke in the 17th century when England had been passing through revolutionary political changes. His theory also supplied the language of the *American Declaration of Independence.* For reference, the relevant passages of the document are reproduced below:

> We hold these truths to be self-evident, that all men are created equal, that they are endowed by their Creator with certain unalienable rights, that among these are life, liberty, and the pursuit of happiness, that to secure these rights, governments are instituted among men, deriving their just powers from the consent of the governed.

These, many people believe, were not just words; they were the convictions of the authors of that monumental document. However, to most people today, these are just words, not only in the US but worldwide even though the socio-economic and political realities of the 18th century were dramatically different from those in the 21st century. To rectify this social degradation, all we need is the honest willingness of the mature citizens who pursue the profession of politics in their lives. For, we now have enough experience about how different political models operate in the real world. More importantly, we have both knowledge and resources to realize the ideals of democracy. The paradigm of modern democracy, stated in the Prologue, is reproduced below.

We, the people living in an internationally recognized territory, have chosen democracy as the principle of governance to protect and promote our security that concerns "life, liberty, and the pursuit of happiness." Security regarding life concerns protection against all kinds of physical and natural violence, including crimes and diseases. Liberty refers to freedoms under law concerning pursuing different types of activity in the territory. Finally, the ability to pursue happiness in life requires that the government provide all necessary goods and services that citizens need in different phases of life. For we all seek happiness in life, but the nature of our need and desire differs decisively between different stages. The children pursue happiness by passing their time in playful activities, while the seniors pursue happiness by resting and socialising. However, independent adults seek happiness in realising their ambitions.

The government is constitutionally obligated to cater these needs and desires to all citizens, not just those who can create wealth. To pursue happiness, junior citizens need schooling facilities. In contrast, all citizens need healthcare, which suggests that the democratic government must be involved in delivering these two services as its constitutional obligation.

The salient features of the system of governance in which this political paradigm can be practiced are summarized as follows: *First, the theoretical foundation of the system of democratic governance is the social contract theory, which is a moral, not scientific concept. Second, in the words of John Locke, the fundamental objective of this contract is to secure three kinds of property—life, liberty, and the estate—meaning all citizens are equally entitled to receive the government's service in this regard. Third, the government is not sovereign; people's sovereign power is vested in this organization. Finally, the adult and independent citizens (voters) periodically choose deputies to run the administration of the government machinery.*

A curious and careful consideration of these features of the theory of democratic governance would direct our attention to "democratic deficit"—a modern political vocabulary used to imply the failure of the government to fulfil its constitutional responsibility—securing the citizens' property rights equally and equitably. These rights basically refer to two political values—equality and liberty—which inspired the ancient Athenians to introduce democracy as the political system for governing their city-state. In ancient Athens, the security of life mainly meant protection from external aggression and internal violence, while liberty implied the protection of the law that would allow every citizen to pursue their own lifestyle.

In modern times, the list of securities has expanded to include providing access to all the basic necessities of life, which include food and drink, accommodation, and medical care. Since the government guarantees the right to own and accumulate wealth, the citizens themselves are responsible for accessing the first two necessities; the government only helps those citizens who cannot access these necessities due to valid reasons. However, healthcare is expensive and very scarce for the average citizens, meaning the government will violate its constitutional responsibility if it denies their right to access to quality medical care.

On the other hand, there is no liberty in the true sense of the term if the junior citizens cannot fully flourish their God-gifted skills. In modern times, access to quality education is a precondition for developing these natural skills. Therefore, liberty, or the right to the pursuit of happiness is now an essential requirement for enjoying freedom promised by the democratic system of government. Thus, citizens worldwide are being deprived of their constitutional right—equitable access to all levels of schooling. The two-tier schooling system, which is a violation of equal citizenship and equitable right, is the norm of the educational system built in the global village.

9.6. Economic Paradigm of Modern Democracy

There is no economy without a state, meaning the political system determines how our *homo economicus*—both in the consumption and production sectors—can pursue happiness in life. Natural selfishness is not the ultimate determinant of what we can aim for and accomplish in our life.

Let us expand this premise to see how the theory of democracy is related to the operation of economic laws. Aristotle defined economics as a science of household management because the Greek households owned all properties and, therefore, it was their job to create wealth creation. The city collected taxes to defray its administrative expenditures.

This definition changed to political economy in the 18th century mainly as a reaction to mercantilism, the commercial policy that the European colonial powers had been using to regulate trade with their colonies (Balaam and Veseth 2020).

Adam Smith was the key figure in exposing the irrational consequences of this beggar-thy-neighbour policy. As a socially concerned philosopher, he was aware of Locke's philosophy about the origin of private property in human society. Smith used Locke's idea of property by extracting it from its political context so that his theory did not clash with the prevailing political establishments. Since the monarchs, emperors, Czars, and military dictators needed the institution of private property for their interest and existence, his book was hailed from all quarters. Today, all monarchs, emperors, and Czars are gone, replaced by democratically elected politicians. We would be so lucky if we could select some socially-concerned politicians in the electoral process.

However, the most remarkable changes in modern times have occurred in the economic sector, described by the p-words, globalization, and global village. If we look closely, we will find two enormously critical ideas behind these theories—a sovereign state and its government—which suggest that all our economic thinking rests on the conception of a nation-state and its political system.

We have summarized above the nature of the constitution of modern democracy. Accordingly, here we are tasked to formulate a paradigm for the type of economics supposed to be learned and taught in this political system. This job does not seem very difficult to accomplish. We can follow the path our past masters travelled to make the study of economics consistent with the political society they lived in. Aristotle defined labour as an instrument of production, which was how the slaves were treated in his society. Classical economists defined labour as one of the factors of production exchanged in the market like any other commodity. In the 18th and 19th centuries, human labour was indeed a commodity as the masses had little political rights. However, today's political reality is distinctly different because all nationals are citizens of a sovereign state, who collectively establish the state and own the government. Accordingly, no citizen, irrespective of their mental and material wealth-holding position, can be treated as an input in any economical venture where more than one individual's services are used.

Thus, the new paradigm of economics must treat the working people as the citizens of a democratic country, not as selling labour in the labour market. This paradigm change immediately expands the scope of economic inquiry because economists need to study the three classes of citizens —junior, independent, and senior, not just the independent class. The health economists, for example, must develop models to provide healthcare, not only to the working people who enjoy health insurance as a part of the company package but also to the junior and senior citizens whom they have excluded. If they do so, they will find it very difficult to retain their current model of health economics.

Thus, this paradigm change is supposed to bring about dramatic changes in our thought, not in the theory developed so far. More specifically, the essence of the basic market model of microeconomics is not supposed to change. However, its structure will change dramatically.

First, for an example, consider Figure 1, which reproduces SN's Figure 2-1. In this figure, which describes their circular micro model, SN divide the economy into two sectors—consumption and production. The consumption sector represents our traditional concept, the household, which consists of all legal residents of the country, called consumers. Firms or businesses represent the production sector. In modern terminology, they are corporations that are artificial persons as they are legal entities independent and distinct from their owners. They enjoy most of the rights and responsibilities that a sole proprietor or a partnership business is entitled to, such as making contracts, borrowing money, hiring employees, owning the asset, and paying taxes. Because of these rights and responsibilities, a corporation may sue someone or another corporation and might be sued in the same way.

The two sectors' activities generate markets for commodities—goods and services—where they are exchanged. Relating to the commodities exchanged in the two sectors, all markets are divided into two kinds—product and factor. The product markets determine the prices of all intermediate and final goods and services. In the case of the final products, consumers generate demands based on their purchasing power. Firms or businesses generate supply based on the costs of production. In this process, the market prices are determined by the commodity characteristics demonstrated by three kinds of demand elasticities—price, income, and cross. The supply elasticities merely exploit these demand elasticities.

The prices of factors used in the production process are determined in the factor markets. Both classical and neoclassical economics have classified all production factors into three categories— land, labour, and capital—which correspondingly earn rent, wages and interests, and profits. All issues concerning the distribution of net revenue from the production process, which are summarized by one phrase, "economic inequality," arise from these classifications. The net revenue is created by the corporation, which is a legal entity, not an actual human being. Accordingly, net revenue, which is the corporation's profit, ultimately accrues to the owners of this corporation because rent, wages, and interest have already been paid out to their owners.

This is the Ricardian theory of distribution, which was factual in his time. Human labour was bought and sold like any other commodity in the labour market. However, retaining this assumption today in the western hemisphere would not only be unreal, but it would also be an insult to western civilization. This assumption suggests that all the efforts made by western leaders and the socially concerned public to establish human labour's dignity mean nothing to the economics profession. This is then the paradigm change in the economics discipline to be studied in countries by the principles of 21st-century democracy. It is critical to note that we are not changing the original definition of democracy developed by Aristotle. What we are changing here is the definition of citizenship, which fundamentally transformed over this long history.

Second, modern neoclassical economics does not care about the security of human life—the fundamental reason for establishing a government in human society. One consequence of this premise is that the commodities are treated as perfectly substitutable in the consumption theory. This method directly contradicts the facts of life. Our consumption habit is naturally determined: we first meet our need for necessities—food, clothing, accommodation, and healthcare. Once these needs are satisfied satisfactorily, our tastes begin to dominate our choices. Thus, the issue of choice, which is thought of as the subject matter of economics, denies the natural system of human preference. When the economic man is treated as a citizen, we first ensure his security of life and liberty to pursue happiness. Therefore, inserting this fact of life in our model will require us to abandon the perception of perfect substitutability in our indifference analysis so that goods can be classified for applying economics laws.

Finally, orthodox economics has freed the government from its fundamental responsibility of taking care of its citizens. Robbins's assertion that economics has little to do with the community's welfare it studies paved the way for distancing the government from its democratic responsibility. Since the government leadership does not need to think about healthcare and education—the two fundamentally scarce commodities in modern times, especially for ordinary people—it gets enough time to manipulate both national and global affairs in the way they like. This could not happen if the leaders of all democratic countries mind their own business. Since the goal of democracy is the same, these leaders must cooperate to make the global village a better place for everyone.

To sum up, we need to change our paradigm to make the study of economics consistent with our political system—democratic governance. This paradigm change concerns the theory of distribution that Ricardo stated in the second decade of the 19th century:

> The produce of the earth—all that is derived from its surface by the united application of labour, machinery, and capital, is divided among three classes of the community; namely, the proprietor of the land, the owner of the stock or capital necessary for its cultivation, and the labourers by whose industry it is cultivated.
>
> But in different stages of society, the proportions of the whole produce of the earth which will be allotted to each of these classes, under the names of rent, profit, and wages, will be essentially different; depending mainly on the actual fertility of the soil, on the accumulation of capital and population, and on the skill, ingenuity, and instruments employed in agriculture.
>
> *To determine the laws which regulate this distribution is the principal problem in Political Economy* [emphasis added]: much as the science has been improved by the writings of Turgot, Stuart, Smith, Say, Sismondi, and others, they afford very little satisfactory information respecting the natural course of rent, profit, and wages (Ricardo 1817, iii).

Ricardo's theory is unacceptable today because the law of universal suffrage in modern democracy ensures that the services of a human being, irrespective of their kind and criticality, cannot be treated as a commodity. Lands made ready for use in the production process, machinery manufactured, and financial resources borrowed from the capital and credit markets are all products of sunk human labour. Because this sunk labour was not a commodity by the law of modern democracy, the labour which uses this sunk labour to produce different kinds of commodities also cannot be considered a commodity.

In the modern economy, all production factors need to be divided into human input and non-human input. The non-human input, which may be encapsulated in the term capital, both equity and borrowed, constitutes production costs. Wages and salaries may be included in this category as partial payments to the share of net revenue each participant is supposed to receive based on their contribution to the production process. However, these payments should not be considered final, which may be augmented with bonuses. Human labour is human labour, whether it constitutes a janitor's service or that of the CEO of a corporation. Under the principle of modern democracy, each employee of a corporation, an artificial person, should receive the share of the net revenue according to the socially determined principles of compensation, not the market-determined wages and salaries.

CHAPTER X
CONCLUSION

This chapter concludes the book that conducted a lengthy and tedious critical review of the definition and scope of economics in the context of democratic governance in the 21st century. There are probably better and more transparent ways to present its ideas than the author has laboured here. Accordingly, it is hoped that the social scientists, who are genuinely interested in the theory of democracy as a system of governance, would try them.

However, let us pause and review the intellectual phenomenon under investigation. And when we do so, we will see that modern political philosophy and social sciences are founded on a wrong perception of the fundamental basis of life in society. It is a general belief in modern academia that human beings are born *free (independent) and equal.* We need no reflection to see that this statement is utterly false. Babies are born both dependent and unequal, who remain dependent on their parents until they can take care of themselves physically and financially. All human beings are born naturally unequal, beginning with the differences in gender and physical and mental merits. The socio-economic status of their parents further sharpens these natural inequalities.

Our past masters—leading figures in religion, politics, and economics—made the *equality premise* the foundation of the system of their thought for very good reasons, including protecting the rights of the weak from the powerful. In this time of globalization, this justification is no longer required in western hemisphere countries because the law and order conditions have improved satisfactorily, though not optimally.

The conceptions of the global village and globalization imply that human beings, living in distant and disperse places on earth, are fundamentally dependent for various reasons. Therefore, as understood during the Age of Enlightenment and Industrial Revolution in Europe, it is not individual freedom that is supposed to be pursued in this 21st-century world. Instead, we need to find ways to make our dependency practical and pragmatic. The junior citizens need equal opportunity to develop their natural potentials. The senior citizens need appropriate security of life, including medical care. Finally, independent citizens need an appropriate work environment to pursue happiness in their lives. To achieve this objective, they must cooperate to create an environment where they can compete. The social environment of fair competition makes us human, while we become worse than beasts when this environment is unfair, i.e., not level playing. We can achieve this goal only by practicing the principles of the social contract developed and refined respectively by John Locke and Rousseau.

Life in society is a matter of social contract. Everything we do in our civilized life has been made possible by social contracts, beginning with marriage and establishing a political society or the state. This idea, in turn, will provide clues about how to deal with the fact that human beings are *born dependent and unequal*.

With this overwhelming premise in mind, this chapter concludes the manuscript by discussing two questions: (i) What is the definition and scope of economics studied under the current system of democracy, particularly in the western world? (ii) Why are we at all interested in this question?

To initiate this discussion, we first need to deal with the second question: Why are we interested in the definition and the subject matter of economics? The answer to this question reveals the motive of the author(s). Motive is the original inspiration that activates our passions that are not natural. We need no willpower or moral support to satisfy the passions that are excited by natural causes. Examples include satisfying hunger, thirst, sex, etc. However, we do need to be socially concerned to actively or passively promote democratic values.

Pareto, cited in Chapter VIII, summarizes the nature of motives an author can pursue in writing a book in two categories. The first category concerns the usefulness of the book's subject matter from both private and public perspectives—practical and normative. The second category is concerned with searching uniformities among concerned variables without worrying about suggesting precepts or seeking happiness, benefits, or humanity's well-being. Pareto's motive to publish the *Manual of Political Economy* belongs to the second category. Robbins's motive in publishing the *Essay* was similar, if not the same. The first part of his *Essay* identifies and describes the unifying force that plays a significant role in the economy founded on the institution of private property. It seems clear that Robbins copied Pareto's idea because the *Manual* was published in 1906 while the *Essay* was published in 1932. Moreover, he has acknowledged his intellectual debt to Pareto in the *Essay*.

Pareto is logically correct in dividing the intellectual motives into two categories, but he is wrong in supposing that this categorization applies across all intellectual inquiries. If Pareto were correct, then we would never have divided the methodology of economics into two compartments—positive and normative economics. In positive economics, identifying uniformities is the fundamental purpose of research because economic theories are nothing but the statements of uniformity among concerned economic variables. The law of demand says that the price and quantity demanded are negatively related, *ceteris paribus*. The government applies this economic knowledge in a variety of ways, including formulating its tax policy. In advanced democracies, there is no tax on food items, but narcotic products are heavily taxed. The efficiency criterion that Pareto had developed is used in welfare economics—the normative part of modern economics. How could one use a criterion for comparing welfare in a political society when welfare was no consideration during its conception process? In the case of Robbins, we can confidently say that he had primarily dealt with the topics of positive economics. His definition of economics has no relation to policy analysis, i.e., normative economics.

Naturally, before discussing the definition and the scope of economics, we must ask ourselves why we are interested in the topic. If we do so, several critical issues will surface that we never think about when dealing with this topic. First, suppose we are doing this research as a member of the department of economics in a renowned university of an advanced democratic country. This employment situation brings up two issues of enormous importance. First, we are employees of a university, which suggests that we must follow its rules. Let us assume that the university we are working in is public-funded, meaning the government compensates us for our services. The government has a definite policy objective for setting up public universities. Since the government machinery is administered by the fundamental principle of democracy, its policy concerning higher education must be guided by the same principle: the well-accepted doctrine of equal citizenship. Any policy found inconsistent with this principle must be declared *undemocratic* and hence rectified or rejected.

If this is our employment situation, how can we remain in our job under the avowed declaration that welfare, whether social or individual, is none of our business? If we do this, we are violating our job contract. This is an intellectual crime that is hardly brought to justice because there are few complaints against this practice. However, questions may be raised from another perspective. Why should the government, our employer, allow us to continue violating our contract? Then, whatever we publish is for the consumption of the public, both national and international. Why would this national and global readership pay any attention to our articulated arguments if composed under a complete denial of individual and social welfare?

However, let us return to our topic—why we want to discuss the definition and scope of economics. The only reason that seems robust enough to escape all controversy is that we believe in the system of democratic governance. And, our motive for investigating the issue is to make the operation of our economy consistent with the fundamental principles of democracy. Equality is the only criterion that will guide us in all kinds of social affairs—politics and economics in particular. This principle entitles us to become part of the state's sovereign authority. The same principle guides us to formulate our professional ethics under which we are supposed to conduct our scientific research concerning economic affairs, i.e., production, exchange, distribution, and consumption of wealth. It may be noted that all these economic activities involve, some way or another, contracts among the participating persons.

Now, let us focus on the first question, which concerns the definition and scope of economics under democracy in the 21st century. Given the background that we live in an advanced democratic country, which is guided by the principle of political equality, we may now discuss the definition and scope of economics by referring to Jacob Viner's famous but misunderstood reflective maxim—economics is what economists do. He seems to be unfairly criticized for this extempore utterance. Viner is criticized for the accusation that his utterance signifies a circular statement. This is because we now need to define who is an economist to understand what economics is. The criticism has resulted from the perception that everyone who has an advanced degree in economics is an economist. This is a wrong perception because anyone with an advanced degree in economics can legitimately claim to be an economist. This truth does not suggest that all the topics examined by them qualify to be included within the subject matter of economic inquiry.

Consider Gary Becker's theory of crime:

The economic theory of criminal behaviour is an application of the neoclassical theory of demand. Formalized by Nobel Laureate Gary Becker in 1968, it states that potential criminals are economically rational and respond significantly to the deterring incentives by the criminal justice system. They compare the gain from committing a crime with the expected cost, including the risk of punishment, the possibility of social stigma, and eventual psychological costs. If Becker's theory is correct, increasing the resources that society devotes to the arrest, conviction, and punishment of criminals may be the best policy prescription for reducing the amount, and social costs, of crime.

Consider an example. Suppose an individual considers violating speed limits. S/he should consider, on one side, the benefit from such behaviour (arriving earlier to his/her destiny or the simple pleasure of driving above the speed limit) and, on the other side, the possible punishment. However, a fine for violating speed limits is not paid with certainty, although there is a certain probability that such behaviour is detected and effectively punished. Furthermore, there might be other elements to be considered, such as reputation (which could go both ways, depending on the social group of reference) as well as possible consequences (for example, loss of one's driving license at some point in the future). If the benefit is more important than the costs, this individual is expected to violate speed limits. If the benefit is not sufficient to compensate for the costs, the individual is deterred and, therefore, no violation of speed limits takes place (Garoupa 2014).

This is not the occasion to judge Becker's theory. However, it is critically important to note that his theory is entirely consistent with Robbins and Samuelson's ideas in their books. No matter how attractive it might appear to the economics profession due to its magnetic mathematical charm, this theory is to be rejected outright because it is inconsistent with democracy's fundamental principle. The criminals violate the rights of their fellow citizens. Therefore, from the perspective of democratic governance, crime cannot be considered a topic of economic inquiry.

When we accept the truth that everything written by the possessors of the economics degree does not qualify to be included in the subject matter of economics, we will see a very different side of Viner's maxim. This maxim directs our attention directly to our textbooks used at universities for teaching introductory courses microeconomics—the foundation of economic discipline.

With this background discussion, we may define economics for the 21st century advanced democracy as follows: *Economics is a social science that studies the production, exchange, distribution, and consumption of wealth following the fundamental principles of democracy.* Popular definitions use the conception "human behaviour." However, this practice seems unnecessary because all social sciences are meant to study human behaviour. In this regard, the scope of economics is delimited by the concept of wealth to be understood in its broadest signification. It may be recalled that reformulating economics in this way will require changing our basic paradigm about the relation among citizens concerning their participation in the production of wealth. By the requirement of modern democracy, human labour can no longer be treated as a commodity, used as input in the production process. Production in the private sector, which requires more than one, and the revenue, must be shared by all employees of the company, including the executive staff. When we change our unempirical premise about production factors, we will see that the neoclassical economics we study today has become perfectly consistent with our political society, making it possible for us to live the modern civilized life.

BIBLIOGRAPHY

- Amadeo, Kimberly (2021). US National Debt by Year Compared to GDP and Major Events: Why the U.S. Debt Has Risen Dramatically Since 1929. *The Balance*. Available from https://www.thebalance.com/national-debt-by-year-compared-to-gdp-and-major-events-3306287#:~:text=The%20U.S.%20national%20debt%20hit%20a%20new%20high%20of%20%2427,GDP%20ratio%20to%20record%20levels (accessed on 24 February 2021).
- Albert Einstein Quotes. (n.d.). BrainyQuote.com. Retrieved January 27, 2021, from BrainyQuote.com. Available from https://www.brainyquote.com/quotes/albert_einstein_385842 (accessed on 27 January 2021).
- Aristotle (350 BCE). *Politics*. Available from http://classics.mit.edu/Aristotle/politics.6.six.html (accessed on 18 February 2021).
- As You Sow (2021). The 100 Most Overpaid CEOs 2019. Available from https://www.asyousow.org/report/the-100-most-overpaid-ceos-2019 https://www.gutenberg.org/files/4705/4705-h/4705-h.htm (accessed on 29 July 2021).
- https://www.asyousow.org/report/the-100-most-overpaid-ceos-2019 (accessed on 10 January 2021).
- Backhouse, R. and Biddle, Jeff (2000). The concept of applied economics: a history of ambiguity and multiple meanings. *History of Applied Economics*, 32 (annual supplement), 2000.

- Backhouse, Roger and Medema, Steven (2009a). On the Definition of Economics. *Journal of Economic Perspectives*, Vol. 23 (1): 221–233.
- Backhouse, Roger and Medema, Steven (2009b). Defining Economics: The Long Road to Acceptance of the Robbins Definition. *Economica,* Vol. 76: 805–820.
- Balaam, David and Veseth, Michael (20202). Political economy. *Encyclopedia Britannica*. https://www.britannica.com/topic/political-economy (accessed on 15 January 2021).
- Bacon, Francis (2011[1620]). *Novum Organum*. A Project of Liberty Fund, Inc. Available from https://oll-resources.s3.us-east-2.amazonaws.com/oll3/store/titles/1432/Bacon_0415_EBk_v6.0.pdf (accessed on 04 December 2020).
- Bensusan-Butt, D. M. (1978). *On Economic Man: an Essay on the Elements of Economic Theory*. Canberra: Australian National University. Available from https://openresearch-repository.anu.edu.au/bitstream/1885/114821/2/b11774587.pdf (accessed on 08 February 2021).
- Bentham, Jeremy (1781). *An Introduction to the Principles of Morals and Legislation*. Available from https://www.utilitarianism.com/jeremy-bentham/#one (accessed on 21 January 2021).
- Burton, Neel (2014). The Problem of Desire: The psychology and philosophy of desire. *Psychology Today*. Available from https://www.psychologytoday.com/ca/blog/hide-and-seek/201411/the-problem-desire (accessed on 20 January 2021).
- Cartwrightby, Mark (2018). Feudalism. *Ancient History Encyclopedia*. Available from https://www.ancient.eu/Feudalism/ (accessed on 30 January 2021).

- Cullinane, John (2012). The economic consequences of Mrs Merkel. The Progressive Policy Think Tank. Available from https://www.ippr.org/juncture-item/the-economic-consequences-of-mrs-merkel (accessed on 28 July 2021).
- Debertin, David (2012). *Applied Microeconomics: Consumption, Production and Markets.* Lexington: University of Kentucky. Available from https://uknowledge.uky.edu/agecon_textbooks/3/ (accessed on 10 February 2021).
- Dewett, K. K. and Nahalur, N. H. (2006). *Modern Economic Theory.* Mumbai, India: S Chand & Co Ltd.
- DeLong, Brad (2017). Should-Read: John Maynard Keynes (1924): Obituary for Alfred Marshall. The Washington Center for Equitable Growth. Available from https://equitablegrowth.org/should-read-john-maynard-keynes-1924-obituary-for-alfred-marshall/ (Accessed on 05 December 2020).
- Denis P. O'Brien, Denis (2003). Classical Economics. In: Warren J. Samuels, Jeff E. Biddle, and John B. Davis (eds.) *A Companion to the History of Economic Thought.* Malden, MA: Blackwell Publishing Ltd. Available from http://aberkane.yolasite.com/resources/A%20Companion%20to%20the%20History%20of%20Economic%20Thought.pdf (accessed on 10 January 2021).
- Dillard, Dudley (2020). Keynes, John Neville. *encyclopedia.com.* Available from https://www.encyclopedia.com/social-sciences/applied-and-social-sciences-magazines/keynes-john-neville (Accessed on 05 December 2020).
- Duignan, Brian (2021). Causes of the Great Depression. *Britannica.* Available from https://www.britannica.com/story/causes-of-the-great-depression (accessed on 10 January 2021).

- Elahi, K. (2005). Economic Inequality and Paretian Welfare Economics: Some Insinuating Questions. *Forum for Social Economics*, Vol. 35(1): 19-36.
- ELH Insights (2021). Meet the biggest hotel chains in the world. Available from https://hospitalityinsights.ehl.edu/biggest-hotel-chains (accessed on 12 February 2021).
- Elkins, Kathleen (2018). Here's the last time the president of the United States got a raise. https://www.cnbc.com/2018/02/16/how-much-the-president-on-the-united-states-gets-paid.html (accessed on 10 January 2021).
- Friedman, Milton (1953). The Methodology of Positive Economics. Available from https://www.sfu.ca/~dandolfa/friedman-1966.pdf (accessed on 04 December 2020).
- Friedman, Milton (1962). *Capitalism and Freedom*. Chicago: University of Chicago Press.
- Garoupa, Nuno (2014). Economic Theory of Criminal Behavior. In Gerben Bruinsma, David Weisburd ed., *Encyclopedia of Criminology and Criminal Justice*. Available from https://link.springer.com/referenceworkentry/10.1007%2F978-1-4614-5690-2_409#:~:text=The%20economic%20theory%20of%20criminal,by%20the%20criminal%20justice%20system (accessed on 08 April 2021).
- Harman, Chris (1989). From feudalism to capitalism. *International Socialism* 2(45): 35–87. Available from https://www.marxists.org/archive/harman/1989/xx/transition.html (accessed on 30 January 2021).
- Harrison B., Smith C., Davies B. (1992) What is Economics?. In: *Introductory Economics*. Palgrave, London. https://doi.org/10.1007/978-1-349-22006-9_1 (accessed on 30 January 2021). Khoury, George (2018). Etymology of Great Legal Words: Contract. Available from https://blogs.findlaw.com/strategist/2018/07/etymology-of-great-legal-words-contract.html (accessed on 04 January 2021).

- Hobbes (1651). *Leviathan or the Matter, Forme, and Power of a Common-wealth Ecclesiasticall and Civil.* London: Andrew Crooke. Available from https://socialsciences.mcmaster.ca/~econ/ugcm/3ll3/hobbes/Leviathan.pdf (accessed on 14 February 2021).
- Horton, Emily (2017). The Legacy of the 2001 and 2003 "Bush" Tax Cuts. *The Center on Budget and Policy Priorities* (CBPP). Available from https://www.cbpp.org/sites/default/files/atoms/files/3-31-17tax.pdf (accessed on 08 February 2021).
- Howson, Susan (2011). *Lionel Robbins.* Cambridge: Cambridge University Press.
- Hume, David (1739-40). *Treatise of Human Nature.* The Project Gutenberg eBook Series. Available from https://www.gutenberg.org/files/4705/4705-h/4705-h.htm (accessed on 04 December 2020).
- Hume, David (1748). *An Enquiry Concerning Human Understanding.* Available from https://www.gutenberg.org/files/9662/9662-h/9662-h.htm (accessed on 28 July 2021)
- Joyce, Hellen (2001). Adam Smith and the invisible hand. Available from https://plus.maths.org/content/adam-smith-and-invisible-hand (accessed on 04 April 2021).
- John Neville Keynes (2018). *New World Encyclopedia.* Available from https://www.newworldencyclopedia.org/entry/Special:CiteThisPage?page=John_Neville_Keynes (Accessed on 05 December 2020).
- Kant, Immanuel (1788). *The Critique of Pure Reason.* London: The Macmillan Company. Available from http://files.libertyfund.org/files/1442/0330_Bk.pdf (accessed on 04 December 2020).
- Keynes, J. M. (1936). *The General Theory of Employment, Interest and Money.* https://www.files.ethz.ch/isn/125515/1366_KeynesTheoryofEmployment.pdf (accessed on 28 July 2021).

- Keynes, J. M. (1924). Alfred Marshall, 1842-1924. *The Economic Journal*, Vol. 34(135): 311-372. Available from https://delong.typepad.com/files/keynes-marshall.pdf (Accessed on 05 December 2020).
- Keynes, J. N. (1884). *Studies and Exercises in Formal Logic, Including a Generalization of Logical Processes in Their Application to Complex Inferences.* The Project Gutenberg eBook. Available from http://www.gutenberg.org/files/59590/59590-h/59590-h.htm (Accessed on 03 December 2020).
- Keynes, J. N. (1904). *Scope and Method of Political Economy*, Third Edition, Revised. London: Macmillan And Co., Limited. Available from https://ia802907.us.archive.org/22/items/in.ernet.dli.2015.553477/2015.553477.The-Scope_text.pdf (Accessed on 05 December 2020).
- Kirsch, Noah. "The 3 Richest Americans Hold More Wealth Than Bottom 50% Of The Country, Study Finds". Available from https://www.forbes.com/sites/noahkirsch/2017/11/09/the-3-richest-americans-hold-more-wealth-than-bottom-50-of-country-study-finds/?sh=70d040293cf8 (accessed on 09 January 2021).
- Kuhn, Thomas (1962). *The Structure of Scientific Revolutions.* Chicago: The University of Chicago Press.
- Lee, Desmond (1987). Translator's Introduction. In Plato's *Republic*. London: Penguin Books.
- Lester, Mark and Beason, Larry (2019). *The McGraw-Hill Education Handbook of English Grammar Usage.* Available from https://www.moys.gov.iq/upload/common/McGraw-Hill_Education_Handbook_of_English_Grammar_Usage,_3rd_Edition_Bookflare.net_.pdf (accessed on 06 November 2020).
- Locke, John (1690). *An Essay Concerning Human Understanding.* Available from https://socialsciences.mcmaster.ca/~econ/ugcm/3ll3/locke/Essay.htm (accessed on 04 December 2020).

- Locke, John (1690). *Second Treatise of Government.* The Project Gutenberg eBook Project. Available from https://english.hku.hk/staff/kjohnson/PDF/LockeJohnSECONDTREATISE1690.pdf (accessed on 03 December 2020).
- Lorkowski, C. M. (2011). Hume, David: Causation. *Internet Encyclopedia of Philosophy.*
- Available on PhilArchive: https://philarchive.org/archive/LORHDC (accessed on 03 December 2020).
- Mack, Eric (2019). *The Essential John Locke.* Fraser Institute. https://www.essentialscholars.org/locke (accessed on 04 February 2021).
- Mäki, Uskali (2003). 'The methodology of positive economics' (1953) does not give us the methodology of positive economics, *Journal of Economic Methodology* 10(4):495-505,. DOI: 10.1080/1350178032000130484 (accessed on 02 April 2021).
- Malthus, Thomas (1798). *Principles of Political Economy with some of their Applications to Social Philosophy.* The Online Library of Liberty. Available from https://oll-resources.s3.us-east-2.amazonaws.com/oll3/store/titles/101/Mill_0199_EBk_v6.0.pdf (accessed on 04 December 2020).
- MacFarquhar, Roderick (1987). "The succession to Mao and the end of Maoism". In Roderick MacFarquhar (ed.). *The Politics of China* (2nd ed.). Cambridge University Press.
- Machlup, F. (1965). Why Economists Disagree. *Proceedings of the American Philosophical Society*, 109(1): 1-7. Available from http://www.jstor.org/stable/985773 (accessed on 04 December 2020).
- Marshall, Alfred (1890). *Principles of Economics (8th ed).* The Online Library of Liberty - A Project Of Liberty Fund, Inc. Available from https://oll-resources.s3.us-east-2.amazonaws.com/oll3/store/titles/1676/Marshall_0197_EBk_v6.0.pdf (accessed on 02 December 2020.)

- Marx, Karl (1859). Preface to A Contribution to the Critique of Political Economy. Available from https://www.marxist.com/classics-preface-to-a-contribution-to-the-critique-of-political-economy.htm (accessed on 25 February 2021).
- Marx, Karl and Engels, Fedrick (1848). *Manifesto of the Communist Party*. Available from https://www.marxists.org/archive/marx/works/1848/communist-manifesto/ (accessed on 04 December 2020).
- Melin, Anders and Sam, Cedric (2020). Wall Street Gets the Flak, But Tech CEOs Get Paid All the Money. Available from https://www.bloomberg.com/graphics/2020-highest-paid-ceos/ (accessed on 12 February 2021).
- Mises, Ludwig von (1949). *Human Action: A Treatise on Economics.* The Online Library of Liberty. Available from https://oll-resources.s3.us-east-2.amazonaws.com/oll3/store/titles/308/Mises_0068_EBk_v6.0.pdf (accessed on 15 February 2021).
- Mill, John Stuart (1848). *Principles of Political Economy with some of their Applications to Social Philosophy*. The Online Library of Liberty. Available from https://oll-resources.s3.us-east-2.amazonaws.com/oll3/store/titles/101/Mill_0199_EBk_v6.0.pdf (accessed on 04 December 2020).
- Mill, John Stuart (1874). *Essays on Some Unsettled Questions of Political Economy*. Available from https://www.econlib.org/library/Mill/mlUQP.html?chapter_num=6#book-reader (accessed on 28 July 2020).
- Morris, William and Brown, Charlotte R (2020). David Hume. *The Stanford Encyclopedia of Philosophy*. Available from https://plato.stanford.edu/archives/sum2020/entries/hume/ (accessed on 02 February 2021).
- Nagel, Ernest (1963). Assumptions in Economic Theory. *American Economic Review, Papers and Proceedings*. Volume 53 (May): 211-19.

- Online Etymology Dictionary. Contract. https://www.etymonline.com/word/contract (accessed on 04 January 2021).
- Plato (375 BCE). *The Republic*. New York: THE COLONIAL PRESS. Available from https://en.wikisource.org/wiki/The_Republic_of_Plato (accessed on 04 December 2020).
- Pareto, Vilfredo (1971). *Manual of Political Economy*. New York: Augustus M. Kelley Publishers.
- Persky, Joseph (1995). Retrospectives: The Ethology of Homo Economicus. *Journal of Economic Perspectives*, Volume 9 (2): 221–23. https://pubs.aeaweb.org/doi/pdfplus/10.1257/jep.9.2.221.
- Rawls, John (1971). *A Theory of Justice*. Cambridge, MA: Harvard University Press.
- Reisman, David (1994). *Theories of the Mixed Economy: Selected Texts 1931-1968*. London: Pickering & Chatto Ltd.
- Ricardo, David (1817). *Principles of Political Economy and Taxation*. Available from https://books.google.ca/books?id=cUBKAAAAYAAJ&q=editions:y8vXR4oK9R8C&pg=PR1&redir_esc=y#v=onepage&q=editions%3Ay8vXR4oK9R8C&f=false (accessed on 04 December 2020).
- Robbins, Lionel (1945). *An Essay on the Nature and Significance of Economic Science.* Second Edition, Revised and Extended. London: Macmillan and Co., Limited. Available from https://milescorak.files.wordpress.com/2020/02/robbins-essay-nature-significance-economic-science.pdf (Accessed on 06 December 2020).
- Robbins, Lionel (1981). "Economics and Political Economy." *The American Economic Review*, Vol. 71(2):1-10.
- Romer, Christina and Pells, Richard (2020). Great Depression. *Encyclopædia Britannica*. Available from https://www.britannica.com/event/Great-Depression (accessed on 22December 2020).

- Rousseau, Jean Jacques (1762). The Social Contract Or Principles of Political Right. Available from https://socialpolicy.ucc.ie/Rousseau_contrat-social.pdf (accessed on 29 July 2021)
- Rousseau, Jean Jacques (1763). *Emile, or On Education*. Available from https://oll.libertyfund.org/title/rousseau-emile-or-education (accessed on 29 July 2021)
- Russell, Bertrand (1945). *A History of Western Philosophy*. New York: Simon & Schuster Samuelson, Paul (1947, 1983). *Foundations of Economic Analysis*. Cambridge, MA: Harvard University Press.
- Samuelson, Paul (1963). Problems of Methodology – Discussion. *American Economic Review, Papers and Proceedings*. Volume 53 (May): 231-6.
- Samuelson, Paul and Nordhaus, William D. (2010). *Economics,* Nineteenth Edition. New York: McGraw-Hill/Irwin. Available from http://pombo.free.fr/samunord19.pdf (accessed on 27 February 2021).
- Statista (2020). Japan: National debt from 2015 to 2025 in relation to gross domestic product (GDP). Available from https://www.statista.com/statistics/267226/japans-national-debt-in-relation-to-gross-domestic-product-gdp/#:~:text=In%202018%2C%20the%20national%20debt,of%20the%20gross%20domestic%20product.&text=Japan's%20national%20debt%20ranks%20first,been%20in%20the%20spotlight%20recently (accessed on 09 January 2021).
- Say, Jean-Baptiste (1880). *A Treatise on Political Economy; or the Production, Distribution, and Consumption of Wealth*. Kitchener: Batoche Books. Available from https://socialsciences.mcmaster.ca/~econ/ugcm/3ll3/say/treatise.pdf (accessed on 04 December 2020).
- Smith, Adam (1776). *An Inquiry into the Nature and Causes of the Wealth of Nations*. Available from http://geolib.com/smith.adam/woncont.html (accessed on 01 September 2020).

- Tanable, Rosie (2016). Alfred Marshall. In Frank Kaufmann (ed) *New World Encyclopedia*. Available from https://www.newworldencyclopedia.org/p/index.php?title=Alfred_Marshall&oldid=1001448 (Accessed on 05 December 2020).
- The Editors of Encyclopaedia Britannica (2019). Laissez-faire. *Encyclopædia Britannica*. Available from https://www.britannica.com/topic/laissez-faire accessed on 21 January 2021).
- Torrens, Robert (1821). *An Essay on the Production of Wealth: With an Appendix, in which the Principles of Political Economy are Applied to the Actual Circumstances of this Country*. London: Longman, Hurst, Rees, Orme, and Brown. Available from https://books.google.ca/books?id=mgpYAAAAcAAJ&pg=PA1&source=gbs_toc_r&cad=4#v=onepage&q&f=false (accessed on 04 December 2020).
- Weldon J.C. (1988) The Classical Theory of Distribution. In: Asimakopulos A. (eds) *Theories of Income Distribution*. Recent Economic Thought Series, vol 12. Springer, Dordrecht. https://doi.org/10.1007/978-94-009-2661-5_2 (accessed on 09 January 2021).
- Wicksteed, Philip (1910). *The Commonsense of Political Economy, including a Study of the Human Basis of Economic Law.* The Online Library of Liberty. Available from https://oll-resources.s3.us-east-2.amazonaws.com/oll3/store/titles/1415/Wicksteed_0587_EBk_v6.0.pdf (accessed on 15 February 2021).
- Whitaker, J.K. (1987). Alfred Marshall. In John Eatwell et al., eds *The New Palgrave: A Dictionary of Economics*. Vol. 3 (K to P): pp. 350–363. New York: Macmillan Press.
- Wrigley, E. Anthony (2018). Reconsidering the Industrial Revolution: England and Wales. *Journal of Interdisciplinary History* 49(01): 9–42.